Henry Edward Manning

Sermons on ecclesiastical subjects

Henry Edward Manning

Sermons on ecclesiastical subjects

ISBN/EAN: 9783744744799

Printed in Europe, USA, Canada, Australia, Japan

Cover: Foto ©Lupo / pixelio.de

More available books at **www.hansebooks.com**

SERMONS

ON

ECCLESIASTICAL SUBJECTS.

BY

HENRY EDWARD,

ARCHBISHOP OF WESTMINSTER.

AMERICAN EDITION.

VOL. II.

NEW YORK:
THE CATHOLIC PUBLICATION SOCIETY,
9 WARREN STREET.

1873.

TO

HENRY DUKE OF NORFOLK,

EARL MARSHAL OF ENGLAND,

AND TO

THE MEMBERS OF THE CATHOLIC UNION,

WITH THE PRAYER

THAT THEY MAY BE STRENGTHENED TO STAND FIRM

IN DEFENCE OF THE HOLY SEE

AS GOOD SOLDIERS OF JESUS CHRIST,

THIS VOLUME IS INSCRIBED.

CONTENTS.

	PAGE
INTRODUCTION	ix

I.
THE TEMPORAL POWER OF THE POPE IN ITS POLITICAL ASPECT:
In the Pro-Cathedral, Moorfields, Rosary Sunday, 1866 . . 1

II.
ROME AND THE REVOLUTION:
In the Pro-Cathedral, Moorfields, Rosary Sunday, 1867 . . 29

III.
CHRIST AND ANTICHRIST:
At the Requiem of those who fell in defence of Rome, in the Pro-Cathedral, Moorfields, 1867 53

IV.
THE SYLLABUS:
In the Pro-Cathedral, Kensington, Rosary Sunday, 1868 . . 77

V.
POPULAR OBJECTIONS TO THE VATICAN COUNCIL:
At the Church of St. Mary, Bayswater, on the Feast of St. Charles, 1869 101

VI.
ROME THE CAPITAL OF CHRISTENDOM:
At the Pro-Cathedral, Kensington, Rosary Sunday, 1870 . . 127

VII.
THE PONTIFICATE OF PIUS IX. AND THE YEARS OF PETER:
At the Opening of the Triduum, in the Pro-Cathedral, Kensington, June 16, 1871 159

VIII.
THE DIVINE COMMONWEALTH:
At the Pro-Cathedral, Kensington, Rosary Sunday, 1871. . 187

IX.
THE TRIUMPH OF THE CHURCH:
St. Mary's Church, Liverpool, Sunday, Sept. 22, 1872 . . 219

X.
THE GLORY OF THE CHURCH ALWAYS PROGRESSIVE:
At the Opening of the Church of St. Francis of Assisi, Manchester, Thursday, Sept. 26, 1872 247

XI.
THE DAY OF THE LORD:
Rosary Sunday, 1872, in the Franciscan Jubilee of Pius IX. . 273

INDEX 305

INTRODUCTION.

THE Sermons contained in this volume relate to the conflict of Pius IX. against the political movements which he has described so often in these years as 'the anti-christian and anti-social revolution.' Seven of them were preached on Rosary Sunday, on which day there has been, in the diocese of Westminster, a special yearly intercession for the Vicar of Jesus Christ. Some of them mark certain notable periods of the conflict, such as the invasion of the Romagnas, the battle of Mentana, and the sacrilegious occupation of Rome; the others treat, at least in outline, of the cause for which the Holy Father has so inflexibly contended.

In the beautiful Cemetery of San Lorenzo, on which Pius IX. has bestowed so much cost and care, there was a simple monument to the memory of the Christian heroes who fell at Mentana in defence of the Holy See. The Italian Junta in

Rome have, we are told, placed upon it the following inscription:

> THIS MONUMENT,
> WHICH THE THEOCRATIC GOVERNMENT ERECTED
> IN MEMORY OF MERCENARY STRANGERS,
> ROME REDEEMED
> LEAVES TO POSTERITY
> AS A PERENNIAL TESTIMONIAL
> OF CALAMITOUS TIMES.
> S. P. Q. R.
> NOVEMBER 2, 1871.

We have here an unconscious confession. The government of Pius IX. is admitted to be a theocracy: Rome is therefore 'redeemed' from God, and brought again into bondage to the prince of this world. This may be taken as the last word of the anti-christian and anti-social revolution: namely, the rejection of God and His Christ.

Here also is an acknowledgment that what the defenders of the Temporal Power have so long been saying is true after all: namely, that the aim of the Italian revolution, cheered and hounded on by the Liberals of Europe, was directed to the end of excluding God from the civil and political society of mankind. The separation of the State from the Catholic Church, which began in the Lutheran Reformation, and was continued by the manifold revolutions springing from the principles of 1789, has now received its completion in the rejection of the Vicar of Jesus Christ. Rome is redeemed from the sovereignty of the Redeemer of the world. We see, therefore, the standards of Christ and of antichrist front to front. The time is now past for illusions. The masks are off all faces; the halters and waverers are out of the lists, waiting for the shock of the great antagonists who know what they mean, and mean what they say. The conflict is no longer between Gallicanism and Ultramontanism, or any internal shades of Catholic policy in feeling or thought, but between faith and unbelief, God and the world.

Since the 20th of September 1870 we have been looking on at the comedy of two sovereigns in one city: of two royal and sacred persons; the one violating every sacred right, the other in just judgment passing sentence on the royal doer of the wrong. This spectacle alone is enough to justify the Divine Wisdom which by a Civil Princedom has provided for the independence of the Head of the Church; and to show that the Temporal Sovereignty of the Pontiff, so long as the world remains Christian, is the only solution of this problem. The Head of the Church can only be a sovereign or a subject. The

King of Italy does not dare to claim the Vicar of Christ as his subject; nevertheless, he has usurped his sovereignty. The problem can, therefore, be solved only by the fall of the Italian kingdom; and that solution seems to be not far off.

It is believed in England that the Italian revolution is the spontaneous act of the Italian people, and that the Roman people have spontaneously accepted the Italian monarchy. This excites in us but little surprise. The steady, traditional animosity in this country against the government of the Pontiff, predisposed Englishmen to believe what they hoped. Their will made them credulous of all they wished to believe; and not only incredulous, but deaf, to all they wished not to believe. In England we glory in the freedom of the press. But a free press may be the harshest of tyrannies. A free press which publishes everything on one side and nothing on the other, which will not even publish corrections of errors or contradictions of falsehoods, is not a free press: its freedom is licence to oppress truth and justice. Such has been the action of many of the chief journals of this country. The English people read them with confidence and credulity, not knowing the hands by which the foreign correspondence and the leading articles on that correspondence are written. They do not know that what they read as the impartial judgment of Englishmen, comes from men whose names would carry their own antidote. The English people have been unconsciously reading with undoubting trust the systematic misinformations of men pledged or paid, or both, to engage the public opinion of this country in favour of the Italian revolution.

In England we cannot conceive it possible that a political party, comparatively few in number, can gain an ascendency over the majority of a people. And yet there is not a revolution in history that has not begun in the action of a minority. If they can only go to the country with a plausible cry, trade on some popular discontent, and gain a momentary political power, by which the public money is at their disposal, all may be done: and there are men enough in army, navy, and every public service, who will go where the sound of money is to be heard, even at any distance. Such has been the growth of the Italian revolution in all its stages through the last five-and-twenty years. It had not one cry only, but two: *Fuor d' Italia gli Stranieri*, and *Abbasso il Governo dei Preti*. These two cries, against Austria, and against the government of the Pope, were sure to find a response wide enough to be mistaken for the voice of the Italian people. As to the first, it truly expressed the desire of Italy, as a like cry would express the desire of other countries whose voice is not heeded. As to the second, it is to be remembered that for half a century an incessant sedition has been actively propagated in all the cities and provinces of the States of the Church. If Belgium had been treated in like manner, no dynasty could have retained its throne. We, in England, guarded by four seas, have been less easily infected by the political propagandism of the revolution. But we must be blind if we do not already discern that our time is coming. We shall pay the penalty of our past. We have countenanced, and flattered, and aided the dangerous political movements of the Continent; and they will pay us back in our own coin. Englishmen have cheered on the revolution against the Pontifical government, believing in their simplicity that they were only pulling down the Pope. Garibaldi and Mazzini have organised their conspiracies not against the Pope only, but against Christianity. Englishmen have been helping on the overthrow of Christianity in Italy. Already the same organisation is spreading among ourselves. But our point now is the will of the Roman people: and I would, therefore, ask any fair man to weigh these facts.

1. Rome was seized in September 1870 by an

overwhelming Italian army. From that day all plebiscites and votings are visibly no longer free.

2. Rome has been from that day under the constant intimidation of a mob gathered from all parts of Italy; the cries of which reveal its will and its intentions. In face of this, no private person is free from danger. Not only were illuminations forced on the unwilling, but counter illuminations were ventured with peril.

3. The Romans were unable to vote in any political elections; both by the fact that they would thereby acknowledge tacitly the authority of the Italian government in Rome, and by the fact that the exercise of the electoral suffrage was coupled with an oath of allegiance to the Italian monarchy. The elections therefore have gone by default, the Romans abstaining from voting.

4. In the plebiscite, it has been ascertained, by every possible test, that not more than 14,000 Romans voted: the rest were men from all parts of Italy, who entered with the besieging army; or soldiers, or *impiegati*, of the Italian government.

5. In the late municipal elections the government candidates would have been rejected, but for the votes of some three or four thousand foreign *impiegati* of the government.

For these and many other reasons we are convinced that the will of the Roman people has never been freely expressed.

What has been said of Rome may be said of Italy. The Italian population is about twenty-six millions. A calculation has been made by Italians fully versed in the political movements of their country, and close observers of recent events, from which it results that not more than three millions spread over the face of Italy are to be counted as the governing party in its present revolutionary state. It may be asked, why do not the majority assert themselves? Any one at all versed in history, or in the events of the movements in France and Spain, well knows that a small organised minority will always and for a long time prevail over an unorganised majority. But it will be asked again, why should the majority be unorganised? The fact is, that majorities are always unorganised. They are content, actively or passively, with the existing order of legitimate governments. The discontented organise themselves in some new forms of aggression, to change or to destroy what exists. The mass of the people are always taken unawares, and are at a disadvantage at the first, and for some time; it may be for many years, until the events of revolutionary changes gradually elicit a counter-organisation, by which at last the will of the people is really known. This I believe to be strictly true of Italy, and of Rome. Already the Catholic sense of Italy has begun to make itself felt. The late municipal elections were carried in many places by the number of those who explicitly voted in the Catholic sense. In Rome, the government candidates would have been beaten if the government *impiegati*, drawn from all parts of Italy, had not voted: even so, if the Romans, who are faithful to the Sovereign Pontiff, had not abstained from voting, the government candidates would have been beaten. It may be asked, why did they abstain? The answer is plain. Hitherto they have abstained from all voting, as a protest against the existing usurpation. In this case they were not directed to vote. They were left to their free choice; and the majority of them persevered in taking no part in what they regard as revolutionary and of short duration. That the sense of religion and of justice in Italy will before long find its organisation, and rise up against the impiety and injustice which now scourges the country, no one can doubt. The time is not indeed ripe as yet; and all things must be worse before they can be better. There is a crisis to be passed, which will, I fear, take a severe account of Italy and of Rome. But God is over His Church, and His eyes are upon His people.

Here we may turn away from this ignoble part of the conflict. The chief work of the government in Rome seems to be the spoliation of convents, the expulsion of religious orders, and the de-christianising of education. We may leave it to fill up the cup of its iniquities. God only can intervene to stay this sacrilege, and He will do so.

There is, however, one point in this history so evidently critical as to form an epoch: I mean the Council of the Vatican; and of this a few words must be added.

No one who was present in the year 1867 will ever forget the moment when the Sovereign Pontiff first announced his intention of convoking an Œcumenical Council. It was in the last Consistory which closed the eighteenth centenary of St. Peter's martyrdom. We were sitting in the *aula* over the portico of St. Peter's, not knowing whether we should ever meet again in Rome; for the September convention was then expiring, and the protection of France in a few months would have ceased to guard the Holy See. It was then that Pius IX., with the confidence of faith which has ever sustained his own calmness and the courage of all about him, declared his intention to convene the Bishops of the whole world once more at Rome. I do not know how any one can fail to see in this a higher power, and a prescience more than his own, guiding the Head of the Church. The state of the Church and of the world demanded a remedy more potent than human legislation. The intellectual and moral aberrations of the last three hundred years had reached a point beyond which there lay only ruin to the civil order of nations. The ultimate power of the Church of God was required to deal with the evils of the Christian world. An Œcumenical Council was therefore convened. The four winds of heaven were holden till the Council had been assembled, and had done its chiefest work. The tempest then fell in a day upon Europe; in the midst of which the government of Italy usurped Rome, and the Vicar of Jesus Christ became morally a prisoner in his own city.

But I do not purpose to dwell on these facts, patent to all the world. I wish to trace out the chief lines of a new persecution which has arisen against the Church. Before the assembling of the Council, it was foreseen that the civil powers would be invoked to control its liberty of action. Of this we were well aware; and I may be excused if I repeat here what I wrote before leaving England for the Council :—

'The tendency of civil society everywhere is to depart farther and farther from the Church. Progress in these days means, to advance along the line of departure from the old Christian order of the world. The civil society of Christendom is the offspring of the Christian family, and the foundation of the Christian family is the Sacrament of Matrimony. From this spring domestic and public morals. Most governments of Europe have ceased to recognise in marriage anything beyond the civil contract, and, by legalising divorce, have broken up the perpetuity of even that natural compact. With this will surely perish the morality of society and of homes. A settlement in the foundations may be slow in sinking; but it brings all down at last. The civil and political society of Europe is steadily returning to the mere natural order. The next step in de-christianising the political life of nations is to establish national education without Christianity. This is systematically aimed at, wheresoever the Revolution has its way. This may, before long, be attempted among ourselves. It is already in operation elsewhere. The Church must then form its own schools; and the civil power will first refuse its aid, and soon its permission, that parents should educate their offspring, except in State universities and State schools. The period and the policy of Julian is returning. All this bodes ill for the Church; but worse for the State. The depression of the moral order of right and truth is the elevation of the material order of coercion and of force. The civil powers of the world do not choose this course; they only advance in it. There is behind them a power invisible, which urges them onward in their estrangements from the Church; and that unseen power is at work everywhere. It is one, universal, invisible, but not holy; the true natural and implacable enemy of the One, Visible, Universal Church. The anti-christian societies are one in aim and operation, even if they be not one in conscious alliance. And the governments of the world, some consciously, others unconsciously, disbelieving the existence of such societies, and therefore all the more surely under their influence, are being impelled towards a precipice over which monarchies and law and the civil order of the Christian society of men will go together. It is the policy of the secret societies to engage governments in quarrels with Rome. The breach is made, and the Revolution enters. The Catholic society of Europe has been weakened, and wounded; it may be, unto death.

The Catholic Church now stands alone, as in the beginning, in its divine isolation and power. 'And now, O ye kings, understand: receive instruction, you that judge the earth.'[1] There is an abyss before you, into which thrones, and laws, and rights, and liberties may sink together. You have to choose between the Revolution and the Church of God. As you choose, so will your lot be. The General Council gives to the world one more witness for the truths, laws, and sanctities which include all that is pure, noble, just, venerable, upon earth. It will be an evil day for any State in Europe if it engage in conflict with the Church of God. No weapon formed against it ever yet has prospered. The governments of Europe have been for the last year agitated and uncertain; the attitude of France is wise and deliberate, worthy of a great people with the traditions of Catholic history at its back. The attitude of other great Powers is also hitherto dignified and serious, proportionate to great responsibilities. Lesser potentates and their counsellors may circulate notes and resolve questions, and furnish matter for newspapers; but they are not the men to move mountains.

'Whilst I was writing these lines, a document has appeared purporting to be the answers of the

[1] Psalm ii. 10.

Theological Faculty of Munich to the questions of the Bavarian government.

'The questions and the answers are so evidently concerted, if not written by the same hand, and the animus of the document so evidently hostile to the Holy See, and so visibly intended to create embarrassment for the supreme authority of the Church, both in respect to its past acts and also in respect to the future action of the Œcumenical Council, that I cannot pass it over. But in speaking of it I am compelled, for the first time, to break silence on a danger which has for some years been growing in its proportions, and, I fear I must add, in its attitude of menace. The answers of the University of Munich are visibly intended to excite fear and alarm in the civil powers of Europe; and thereby to obstruct the action of the Œcumenical Council, if it should judge it to be opportune to define the Infallibility of the Pope. The answers are also intended to create an impression that the theological proofs of the doctrine are inadequate, and its definition beset with uncertainty and obscurity. In a word, the whole correspondence is a transparent effort to obstruct the freedom of the Œcumenical Council on the subject of the Infallibility of the Pontiff; or, if that doctrine be defined, to instigate the civil governments to assume a hostile attitude towards the Holy See. And this comes in the name of liberty, and from those who tell us that the Council will not be free!

'I shall take the liberty, without farther words, of dismissing the Bavarian government from our thoughts. But I must declare, with much regret, that this Munich document appears to me to be seditious.

'Facts like these give a certain warrant to the assertions and prophecies of politicians and Protestants. They prove that in the Catholic Church there is a school at variance with the doctrinal teaching of the Holy See in matters which are not of faith. But they do not reveal how small that school is. Its centre would seem to be at Munich; it has, both in France and in England, a small number of adherents. They are active, they correspond, and for the most part write anonymously. It would be difficult to describe its tenets, for none of its followers seem to be agreed on all points. Some hold the Infallibility of the Pope, and some defend the Temporal Power. Nothing appears to be common to all, except an animus of opposition to the acts of the Holy See in matters outside the faith.'[2]

[2] *Petri Privilegium*, pp. 128 seqq. *The Œcumenical Council and the Infallibility of the Roman Pontiff.* London, 1869.

When these words were written, it was already believed that the Bavarian government, through Prince Hohenlohe, had begun a systematic agitation against the Council. It was known that he had addressed a circular note to the European governments. But the text of that note was not, so far as I know, ever made public. I am able now to give the text in full. It affords abundant proof of the assertion here made, that a deliberate conspiracy against the Council was planned with great artifice, and speciousness of matter and of language. Moreover the date of this document shows how long before the opening of the Council this opposition was commenced. The Council was opened on December 8th, 1869; Prince Hohenlohe's note is dated on the 9th of the April preceding, that is to say, about eight months before the Council began. It runs as follows:

'Monsieur,—It appears to be certain that the Council convoked by his Holiness Pope Pius IX. will meet in the month of December next. The number of prelates who will attend it from all parts of the world will be much greater than at any former Council. This fact alone will help to give to its decrees a great authority, such as belongs to an Œcumenical Council. Taking this circumstance into consideration, it appears to me indispensable for every government to give it their attention; and it is with this view that I am about to address to you some observations.

'It is not probable that the Council will occupy itself only with doctrines appertaining to pure theology; there does not exist at this moment any problem of this nature which requires a conciliar solution. The only dogmatic thesis which Rome would wish to have decided by the Council, and which the Jesuits in Italy and Germany are now agitating, is the question of the Infallibility of the Pope. It is evident that this pretension, elevated into a dogma, would go far beyond the purely spiritual sphere, and would become a question eminently political, as raising the power of the Sovereign Pontiff, even in temporal matters, over all the princes and peoples of Christendom. This doctrine therefore is of such a nature as to arouse the attention of all those governments who rule over Catholic subjects.

'There is a circumstance which increases still more the gravity of the situation. I learn that among the commissions delegated to prepare matter, which later on is to be submitted to the deliberations of the Council, there is one which is occupied only on mixed questions, affecting equally international law, politics, and canon law. All these preparations justify our believing that it is the fixed intention of the Holy See, or at least of a party at present powerful in Rome, to promulgate through the Council a series of decrees upon questions which are rather political than ecclesiastical. Add to this that the *Civiltà Cattolica*—a periodical conducted by the Jesuits, and bearing an official character through the brief of the Holy Father—has just demanded that the Council shall transform into conciliar decrees the condemnations of the Syllabus, published on December 8th, 1864. Now the articles of this encyclical being directed against principles which are the base of modern public life, such as we find it among all civilised nations, it follows that governments are under the necessity of asking themselves if it is not their duty to invite the serious consideration, both of the Bishops who are their subjects, and of the future Council, to the sad consequences of such a premeditated and systematic overturning of the present relations between Church and State. It cannot indeed be denied that it is a matter of urgency for governments to combine, for the purpose of protesting, either through their agents in Rome, or in some other way, against all decisions which the Council may promulgate without the concurrence of the representatives of the secular power, in questions which are at the same time of a political and religious nature.

'I thought that the initiative in so important a matter should be taken by one of the great Powers; but not having as yet received any communication on this subject, I have thought it necessary to seek for a mutual understanding which will protect our common interests, and that without delay, seeing that the interval between this time and the meeting of the Council is so short. I therefore desire you to submit this matter to the government to which you are accredited, and to ascertain the views and intentions of the court of —— in respect to the course which it deems it advisable to follow. You will submit for the approbation of M. —— the question whether it would not be advisable to fix beforehand the measures to be taken, if not jointly, at least identically, in order to enlighten the Holy See as to the attitude which the governments of the Continent will assume in reference to the Œcumenical Council; or whether conferences composed of representatives of the States concerned would not be considered as the best means to bring about an understanding between their governments.

'I authorise you to leave a copy of this despatch

with the Minister for Foreign Affairs at ⸺, if he desires it; and I wish you to inform me as early as possible of the manner in which this communication shall have been received.

'I have the honour, &c.

'Munich, April 9, 1869. HOHENLOHE.'

Who can doubt by what hand this truly theological document was written?

The indiction of the Council was no sooner published than the well-known volume called *Janus* appeared. It was said to be the work of many hands, and of various nations—of two at least. The chief object of its animosity was Rome, and its detailed hostility was levelled against the Infallibility of the Roman Pontiff and the Syllabus. The book was elaborately acrimonious and extravagantly insolent against Rome. Its avowed aim was to rouse the civil governments against the Council. The Sovereign Pontiff had, with great wisdom and justice, dealt with the governments of Europe on the ground chosen by themselves. They had renounced the Catholic relations of union hitherto subsisting between the civil and spiritual powers. Pius IX. took them at their word. He convened the spiritual legislature of the Church; he did not invite those who have gloried in their separation from it. This, again, sharpened the jealousy and suspicion of the governments. At this time came forth certain publications—to which I will not more explicitly refer—avowedly intended to excite the civil powers to active opposition.

About the month of September 1869, as I have already said, a document containing five questions was proposed by the Bavarian government to the Theological Faculty at Munich. No one could for a moment doubt by what hand those interrogatories also were framed: they were intended to elicit the answer, that the action of the Council, if it were to define the Infallibility of the Roman Pontiff, would be irreconcilable not only with Catholic doctrine, but with the security of civil governments. In due time the answers appeared, leaving no doubt that both the questions and the replies were inspired by one mind, if not written by one and the same hand.

We have already seen that Prince Hohenlohe, President of the Council and Minister of Foreign Affairs in Bavaria, addressed a letter to the French and other Catholic governments, calling on them to interfere and to prevent the 'fearful dangers' to which the Council would expose the modern world. Next, the Spanish Minister, Olozaga, hoped that the Council would not meet, or at least would 'not approve, sanction, or ratify the Syllabus, which is in contradiction with modern civilisation.' He then threatened the Church with the hostility of a league formed by the governments of France, Italy, Portugal, Spain, and Bavaria. An Italian infidel then took up the game and proposed an Anti-Œcumenical Council to meet at Naples. A French infidel was invited, who promised that his soul should be present, and said: 'It is an efficacious and noble idea to assemble a council of ideas to oppose to the council of dogmas. I accept it. On the one side is theocratic obstinacy, on the other the human mind. The human mind is a divine mind, its rays on the earth, its star is above. . . If I cannot go to Naples, nevertheless I shall be there. My soul will be there. I cry, Courage! and I squeeze your hand.' The reader will forgive my repeating this trash, which is here inserted only to show how the liberals and infidels of Europe rose up at the instigation of Dr. Döllinger to meet the coming Council.

About the month of June in 1869 another despatch was addressed by Prince Hohenlohe to the other governments, inviting them to make common cause against the Council. It was extensively believed to be inspired by Prussia, the policy of which was thought to be, to put in contrast the liberty accorded to its own Catholic subjects in respect of the Council with the pedantic meddling of the Bavarian government. At this time General Menabrea, under the same inspiration, addressed a circular to his diplomatic agents, proposing to the Powers to prevent the assembling of the Council, on the ground of their not having been invited to it. It was supposed at that time that this policy also was secretly supported by Berlin. A joint despatch was sent by Prince Hohenlohe and the Italian government to the French government, urging the withdrawal of the French troops from Rome during the Council, *to insure its freedom of deliberation!*

Such were the preparations to oppose the Council before it had assembled. It met on December 8th, 1869. In the following January Dr. Döllinger received the freedom of a German city in reward for his attacks on the Catholic doctrine of the prerogatives of the Holy See.

When the well-known *postulatum* of the Bishops, asking that the definition of the Papal Infallibility should be proposed to the Council, was made public, Dr. Döllinger openly assailed it; and the French Minister of Foreign Affairs, Count Daru, addressed a letter to the Holy See with a view to prevent the definition. Rome was at that time full of rumours and threats that the protection of the French army would be withdrawn. I had personally an opportunity of knowing that these threats were not mere rumours.

At the same moment while France was attacking the definition of the Pope's Infallibility, the Protestant Chancellor of Austria, Count von Beust, addressed himself to the Canons of the Schema, published in the *Augsburg Gazette*, which he declared would 'provoke deplorable conflicts between the Church and State.' Every European government from that time put a pressure more or less upon the Council to prevent the definition.

The source of this opposition, then, was Munich. The chief agent beyond all doubt was one who in his earlier days had been greatly venerated in Germany and in England. Truth compels me to ascribe to Dr. Döllinger the initiative in this deplorable attempt to coerce the Holy See and to overbear the liberty of the Bishops assembled in Council. Prince Hohenlohe is assuredly no theologian. The documents published by him came from another mind and hand. Such was the opposition before and during the Council.

What I have hitherto said to prove the conspiracy of certain European governments, and the intrigues of the Old Catholics against the Council, both before its assembling and during its sessions, would not have been needed if the *Diary of the Council* by Professor Friedrich had sooner come into my hands. I have been feeling in the dark for proofs which he brings to light by a series of astounding confessions. I had always believed in the conspiracy; but I never knew how systematic and how self-confident it was. I had always known that the Gnostic vain-glory of German scientific historians was its chief instigator; but I never before imagined the stupendous conceit or the malevolent pride of its professors. A critique of Professor Friedrich's *Diary*,[3] by some strong German hand, has appeared lately in one of our journals; and I cannot refrain from giving certain passages in final confirmation of what I have said above.

And first as to the governments. Professor Friedrich puts into the mouth of a diplomatist the following words: 'The means by which the greatest amount of influence might be brought to bear on the Council, would be a determined and plain manifestation of the public opinion of Europe in favour of the minority. Clearly the *Curia* could not prevent this; and it would add strength and numbers to the opposition, by giving it the assurance that, if at the last moment it found itself obliged to protest and appeal

[3] Appendix to *Tablet* Newspaper, Oct. 5 and 12, 1872.

to the nation, the governments and all intelligent laymen would support it. This measure would also secure weak and doubtful Bishops' (*Diary*, p. 184). On the 26th of December 1869 Friedrich wrote: 'That he was considered by many persons to be residing in Rome as the representative of an approaching schism, if the majority obtained the upper hand in the Council' (p. 41). He says in another place: 'It would not be the first time in the history of the Church that a schism had broken out. Church history recounts many such, besides that of the Greeks' (p. 196). The critic of Professor Friedrich's book writes as follows: 'The alliance between "German science" and diplomacy was not productive of all the results which at first had been looked for. Friedrich expresses himself very bitterly on this point; nevertheless he endeavoured all the more to excite German science to fresh efforts. Under date of the 27th of March (p. 202), he writes: "The governments are by degrees acting an almost ridiculous part towards the Council. First boasts; then embarrassment, connected with meaningless threats; and at last the confession that the right time has passed by, and that the *Curia* has command of the situation. If German science had not saved its position, and been able to establish a firm opposition in the Council, even in contradiction to its own will, and kept it alive; and if our Lord God had not also set stupidity and ignorance on the side of the *Curia* and of the majority—the governments would have been put to shame in the sight of the whole world. Prince Hohenlohe, in fact, is the only statesman possessed of a deeper insight in this question, and by degrees he has come to be looked upon as belonging to the minority."'

A few words must be added as to the pretensions of 'German science.'

Some years ago an address was delivered to the University of Munich, in which were found certain extravagances which were believed, at least so it was hoped, to be rhetorical phrases. It was said that the candlestick of theology had been removed from Italy, and that its place now was in Germany alone that scientific theologians hold now the office of the prophets under the old law; that it is by them that the public opinion of the Church is elaborated and formed; and that by this public opinion the doctrinal office of the Church is governed, and to it the authority of the Holy See must ultimately conform itself.

We never supposed that these dreams would pass beyond the lecture-room of a professor. But the *Diary* before us shows that these mental intoxications have been in close contact with the Vatican Council.

Professor Friedrich shall give his own account of himself. A more mournful and odious exhibition of conceit and feebleness can hardly be found. He declares himself to be the sole representative of German science at the Council (p. 329). According to page 37, until the arrival of Hefele, it was represented by him alone; the rest of the theologians 'having come to Rome without any scientific preparation, and practising theology only in a haphazard manner.' But Hefele maintained in the Council that the Council of Florence was œcumenical; on which Friedrich declared that he should be destitute of all help, and should still be the solitary theologian who alone had any scientific education. After speaking of the Bishops of the majority in terms of gross depreciation, Friedrich adds: 'And if even among this class of people some really excellent characters are to be found, ... ignorance of the history of the Church, and especially of the Councils, is a great hindrance in their path; for in these critical circumstances it is only from such sources the light can come which can guide us out of our difficulties.'

Of the Bishops of the minority he goes on to say (May 15, 1870, p. 247): 'It is often a sort of silent satisfaction to me when I hear from one person or another, after the lapse of two or three, or even more weeks, things that were derived from myself only; and which through myself alone came to the knowledge of these gentlemen. They even accept and reproduce my own ideas. They do not know, however, by whom this thing or that was put in circulation. And that is very well; for, as matters stand at present, it would cause great suspicion if it were to be discovered that anything took its origin from my witches' kitchen.' At page 318 he says: 'I am still very curious to know what part I shall one day play in an Ultramontane history of the Vatican Council.' This self-importance besets the man like a possession. At page 7 he talks of Jesuit poison. At page 61 he says the Pope himself was afraid of him. At pages 161 and 190, that he was pursued with unceasing hatred because he was a Munich professor; but at page 227 he is indignant that the Jesuit Father Schrader had no idea that he was in Rome. At page 317 he is angry with the *Univers* for the same reason. At page 318 he will not believe that the Pope had not been told that he had been in Rome a long time. But we must come to graver matter.

Friedrich says, at page 82, that in all Councils, Trent included, science formed the highest court of appeal; but at page 239 he affirms that, 'in all this the Vatican Council was entirely deficient; that theological science was wholly excluded; that therefore the Council could never be regarded as truly œcumenical.' At page 203 he says: 'Even at the time when I felt the greatest anxiety and perplexity on the subject, it was always clear to me, and I had no scruple in saying so repeatedly, that it would be *theologians exclusively who would have to decide whether the Council was œcumenical or not.* I have always felt firmly convinced that its œcumenical character would be denied; and no one must imagine that the power of theology is of as little account as it is attempted here to make it appear. The time will come, and I see it already approaching, when neither the *Index*, suspension, nor even excommunication itself, will have any effect.' He then adds: ' As for myself, I am firmly persuaded that the Holy Spirit will first constrain the Bishops by His power to make themselves capable, before they can be rendered His organ for any definition of faith. That we theologians will have to take a part in the decision of the principal question, is also equally clear to me.'

The Council of the Vatican was not convened an hour too soon. If the Gnosticism of what has well been called the Professordom of Germany had been allowed to spread its mixture of conceited illuminism and contemptuous rationalism for a few years longer, the faith of multitudes might have been irremediably lost; and Germany, which now presents the noblest fidelity and constancy in its Episcopate, in its Priesthood, and in its laity, might have been a prey to the Old Catholic schism, or to the tyrannical liberalism of those who deify the civil power.

We will now look at the events which followed the Council. It was no sooner suspended than at Munich began the 'old Catholic' schism. As a religious movement it was unworthy of notice. This even its leaders evidently felt. The exposures of Frohschammer, and the language of the *Augsburg Gazette*, showed that, as a religious movement, it was sterile, and doomed to extinction. But as a political movement it had better hopes. It was certain that all the unbelievers, all the rationalists, all the worldly, all the anti-catholic politicians, all the freemasons, all the so-called liberals, all who hate the supernatural, especially in the forms of what they call Sacerdotalism and of Ultramontanism—that is, of Christianity in its fulness of grace and of authority, would flow together into one common tide of hostility to the Vatican Council, and to the definition of the Infallibility of the Roman Pontiff. But they could not unite in a doctrinal or a religious controversy against it. Every time they met to do so, they separated in irreconcilable religious confusions. Frohschammer told them plainly that he was the only consistent 'old Catholic:' that to reject the Infallibility of the Pope, and to retain the infallibility of the Church, was to stultify themselves; that 'scientific history' either refutes both, or neither; that to hold the Council of Trent, and to reject the Council of the Vatican, was still more incoherent and unworthy of 'cultured men.' Others, again, laid down as the programme of 'old Catholicism' the rejection of the celibacy of the clergy, compulsory confession, the Immaculate Conception, and the like. This to the Tridentine 'old Catholics' was fatal. On the basis of revelation, or religion, or doctrine, no common ground was to be found. It was therefore necessary to find a common ground outside of religion. It was ready to their hand in the political animosity against Rome with which the Bavarian government had been inspired by Dr. Döllinger. As a religious movement, therefore, the 'old Catholic' schism may be considered to be at an end. Its last act has been to involve itself in the excommunication by which the Jansenists of Holland have been formally cut off from Catholic unity. The mission of the Jansenist

Archbishop of Utrecht to Munich closes this part of the history. But the true character and work of this schism is to be traced in the politics of the German Chancellor.

For some time after the closing of the war in France, it appeared that the government of Prussia was disposed to act with calm and reasonableness. Certain professors holding chairs by the nomination of the government were suspended for refusing submission to the Vatican Council. The government declared that the public law of Prussia recognised the Council of Trent; but that it had never incorporated the Council of the Vatican in the public law of the State. This was in one sense true, in another it was obviously unreasonable. The public law of Prussia recognised not Councils at any time, but the Catholic Church, and therefore whatsoever the Church, whether in or out of Council, should declare to be the Catholic faith. No such plea was set up at the time of the definition of the Immaculate Conception. If, then, the government of Prussia had said, 'Give us official knowledge of any new definitions which enter into your faith, and we will recognise them as obligations on the professors appointed by us,' it would have acted with justice, and would have shown a desire to maintain the relations of peace then existing between Prussia and the Catholic Church. But this the government did not say. It endeavoured by a high hand to maintain heretical professors as the instructors of Catholic youth: from which it may be inferred, without injustice to the Prussian government, that it desired to quarrel. This was speedily followed by the legislation which excludes the Catholic clergy from the management of schools: and this again by the nomination of Cardinal Hohenlohe as ambassador to represent Germany at the Holy See. Whether this proposal was intended to throw on the Sovereign Pontiff the odious necessity of a refusal, which to the public opinion of Europe should have the appearance of discourtesy, unreasonableness, and an implacable opposition, I will not venture to say. It is certain that Pius IX. could return no other answer. Cardinal Hohenlohe is already so united to the sovereignty of the Holy See that he could not represent any other sovereign. He is also one of the Sacred College, whose office it is to elect the Pontiff. No ambassador of any civil power can be admitted to such a trust. Every Catholic nation in the world would rise up to protest against it. Every Catholic throughout the world would be bound to denounce the attempt to introduce in the Conclave the national influence of any government. The utmost that has ever been allowed as a concession to Catholic nations, while they were faithful to the Holy See, was a *veto* upon some one member of the Sacred College whose election they supposed to be adverse to their welfare. But this veto could only be exercised before the election. The Pontiff once elected, all vetos were null. It is an historical error to say that French cardinals have been ambassadors of France at Rome. They were not ambassadors. They were only *chargés d'affaires*: and even this was an anomaly sufficiently inconvenient, and tolerated only because the crown and people of France were at that time altogether Catholic. What parity, then, is there in this respect between France and Prussia? Nevertheless, down to this stage of the controversy there was nothing on the part of the Prussian government to forbid a hope of reconciliation. It is perhaps not safe for us to speak confidently on the state of public feeling in any country except our own. And even here we know how hard it is to form a correct and adequate judgment. Nevertheless, I must venture to say, that there were abundant evidences to show that the Catholics of Germany would have accepted, some with zeal, others with passive acquiescence, the political unity of the German empire. The love of Fatherland had united them through the sufferings and losses of the war in

France. They were willing to consolidate their great victories by the unity of Germany. The differences of religion had not hindered their fighting and dying side by side; neither would this have hindered their living together in a solid political unity. Only one man could hinder this consummation: and he has hindered it. He has made it impossible in conscience for Catholics to obey. They would have been good subjects if he would have let them; but by some inexplicable policy he has refused to let them be loyal. He has forced on them the alternative of violation of conscience or opposition to his laws. We, in this country, should have thought that the history of England and of Ireland would have rendered impossible so stupendous a political error. The Catholic religion would have consolidated the civil obedience of Germany to the empire. It has been the only element which has made Ireland submissive. Religious persecution has made Ireland ungovernable even by the imperial power of England: it is the cessation of anti-catholic legislation which is slowly drawing Ireland to a willing union with Great Britain. The German Chancellor appears to be reversing this policy: and in the very moment when he has completed the political unity of his country he has opened its religious division with an intensity which can be overcome only by one of two policies. He must retrace his steps, or he must carry through in the nineteenth century a persecution which, after two hundred years of unequalled cruelty and injustice in England and in Ireland, has utterly failed, and has been abandoned as wicked and foolish. It may be that, flushed with the overthrow of Austria in the east, and of France in the west, he may contemplate the overthrow of Bavaria in the south, and that he may desire a religious quarrel as a pretext for a political and military conquest. But this is a policy which cannot last.

I have said, that, at the outset, the acts and speeches of the Chancellor of the Empire gave reason to believe that his broader intuitions, and calmer consciousness of strength, would have led him to adjust peacefully and solidly the relations of the German Empire with the Catholic Church. We were led to hope this for many reasons, among which this was one: kingcraft has become a losing trade. The governing powers of the world are weak; and the millions of all countries have become in every ten years since 1789 more and more ungovernable. The political constitutions of Europe have ceased to be commensurate to the needs of the people. The population of every European state has outgrown its institutions in number, needs, and power. The governing classes everywhere are a numerical minority, and are exposed to the odium and animosity attaching to privileged classes. They possess political ascendency, without possessing also real effective power to maintain themselves against popular animosity, or revolutionary movements. The discontented classes are in a great majority everywhere. At this crisis of European society an organisation arises in every country, united by a common aim, namely to destroy utterly the old Christian and civilised society of the world. In 1848 it challenged the aristocracies of Europe to fight for their existence. It now challenges legislatures, and authority as such, in every form, to defend itself by force, or to be swept off the face of the earth. The war in 1848 was against privileged classes. The war now is against the society of mankind; against property, nation, and family.

I shall be told that these are the utterances of madmen. That may be. But madmen can set the house on fire, and are more likely to do so than men of sound mind. We have these madmen by hundreds of thousands in all countries of Europe. When then the German race united itself into one great empire, I believe the Catholics of many countries looked on with hope and sympathy. They hoped for three results, which would have been blessings to Christian Europe. First, that a powerful empire would block the path of war between the great empires of East and West, and thereby give security for peace. Secondly, that the civil authority of Germany would be so strong as to guarantee the social order of central Europe against anti-social revolutions; and thirdly, that the peaceful and loyal Catholic populations of Germany would live securely under the shelter of a great empire, whose every interest would bind it to respect the liberty of the Catholic Church. There would, we believed, be no more contented and faithful subjects of the Emperor William than the Catholics of Germany; no more friendly and respectful well-wishers than the Catholics of almost every country in Europe.

All this has been deliberately ruined by the later policy of the Prussian government. This policy seems to be a medley made up at Munich and at Florence; a conspiracy of Janus and Cavour. The simultaneous action of the German and the Italian governments against religious education and the religious orders points to a common policy; in which, however, the German government has pre-eminence of injustice. The Italian government has indeed, at the time I am writing, seized the House of the *Gesù;* but the German government has by a legislative act expelled the Jesuits from its territory. This is an ignoble act, view it how you will. A body of men, without accusation, without evidence, without judgment, and therefore without fault; citizens invested with every civil right enjoyed by every subject of the Prussian Crown, from the Imperial Chancellor to the boatman upon the Rhine, driven into exile from home and country by a blind and passionate vote. And not the Jesuits only, but 'the Liguorian Brothers,' whosoever they may be, and 'all kindred societies,' are likewise under the ban of the empire. The Prussian government has therefore created a new crime, that is, freedom of conscience. It has tarnished the name of Emperor William with the imputation of tyrannical acts worthy of Henry VIII. But this is not all. There is no resting-place in this descent; nor any power to check the course of persecution once begun. The illusion of a free Church in a free State deceives nobody at Berlin. The banishment of the Jesuits is but a skirmish of outposts. The true battle is against the Bishops of the Church, and in them against the Church itself. To the Bishop of Ermland belongs the honour of being the first struck at in this conflict. The children of St. Thomas of

Canterbury will pray for him in his fidelity to one of the chief liberties of the Church for which our great Martyr died. It was precisely for refusing to absolve from excommunication those who were unworthy of absolution that St. Thomas won his crown. In the northern transept of his Cathedral, and at the last moment of his life, one of his murderers cried out, 'Absolve the Bishops, whom you have excommunicated.' He answered, 'I will do nothing more than I have already said and done.' This is literally the cause of the Bishop of Ermland. And for this the government pretends to inhibit him from the exercise of all episcopal acts; that is from the exercise of the authority which he has received, not from men nor by men, but from the Holy Ghost. Such is the account which has reached us. It is not indeed easy, as I have said, to know the truth in respect to foreign affairs. The inculpable blunders and the culpable misrepresentations of journalists and correspondents have reached to such a pitch that we must always speak with caution. Nevertheless, I believe what has hitherto been said to be within the truth. It was some time ago announced that if the Bishop of Ermland should refuse to withdraw the excommunication, he would be stripped of the temporalities of his See. As it is certain that not a Bishop in Germany would so prostitute his divine authority, they must be stripped of their temporalities, one by one, as occasion shall arise. It is more probable that another vote of the Reichstag will save all trouble by proclaiming a separation of the Church from the State; but when that shall come, it will not be a free Church in a free State. A power which has exiled Jesuits for no crime but their existence as Jesuits, has effaced religious liberty and freedom of conscience from the statutes of the empire. It is more likely to offer to the Church subservience as the condition of existence; that is, of a Church in bondage to a State not free; for when conscience is under the coercion of human laws, to prate of freedom is hypocrisy. The attack upon the Jesuits and kindred orders, therefore, is a transparent feint. The real attack is upon the Church. The pretence of distinguishing between Ultramontanism and Catholicism is too stale to deceive any Catholic. The Holy See is Ultramontane, the Vatican Council was Ultramontane, the whole Episcopate is Ultramontane, the whole Priesthood, the whole body of the Faithful throughout all nations, excepting only a handful here and there of rationalistic or liberal Catholics, all are Ultramontanes. Ultramontanism is Popery, and Popery is Catholicism. Even English Protestants are not to be caught with such chaff. They do not believe in a Catholic who says that he does not believe in the Infallibility of the Pope. They know that this was explicitly or implicitly contained and affirmed in the Supremacy of the Pope for which our martyrs died. They know that their fathers persecuted ours for this, which they call Popery. There is no Catholicism to attack except Ultramontanism; and it is Catholicism that is attacked now: witness the exclusion of the clergy from the schools; the maltreatment of the Bishop of Ermland, and of Mgr. Namzanowski; and finally the official threats of laws now preparing to regulate the Catholic Church in Germany. The air is full of rumours, which may be false and foolish; but they may be true. The Prussian journals tell us that by the new laws the examination of candidates for Ordination is to be held in the presence of a government commissary; that Episcopal Seminaries are to be subject to the government; that the manuals of theology are to be examined and approved by the government; that no successor to Pius IX. is to be recognised in Germany unless he consents to rescind the acts of the Vatican Council. These are not the ravings of madmen, but the deliberate threats of 'Liberals.' One mask at least is taken off. The most despotic tyranny is the Liberalism of the nineteenth century. It no longer comes to us in sheep's clothing. We see it for what it is. But do these men really believe that they will have their will? If eighteen centuries of experience are not enough, when will they at last learn that it is 'hard to kick against the goads'? They may inflict much misery, and shed much blood, and make the fair Christian civilisation of Germany like Russian Poland or Siberia; but the desolation of their Fatherland, the hatred of their own flesh and blood, with the just judgment of God, will be their only reward. Among other rumours that come to us, the two following are perhaps the most significant. An Austrian diplomatist of the highest rank is reported to have said that Italy will never be able to deal with Pius IX. until it has cut off the supplies of Peter's-pence, and forbidden the concourse of the faithful from all nations to the Vatican. This again is a revelation, precise, direct, and emphatic, of the spirit of Antichrist: 'This man doeth many miracles: if we let him alone, all men will believe in him.'[3] This also is the freedom of religion and of conscience of which modern progress is so proudly boastful. The other rumour I give as it comes to me. I have no means of testing its truth; but as it is believed in Berlin, it may as well be known

[3] S. John xi. 47, 48.

in London. It is said that Prince von Bismarck has addressed a diplomatic note to the German *chargé d'affaires* at the court of Victor Emmanuel. In it the Chancellor dwells on the impossibility of the co-existence of two sovereignties in Rome; and recommends the removal of the Pope from Italy. The *Capitale* quotes the German *National Zeitung* as saying, 'An institution like the Papacy, closely connected with the character and history of the country, cannot be disposed of by a law of guarantees, or the reduction of its real power within a narrow circle, *while it is left an unlimited sovereignty in the region of the ideal.*' That is to say, so long as the minds of men are free to believe that Christ has a Vicar upon earth, the German and Italian revolutions are baffled of their completeness. We must make penal laws against the mental freedom of men; we must persecute the inward thoughts of men; we must make faith a felony and a treason; we must erect a Liberal Inquisition to extirpate the Catholic Faith; we must encounter the Infallibility of the Church by the Infallibility of the State 'in the region of the ideal;' and make it penal to differ from the theology of the civil power. The *National Zeitung* continues: 'The last struggle between the Vatican and the Quirinal has not yet come off. . . . The

Italian government will be more or less obliged to follow in the road which the government of Germany has been treading in the last year. Germany and Italy are two creations incompatible with an infallible Papacy.'[4] That is to say, they are formally Antichristian. I commend this to any who still believe in Liberalism, or have ever been deceived by the imposture of 'a free Church in a free State.' In confirmation of what is here said, I add the judgment of a very competent writer in Germany:—

'Herr Wagener, a member of the Reichstag, and honoured by the Berlin correspondent of the *Augsburger Allgemeine Zeitung* (No. 172), as one of the most confidential intimates of Prince Bismarck, has revealed to us the full import of these events. In his speech on the 14th of June the same officious correspondent tells us that "he expressed with palpable clearness the will of the Chancellor of the Empire." "The German Empire," he remarked, "is at open war with that party which is now in power at Rome, and by this law we have put ourselves in a state of siege" (*Sten. Rep.* 1,009). A similar character is assigned by another exasperated antagonist of the order, Dr. Volk, to the course of action set on foot by the law against the Jesuits. " This question is a contest be-

[4] *Tablet*, Aug. 31, 1872, p. 259.

tween the Roman Catholic Church, subdued as it has been by the Jesuits, and the German Empire. Such is properly the fight in which we are engaged" (*Sten. Rep.* 1,022). The well-known canonist of the court, Dr. Dore, also spoke of the war between the Pope and the German Empire. The tone of the press is still more explicit. Its constant strain is: "Down with Catholicism!"

'Wagener's expressions were taken up by the members of the Centre as a declaration of war. "The deputy Herr Wagener," replied Windthorst, "has intimated to us repeatedly and in the most unmeasured terms that he and his—' *We*' (the party of Bismarck)—are bent on war to the knife with us, the representatives of the greatest part of the Catholic people. Gentlemen, the Catholics of Germany do not wish for a war, they wish to live in peace. If you will not allow them to do so, if you wish to declare war against them in such a brutal manner—well! you shall have it, since we are forced to defend ourselves with all the energy we can" (*Sten. Rep.* 1,013). Then the orators of both sides declared, one after the other, "The war has begun."

'We have, therefore, the most interesting spectacle—a war between the two greatest powers of the

Continent, between the most powerful State and its greatest Church; and the most important action that has occurred till now has been the debate on the law against the Jesuits. Although it has been said at different times during the debates that the assailants did not wish to fight against the Church, but only against that party which is now dominant at Rome and in the Church, it comes in the end to the same. Did not Prussia also say in the beginning of the French war that she did not march against the French people, but against its ruler? It would seem that in Germany the attack is not aimed against the Jesuits only. "The law against the Jesuits," said its proposer, Dr. Mayer, "is but the taking up of our *first* position in this war" (*Sten. Rep.* 1,063). Other measures have already been taken against the Catholic Episcopate and clergy, or are prepared for the future. At Berlin they already are turning their thoughts to the question of the next Conclave, in order to secure a pliable Pope, who may allow the foundation of national churches. For, according to the view of one of the principal counsellors of the government, Dr. Gneist, interference with the jurisdiction of the State is "inseparable from the essence of a Universal Church;" religious peace is endangered by "the immutable position of the Universal Church, and peace is here only possible by an appeal to the majesty of the State" (*Ibid.* 422-423).

'The gravity of the struggle against this character of the Catholic Church has not been under-estimated in the Reichstag. Wagener himself, who so courageously gave the signal for the combat, confessed "that the expeditions against Rome in matters spiritual to which we now are called, are attended with as much danger as were military operations against Rome in the middle ages" (*Ibid.* 382). "For my part," exclaimed another exasperated enemy of the Jesuits, "I have entered upon this contest with feelings of reluctance; since I see that it will be the cause of involving the consciences of many in conflicts which I should regret" (1,079). Moreover the Prussian Court canonist, Dr. Dore, said, "The combat upon which we are entering is one of greater difficulty than attended the conquest of France; the way is dangerous and long" (1,130). But the unprecedented victories of Prussia in the French war fill him with hope of the good success of this undertaking also: "This German people," he exclaimed, amidst the loud applause of the house, "will vanquish the Jesuits and the Vatican, as it has vanquished Paris" (1,130).

'I cannot for my part share in this sanguine hope of victory. I rather believe that Prussia will not gain in this war with the Vatican the same laurels which she has wrung from France. The war against France was the occasion of the union of the German nation, and it is only to this united action of Catholics and Protestants that the conquest of Paris is to be ascribed. The war against the Vatican will disunite the nation, and will rend asunder its most intimate links. Such discord is not a pledge of triumph; it is an ominous sign of the downfall of the Empire. I am still more confirmed in this opinion when I consider attentively the success which the government hitherto has obtained in the first skirmishes of this campaign. Has, it may be asked, the protection of the Old Catholics by Berlin secured a victory for that party, or even prevented its great pretensions from coming to naught? Has not the government been obliged in the Braunsberg affair (in which it wished to force the Catholic pupils to listen to religious instructions from a priest who has been declared a heretic and excommunicated) to cease from insisting on this exaction as too signally violating liberty of conscience? Has that despicable pulpit-law at all diminished the influence of the clergy in elections? or has it not rather exasperated this already powerful section of Catholic Germany against the government, and made them act with greater caution, but with more success, in this matter? Did not the government, on the 1st of July, quickly pay the salary to the unyielding Bishop of Ermland, although he had been frequently threatened with its withdrawal? But the greatest miscarriage seems to have happened in the proceedings against the Catholic military chaplains, the treatment of whom has been the occasion of introducing religious discord even in that army otherwise so celebrated for its union. Moreover, I doubt very much whether the government will have better success with the present law against the Jesuits. "This measure," said Dr. Lasker, the leader of the national Liberals, a man otherwise much attached to the policy of Bismarck, "is not calculated to reconcile hearts, but rather to farther estrange them." "It is," as another notable speaker, Dr. Reichensperger, said, "a declaration of bankruptcy from modern Liberalism" (1,131). So much does this law belie the principles at other times so highly extolled by Liberalism. Therefore it has been received by the press with coolness and even with contempt; with the exception, of course, of numerous officious correspondents of such newspapers as, being bought over into complete subjection by the immense amount of money freely dispensed by Prince Bismarck, continually distract the public opinion of Germany. At Berlin itself the social democratic party — in other things very hostile to religion — has held a large meeting against this law. But, after all, even the defenders of the law themselves could not deny its preposterousness; they tried to excuse it on the plea of extreme need in the urgency of the straits to which the Society of Jesus has brought the German Empire. A marvellous confession! The German Empire,—defended by a million of bayonets, and with a legion of secret and public policemen at its disposal; celebrated, sung, and idolised only a few days ago by an innumerable crowd of panegyrists as the first Power of the world,—reduced to straits by two hundred defenceless priests! The home of intelligence, with innumerable schools for the people under its inspection, with so many celebrated universities and colleges, and a great number of other scientific establishments; backed in its contest against the "Ultramontanes" by almost the whole press and even the theatre—brought to straits by the learning of two hundred men, who have not a single school in Prussia and Southern Germany! Indeed, it is too much to ask a stranger to believe it without evidence; if anywhere, surely here, he must lay claim to the right of examining.'⁵

The following summary of the utterances of the German newspapers and political writers, carefully made by a very competent hand, is too valuable to be omitted. I therefore insert it as it stands. One thing is worthy of remark, namely, that the true character of Liberalism is a hypocritical pretence of fairness while it is weak, and an insolent tyranny when it is strong :—

'What it is necessary above all things to bear in mind in considering the action of the Prussian government, what arises incontrovertibly from the review of the situation, is, that the attacks on the Catholic Church are not isolated acts of hostility, such as have frequently occurred under un-catholic auspices, but stages in a deliberate *plan of operations* designed thoroughly to stamp - out Catholic Christianity in Germany and in the world. Of course this implies, and by the Freemasons is meant to imply, the extinction of Christianity itself. It is needless, however, to go beyond the *avowed* designs of the Prussian government. As the *Allgemeine Zeitung* of Augsburg wrote on the 30th of

⁵ Special Correspondent of the *Tablet*, from Germany, Aug. 10, 1872.

June, "Whereas the State is the lawful organisation of the community, it is impossible that it can abandon the definition of 'the independence of the Church' to any ecclesiastical party. *Religion is exhibiting itself anew as too great a power to be classed among the private predilections of individuals.* . . . In this sphere, accordingly, people are anxiously looking for an ecclesiastical—Bismarck." In other words, the civil power is to define the relations of Church and State, and to dictate to men what to believe and what to think. It is to be supreme over intellect and conscience. We are not, however, left to conjectures to understand the policy which is to be applied to the Church. The leading organs of all the anti-catholic parties, in other words, the mouthpieces and representatives of the Reichstag majority, have openly explained the procedure which is to make the Catholic Church of the future reverence, as an old Pagan would say, "the Divinity of the Emperors." The *Allgemeine Zeitung*, the *National Zeitung*, the *Spenersche Zeitung*, and similar journals, are weekly and daily engaged in developing the plan and spreading the knowledge of the necessary steps among the anti-catholic populations who are to support the measures of the government. Nor does it detract from the importance of these journals, that, though some of them are not the government, they are the masters of the government. They are, in a word, the so-called national Liberal party or *intolerant Germanism and intolerant Liberalism combined*. Every measure they have demanded up to the present has been accorded. They have favoured Döllingerism. They have suppressed the separate department for Catholic affairs. They have banished the Jesuits. It is only rational to suppose that they are as likely to have their own way in the future as in the past. Their declarations of a policy may, accordingly, be taken as authoritative declarations. Knowing what they design, we know what the Catholics have to expect.

'The Berlin correspondent of the *Allgemeine Zeitung* writes on the 18th of July, to say that the forthcoming law to regulate the relations of the State and the Catholic Church is being prepared with the utmost zeal. Among the provisions are regulations by which "all Catholic Bishops and Catholic professors of theology are to be required to sign engagements binding them to a definitely formulated line of conduct" towards the State. "*Every refusal will entail exclusion from the Episcopacy and the professoriate.*" " The seminaries are to be withdrawn from episcopal supervision and made dependent on the approbation of the State." "The teachers and the taught in the ecclesistical seminaries are to be alike subjected to examination by government commissioners." The reason of these provisions had been previously set forth in the *Allgemeine Zeitung* of the 7th of July, in an article on *die Bildung des Geistlichen.* "The prohibition of the Order of Jesus is an important sign that the German Empire is taking up position against the enemy. *It will be of little use, however, unless more positive measures follow.*" "What need is there for Jesuit colleges in Bavaria, when in neighbouring Innspruck there is a theological faculty of Jesuits, when the young clerics can get schooled there or in Jesuit colleges at Rome, and when Jesuit manuals of dogmatic and moral theology lord it over the ecclesiastical seminaries of Germany?" It is thus already avowed that the legislation which pretended to attack the Jesuits alone, cannot stop short there.

'It is in the following terms that the *Spenersche Zeitung* of the 25th of July recommends the deprivation of the Bishop of Ermland. Such a measure it says will produce hardly any public inconvenience. It is true that the priests appointed by a Bishop repudiated by the State will have no more legal status than their diocesan. The marriages performed by such priests will have no civil consequences. "But temporarily couples can be married by priests in the neighbourhood. *Finally, the difficulty must be met by civil marriage*, whether by the action of the Landtag or the Reichstag."

'The Berlin correspondent of the *Allgemeine Zeitung*, writing on the 21st of July, reports with satisfaction that the army will not be neglected in the struggle against the Church. "The military authorities are acting with like resolution against the military chaplains who refuse to submit themselves unconditionally to the orders of the Minister of War, by distinguishing between military and spiritual obedience. There cannot be a doubt that this resolution will result in *the total suppression of Catholic chaplaincies in the army*."

'A very important series of articles in the *Allgemeine Zeitung* of the 24th, 25th, and 26th of July, entitled *Zur religiösen Einigung der deutschen Nation*, is devoted to the double thesis that the Catholic Church is the mortal foe of Germany, and that every nation has a religious development suitable to itself. "To-day it is not on the border and in weaponed hosts that the enemies of the Fatherland stand. In the very midst of us have they risen, some with audacious forehead opposing the will of the whole nation, some with secret cunning creeping about from congregation to congregation and from city to city. . . . That this is so requires no proof; we all know it. . . . The only question is, how to master these enemies. . . . Let us only consider our own people, leaving out of consideration foreign peoples and the forms which the Christian religion has assumed in them. . . . . Let the representatives of the Romish Church ignore deep national distinctions, as the Romish Church has affected to ignore them for centuries: the German nation will not allow itself to be deceived; it will rather take up the combat against its nearest and most dangerous enemies, against anti-national hierarchy, against anti-national hypocrisy, against international superstition and intolerance, against anti-national lies and cozening, against anti-national Rome with all its champions, partisans, and train-bearers, Catholic and Protestant." After this mild introduction, the *Allgemeine Zeitung* proceeds to observe that "sufficiently long" has Germany endured the moving spectacle of "science and art, trade and industry, and all our modern State-life being cried down as the enemy of religion and the work of Satan;" and accordingly the *Allgemeine Zeitung* is of opinion that a wider, and higher, and nobler, and broader, and deeper Christianity is required, which is to achieve the desirable end of "embracing everything," and which the great, deep, broad, and in all things noble German nation is to proceed to substitute for the falsified Christianity of Rome. The *Allgemeine Zeitung* explains how this is to be done. "*Above all things is it necessary to deny now and for ever, resolutely and once for all, the pretension of the Hierarchy to be an intermediary between God and us.*" In the second place, the "Priesterthum," which has been so powerful a support of the Hierarchy, must get the same treatment. "This edifice, this fortress of the Romish Hierarchy must we keep in view, must we with the weapons which have been given to us storm and destroy down to the very ground (*von Grund-aus zerstören*), &c."

'The precise manner in which the Catholic Church is to be "stormed and destroyed down to the very ground" has recently been explained in the semi-official *Jahrbuch für Gesetzgebung, Verwaltung und Rechtspflege im Deutschen Reich*, in a special treatise entitled *Das Deutsche Reich und die Katholische Kirche*, from the pen of the distinguished Dr. Friedberg of Leipsig, who enjoys the reputation of being an "aide-de-camp of Bismarck," and who possesses the very highest kind of influence among the so-called national Liberals. The object of this important treatise is declared to be, "to make clear the principle and the present relation of the modern State and the modern Catholic Church;" and to show how it has become "the duty of every statesman to take position in the great struggle upon which the German Empire has entered, and whose leading issues the present generation seems called to decide." The modern State being declared to be based "on the principle of free individuality," Herr Friedberg continues, "therefore it follows that the teaching of the Catholic Church and the conception of the modern State are absolutely irreconcilable (*absolut unvereinbar sind*). To-day must we say out the dreadful word: *so long as the Roman Catholic Church upholds the traditions of the Middle Ages and rejects every pacification with the modern State and modern civilisation, so long is a peaceable union between the State and the Catholic Church not to be looked for, and so long must the Catholic Church be regarded as an institution dangerous to the State.*" Herr Friedberg makes the following suggestive observations on the Jesuit controversy. "It is true that during the Jesuit debate in the last session of the German Reichstag, not only a number of deputies, but even the President of the Federal chancery, declared that in the war against the Jesuits there was no thought of war against the Catholic Church. *We are unable, however, to view the measures against the Jesuits as a terminus in the struggle of the modern State against the Catholic Church. . . . .* Can there be a more striking proof than that the Catholic Church of the present is completely identified with the Jesuit Order? Terribly grave though the saying be, we must say it out: *the nowaday Jesuit Ultramontane Roman Catholic Church is dangerous to the State* (staatsgefährlich)." Herr Friedberg makes the following confession about Döllingerism. "The Old Catholic movement, generated by the opposition to the dogma of Infallibility, seemed at first to be about to take enormous dimensions, and enjoyed the favour of the governments." Unfortunately Herr Friedberg must add, "*the Old Catholic movement did not attain the hoped-for significance.*" But though Döllingerism has failed, none the less has it become inevitable that "the State cannot retire from a violent struggle (*heftigem Kampfe*) with the Catholic Church. It is true that, as Herr Windthorst declared in the course of the Jesuit debate, the principles of the Vatican Council are already contained in the Bull *Unam Sanctam* of

Boniface VIII. *But these old assertions of Papal omnipotence have become in our day eminently dangerous to the State."* The national Liberals have thus given up their first pretence that the Vatican decrees were innovations; but openly declare that the absence of the original pretence will not make them desist from this war against the Church. The next portion of Herr Friedberg's treatise contains the whole plan of campaign against the Catholic ecclesiastical and religious system. He asks the two questions: how is the State to guard itself against the Church? and whether is the proposed legislation to be the work of the Empire or the different governments of Germany?

'In the first place, the State is to proceed against the Church, "by drawing a firm boundary-line between it and the Church, and by guarding its dominion from every ecclesiastical influence. By this is to be understood (1) the introduction of compulsory civil marriage; (2) the abolition of the obligation of baptism, *Taufzwang;* (3) the separation of Church and school; (4) the secularisation of the care of the poor, *Armenpflege*. Moreover, the State must have (5) a penal law to prevent the misuse of the clerical office; and farther, the State must take care (6) that no persons enter the pulpit, who are of a disposition hostile to the State: that is to say, the State must control the education of the clergy, who, even when the school shall be taken from them, will remain in an eminent degree the teachers of the people; the State must overlook the examination of the clergy, and must suffer no clergyman to be appointed who meditates civil or political opposition to the government, *welcher der Regierung in bürgerlicher oder politischer Beziehung Anstoss bereitet.* The State must (7) supervise the management of the Church property. The State must not (8) allow ecclesiastical penalties to produce civil consequences, and especially must prevent ecclesiastical penalties from being used to exercise a pressure on State officials. The State must (9) require every ecclesiastical regulation (*jede kirchliche Verordnung*) to be submitted to it; and must (10) make the existence of every religious order dependent on its approval; and must not (11) endure the Order of the Jesuits. Finally, (12) the State must have an effective remedy against misuse of the clerical office, which may hinder every encroachment on the part of the Church, by fines that will be felt, coupled with removal from the clerical office, so as to produce *a salutary system of deterrence by fear* (*ein heilsames Abschreckungssystem*)."

'Such is the system which the author recommends for the Church.

'With regard to whether this system is to be the work of the Reichstag or the local parliaments, Herr Friedberg naturally concludes in favour of the *Reichstag*. What makes Herr Friedberg's treatise so important is, that it is really meant, and has been accepted as the legislative manual of the national Liberals. In the words of the *Allgemeine Zeitung*, "whoever wishes to see clearly in these questions and to be able to give a well-founded vote, should take in hand this treatise, which has been published in a separate form, and make it the subject of careful perusal."

'But indeed the German authorities are hardly waiting for the full and perfect legislation which the *Jahrbuch für Gesetzgebung* inculcates. Thus the authorities in Schleswig-Holstein have addressed a circular to the *Landräthe*, explaining the scope of the words "kindred congregations" in the ukase against the Jesuits. The explanation makes it evident that the design of the government is absolutely to prevent the exercise of every function which is not actually sacramental. Catholicity is to be locked up in its churches, while anti-catholicity is to be put in possession of everything else, preparatory to putting it in possession of the churches also. The authorities, accordingly, instruct the subordinates that every congregation is to be considered affiliated to the Jesuits, and consequently prohibited, which is under the direction of a foreign superior; it is added, with unlimited power, and independent of the Bishop of the diocese; which is under the duty of passive obedience to the rules of the Order; or, finally, which pursues a Jesuitical aim, such as missions among the people or among Protestants, 'pædagogic action,' and so forth. Tried by these tests, the authorities have ascertained the Jesuitical character of the Redemptorists, the Brothers of the Christian Doctrine, the missionary priests of the Congregation of St. Vincent de Paul, the Barnabites, the Theatines, as well as the Redemptorist nuns, and the nuns of the Sacred Heart.

'Nor is it to be supposed that the national Liberals intend to content themselves with banishing, or reducing to servitude, the priests and Bishops of the Church. The laity are also to be taught to feel that that alone is legal of which national Liberalism approves, and that alone is right which Freemasonry practises. The lay societies of Catholics for the defence of Catholic interests are threatened as follows in the *Spenersche Zeitung*: "An association of German Catholics has been established at Mayence, and has published its statutes, as well as a protestation and an appeal to the Catholics of Germany. In brief, *this association designs to supply by a new organisation the want of the political Propaganda, at present paralysed, of the Order of the Jesuits* . . . *The absolutely illegal character which distinguishes it* is manifested above all in the protestation it has published against the decisions of the Parliament, but in reality against the three supreme authorities of the Empire. *These counts and barons, transformed into agitators, are only distinguishable from Karl Marx in that their fanaticism makes them much more impudent* . . . . But the German Empire and its members will bo under the duty of watching the proceedings of this new Jesuitical organisation, and of applying the laws concerning the abuses committed by associations."

'At the same time, the most ordinary liberty of the press is more than threatened; and following fast on the numerous seizures and suppressions of Catholic journals, the *Spenersche Zeitung* openly writes: "While the present clerical agitation aims, by the foundation of Catholic unions and the like, to bring upon the Landtag a new flood of petitions and resolutions upon the oppression of the Catholic Church, *the government is also busy collecting ma-*

terials in order to restrain the activity of the Catholic Bishops in Prussia, especially in the matter of furthering newspapers of an Ultramontane character, and consequently hostile to the Empire."

'When we see, in addition, all the leading journals of the German Empire, like the *Provinzial Correspondenz*, insisting on the necessity of the Pope being the nominee of the Secular Powers, and the *National Zeitung* warning Italy that the way to put an end to an institution like the Papacy is, not by "according it a boundless domination in the sphere of the ideal," and that "*Germany and Italy are two creations incompatible with the Infallible Papacy,*" it is easy to recognise the comprehensive plan of this systematic campaign against the Church. In a word, the German Empire desires to destroy the Church "in its head and its members," and will attempt the satisfaction of this desire to the utmost extent of German ability.'

Such, then, is the present attitude of Germany. The great Empire in the pride of its strength is confronting a greater Empire, 'of whose kingdom there shall be no end;' a rash and perilous conflict, in which no human power yet has obtained victory or glory.

Those who a year ago were well content, and even

hoped, to see the consolidation of a strong and peaceful German Empire, are now no longer able to desire it. They believe that its master-builder has undone the work of his own hands. The political unification of Prussia, Bavaria, Würtemberg, Saxony, and other states, with the strong repulsions, antipathies, and jealousies which have hitherto held them asunder, and have been at last suspended only by the war of France against the Fatherland of their common race; this work was in itself arduous and difficult in the extreme. It was enough for the undivided powers even of Prince von Bismarck. But with this already at stake, what spirit of evil counsel should have misguided him to reopen the religious division of Germany, and to rekindle the memories of the thirty-years' war, it is not easy to divine. I have indeed heard his admirers say that the imperial Chancellor has counted the full cost, and is prepared to wage this war to the bitter end; that the subjugation of the Catholic Church is essential to his imperial policy; that the unity of Germany must be consolidated even upon the stones of the altar. There is much wild talk in the wind. One day we are told that Germany is to be detached from Rome, and a national German Church erected. Another day, that Germany is already engaged in measures to control the Conclave in the election of the next Pontiff. But the age of national churches is at an end. England has tried its hand at this experiment in Ireland, and has pulled down its own work. It has tried it also in England, but its most cherished work is pulling itself down to the ground. King William of Prussia tried it also in the fusion of Lutheranism and Calvinism in the Evangelical Church, which is now doomed to dissolution. National schisms from Catholic unity were possible when nations and governments were Catholic. There is now neither a Catholic government nor a Catholic nation. There is now no national Church in existence. The Established Church of England does not contain half the English people. No scheme of national religion could satisfy and embrace the whole. Every scheme of comprehension would cause new defections. Even the non-catholic peoples of Europe reject secular legislation, and government-meddling in religion. What infatuation, then, can have deceived men into dreaming that Catholics can be seduced or persecuted into a national Church? The civil powers of Europe in separating themselves from the unity of the Church, and opposing themselves to the Holy See, have for ever lost all action upon the conscience of their Catholic subjects. The Prussian government by its opposition to the Œcumenical Council, by its expulsion of the Jesuits and other religious, and by its menace of coercion against the Bishop of Ermland, has roused in Germany an opposition against which the whole weight of the German Empire is powerless. Any attempt to separate the Catholic Church in Germany from the Holy See would have two direct consequences. It would throw it more completely upon Rome as its only centre; and it would purify the Church in Germany of a multitude of faithless Catholics like those who in the Reichstag revealed their unbelief; of a multitude of Gnostics, such as those who liken the German professors to the Prophets of the Old Testament; of a multitude of worldly men who by their politics and their patronage have infected the Catholic spirit of many in Germany. This sifting is not far off. Men forget in the midst of their tumults that there standeth One among them whom they know not, 'whose fan is in His hand, and He will thoroughly purge His floor.'[6] We have, therefore, no fear of national churches or of German patriarchates. What was imposssible in the reign of Frederick II. is more than ever out of all human power now. Whosoever shall attempt it will be broken upon the Rock which cannot be moved; and the fidelity of the

[6] S. Matt. iii. 12.

Church in Germany will be tested and revealed as the gold is tried in the fire. It is strange how the highest intellects in politics become suddenly blind when they deal with the Catholic Church. They seem never to learn, that when the civil power attempts to coerce the Church, it throws it more and more intimately upon the centre and source of all spiritual freedom. The Council of the Vatican did indeed extinguish Gallicanism as a theological error; but it was chiefly the revolution of 1830, and the separation of the Church from the State, which expelled Gallicanism from the pastors and people of France. Already the policy of Berlin has united German Catholics with a sevenfold closeness of fidelity to Rome. It has also compacted the Church in Germany into a solid unity of resistance which revives the memory of forty years ago. Once more the Archbishop of Cologne, with the whole Episcopate of Germany assembled at the tomb of St. Boniface, has published to the world a defence of the liberties of the Church which will be re-echoed in all the world. The laity also of Germany the other day met in Cologne, and with one voice made a noble protest against these violations of conscience and of liberty on the part of the civil power.

As to the other part of the programme—the

manipulation of the Conclave—I have not a doubt that the influence of Prussia will be most powerfully felt by the Sacred College. I can conceive nothing more certain to close, not only the doors of the Conclave, but the minds of Cardinal Electors, against all insinuations and all threats. The insolence of pamphleteers and journalists—for I cannot conceive that any statesman can have so far forgotten himself—has already roused them to a vigilance which will baffle all intrigue. Neither Italy nor Germany, but the Holy Ghost will elect the successor of Pius the Ninth, happily reigning, and in the vigour of old age outliving, one by one, those who have wronged and betrayed him.

But while we are intently watching the attitude of these two great antagonists, a change has passed upon the whole face of Europe. Hitherto the world has known two great powers, Civil and Spiritual, or the State and the Church. Their contests make up the greater part of the history of the world. But this duel is nearly at an end. A third power has arisen, which is at war with both. For generations there has been accumulating in every European country a multitude who are neither reached by the beneficent legislation of the State nor won by the spiritual action of the Church. They may now be counted by millions. They are the raw material of sedition and irreligion, of conspiracies, revolutions, and communes. Society has done little for them; religion they have cast off. They have therefore grown up outside of the social order of states and the communion of religious bodies, with hard labour and scanty food, with little education, and without faith. The inheritance made for them is one of privation. Their experience of society is of a power which exacts labour, and inflicts punishment. Their experience of religion is of restraints without intelligible reason, and of catechisms which they cannot understand. What wonder if they become anti-social and anti-christian? This state becomes a bitter heirloom to their children; and now for centuries millions have been born into it in almost every European country. They have common griefs, common sufferings, common resentments, common antipathies, common sympathies; the bonds of a common humanity, deprived of the culture and of the benefits of civilisation, bind them together in every nation, and thus bind in one the suffering and the dangerous classes of all nations. The International is not a creation of Carl Marx or of Vesinier. It is a growth in the wilderness of man which the State has not cultivated, and the Church has laboured in vain to reclaim. But creation or growth, the International exists, and in every ten years attains extension, solidity, and organised unity of power. This has been the work of the secret political societies, which from 1789 to this day have been perfecting their formation, and in the last six or seven years have drawn closer together in mutual alliance and co-operation. In 1848 they were sufficiently powerful to threaten almost every capital in Europe by a simultaneous rising. In 1871 they obtained their greatest momentary success in Paris. The International is now a power in the midst of the Christian and civilised world, pledged to the destruction of Christianity and the old civilisation of Europe. It has just now held its Congress at the Hague.[7] It is the antagonist of both the natural and the supernatural order. It denies God, law, property, the family, the relations of parent and child, the continuous life of nations, the natural authority of human society. I will not say that this is the ὁ ἄνομος, the lawless one of St. Paul; but assuredly the world has never seen anything so like it. Hitherto all forms

[7] The division of the International into the political and economical, and the general and sectional moieties, may for a time retard its action; but these sections will easily coalesce again on any occasion. Much unwise confidence has been inspired by this internal division.

of evil have been parasites of the Christian world. The International is a new creation or upgrowth from beneath, which cannot coexist with the Christian society of mankind. Its mission is to destroy it utterly: if need be, by fire.

What Mahometanism was in its day, the International is now; but in this far more formidable than Mahometanism: it is within the Christian world, mingled with it everywhere, within all its lines, behind all its defences, cognisant of all its movements, accurately informed of its strength and its weakness. It shares all its resources, all its communications, all its social influences. The Church thoroughly knows its existence, and tracks its operations. The governments, with an incredible infatuation, long refused to believe in its action, and even in its existence. The International desires nothing better. It acts upon the public opinion and upon the governments of Europe without revealing itself. It is invisible and impalpable, but ever active, kindling strife between the people and their rulers, between government and government, and, above all, between governments and the Catholic Church. So long as the civil and spiritual powers of the world are united, anarchy and lawlessness have no opportunity. When these two powers, divinely created for the peace and stability of the world, are in conflict, and in proportion as they weaken each other, disorder has its hour of hope. It has no need to assail either, so long as it can compel both to destroy one another. Such is the conflict now rising in Germany. The 'Old Catholic' heresy could never have prevailed to launch the Prussian government upon a policy fatal to the German Empire, if a mightier power, vowed to its destruction, had not driven both the political parties in Germany into a frenzy of suspicion and of fear. Strange spectacle—a mighty military empire, in self-defence, driving a handful of helpless scholars into exile, and turning pale with fear at a quotation from the fourth chapter of the book of Daniel. Stranger recognition of the power of spiritual authority over all material might! No weapons can prevail over a solitary truth; and no truth fails to avenge itself on those who strive against it. Already these acts of injustice and violence have produced in Germany a reaction which cannot long be disregarded. From two distinct sources, most diverse in character and race, though both German, and wholly unknown to each other—the one an Ultramontane Catholic, the other an advanced Free-thought Protestant—I received the same judgment as to the consequences of the present policy. Both alike foretold the complete dissolution of the Evangelical state religion in Prussia, and finally of dogmatic Lutheranism. The withdrawal of the State from all religious communions will throw them upon their own centre and their own resources. There is but one which, in its origin, began the world all alone; has endured all that man could do against it; has overcome all human power; and can survive and renew itself after all spoliation and all persecution. All else must return to the dust out of which it came. The disestablishment of Protestantism in Germany, like the disestablishment of Protestantism in Ireland, will close a chapter in the history of human error.

It may well be asked, What has wrought this change in Germany? A year ago, the Catholics in Germany were returning with victory and with joy to their Fatherland, many exulting, and others at least acquiescing, in the German Empire. With them returned also the Catholic chaplains and the sisters who, in the soldiers' hospitals and on the fields of battle, had exposed their lives with the armies of their country. The laws of Prussia were then sternly just to both Catholic and Protestant alike; and both the Catholic clergy and the ministers of the Protestant communions were loyal and contented subjects. What, then, has changed peace into conflict? I must believe it to be chiefly the work of one man, who, first poisoning the mind of his own government, has ended in poisoning the other governments of Germany. Like all leaders of revolt against the authority of the Church of God, he has invoked the powers of human rulers to avenge his griefs. Henceforth his name, once venerated in the Church, will go down to history as the instigator of persecution against the faith of Jesus Christ, and as the Achitophel who cast the seeds of dissolution into the first foundation of the German Empire.

History seems for some men to be written in vain; and the lessons of experience seldom outlive the first generation of those whom suffering has made wise. The governments of Naples, Vienna, France, and Spain, in the last century, wrested from Clement XIV. the suppression of the Jesuits. In less than a generation the armies of revolutionary France scourged and overthrew every one of these dynasties. At this moment Italy and Germany are beginning once again the same policy of violence, and there is in the midst of them a Nemesis with its iron scourge, and lips compressed in silence, waiting for its hour to strike. That avenging power is no angel of justice tempered with mercy, but man without God, pledged to destroy the Christian and civilised order of the world, and to strike down, on either hand, both Churches and States.

This grave and ominous conflict has however been relieved by one amusing episode. Certain estimable members of the two Houses of Parliament, together with a Protestant Archbishop, and a President and other members of some Free Church bodies in England, borrowing the graceful custom of German students, serenaded the Imperial Chancellor on the expulsion of the Jesuits without trial or fault, and on the penal laws projected against Catholics, to the well-known air of 'Civil and Religious Liberty.' The Chancellor from above answered with a gravity and elevation proportionate rather to the Reichstag than to so youthful an indiscretion. From this frolic, however, we may gather what our 'friends of religious liberty' would do in these kingdoms if they could. But the public opinion of England is too just and calm, and has not followed them in applauding the penal laws of Germany.

But we are told that all this is the fruit of the Vatican decrees. The Council has introduced, it is said, a new religion, changed the relations of the spiritual and civil powers, turned the Syllabus into dogma of faith, and invested the Pope with omniscience. Do men really believe what they say? or is all this written and said only to create odium, suspicion, and hostility? But, to let all this cant and rubbish pass, I am ready to admit that the Vatican Council and the Definition of Infallibility have been the occasion of the conspiracies of Janus, and the political intrigues of the Old Catholics. The woes denounced by our Divine Master against the Pharisees, Sadducees, and Herodians, at His last visit to the Temple, were the last rebuke that stung them to compass His death. In like manner, no doubt, the inflexibility of the Council and the Definition of the Infallibility stung those who were thereby baffled and defeated to avenge themselves. But they who steadfastly urged onward the Definition to its completion were well forewarned. They were threatened, week after week, with the withdrawal of the French protection, and with the approach of revolutionary hordes. They knew the alternative to lie between any extreme of temporal persecution and the compromise of a doctrine of revelation. The very imminence of the dangers revealed the necessity of proclaiming the truth. The divine authority of the Church throughout the world, the divine certainty of all faith were at stake. Even though it should cost the usurpation of Rome, or a century of persecution, the Council could not waver in its office as

g

the Witness, Judge, and Teacher of the truth as it is in Jesus. Therefore, though kingdoms and empires combine to persecute, necessity was laid upon the Bishops of the whole world to declare a truth, vital at all times; more than ever vital now, because never so insolently denied. The storm it has evoked is the test and the measure of the need. If the Vatican Council had to be convened to-morrow, with the usurpation of Rome and the persecution of Germany before its eyes, all the more would it promulgate to the world the divine institution of the Holy See, the supreme jurisdiction and infallible assistance given to Peter, and in Peter to his successors for ever. We are told also that the Church by the Syllabus and by the Definition has separated itself by an impassable chasm from the Christian religion and the thought of man. If the Syllabus and the Definition be false, this would be certainly true; but what if they be true? It is strange that acute reasoners do not see how this is to beg the question. What if the Syllabus and the Definition be the true application of Christianity to the moral, political, and spiritual errors of human society? Then there is no chasm between them and the Christian religion, but an union even to identity. And as for the thought of man, it is thereby convicted of aberration. The Word of God teaches us a truer estimate of the thought of man. They 'have become vain in their thoughts.'[8] The thought of man is normal only when conformed to the Word of God. And here we have the same *petitio principii* over again. In truth, men have made up their mind that the Catholic Church is a troubler of the world and a teacher of falsehood. It is manifest that either the Church or the world has gone wrong. *Aut mundus errat, aut Christus frustra mortuus est.* If, indeed, the thought of the world be the rule of faith, we may be forgiven for rejecting it. The universal and ever-multiplying confusions both moral and intellectual outside the unity of the Catholic Church, the rapid progress of unbelief, the irresistible advance of speculative and practical atheism, demonstrate that the unassisted thought of man is not the witness, or the judge, or the teacher of the Christian Revelation. But no serious or grave man would deny this; and if not, why contend against the Holy See for resolving its rule of faith into the witness, and judgment, and teaching of the Universal Church, assisted by the Spirit of Truth, and infallibly enunciated by the voice of its Head? Such is the Definition. And in what does it bar the progress of human thought? Truth

[8] Rom. i. 21.

bars the way to error; every known truth closes some path to falsehood; but every truth is also progress to the thought of man. The revelation of Christianity was the largest, noblest, highest progress ever made by the reason of mankind. The infallible certainty of faith, by guaranteeing the human reason from aberration and from retrogression, guarantees for ever the progress of Christian and human thought in the knowledge of God and of man.

Where, then, is the judge who shall decide which has erred, the Church or the world? If the Church has erred, 'Woe to the world because of scandals.'[9] There is no salvation left for it. But a church that errs is not the Church of God; for if it errs, it cannot be God's witness to mankind. But if God so leave Himself without a witness, 'Woe to you, blind guides.'[10] The blind are leading the blind, and all truth, morality, law, civilisation, and order will fall into the ditch. It is of this the Syllabus has warned the world. The Deism, Atheism, and Rationalism, the deification of the State, the denial of the basis of all morality, now infecting the Christian world, and sapping the foundations of public and domestic life, have separated the nations of Europe, with their laws and their governments, from the revelation of Chris-

[9] S. Matt. xviii. 7.   [10] Ibid. xxiii. 16.

tianity, from the Sovereignty of God, and therefore from their own progressive welfare. There are now no Christian governments, no Christian nations; and therefore no Christian world. The Christian Church, indeed, is still in the world, and therefore the world will not believe itself to be fallen from Christianity. It resents the warning, it hates the voice that passes judgment on its intellectual aberrations and on its pride of life. But we cannot therefore be silent, even though men will not hear, and governments are offended, and the world still goes its way. The Church exists by the truth and for the truth; and even if it be abandoned by the multitude for the truth's sake as its Divine Head was, in the desert, it can only repeat its doctrines, and ask of those who stumble at the Word of God, 'Will ye also go away?' The tide of unbelief has been running for three centuries against the Christian society of Europe. It has now almost accomplished its work. The Church stands out more than ever visible to the world, as the old civilisation is washed away from the rock on which the Church is built. The political society of the world is no longer Christian. Religion has been eliminated from legislation, science, history; from the public laws and institutions of nations; and now it is being expelled from the public schools and public education of the people. Against this de-christianising of the society of man the Church opposes itself with all its power and all its inflexibility. It will not reconcile itself with this progress from national Christianity to national Atheism. It will even cast itself across the path of nations in their fatal departure from God. If its members be crushed here and there, it will rise again. It willingly gives of its life-blood for the salvation of society. What befell in Ireland, in England, in France, will, it may be, befall in Italy and in Germany. The public life of nations will be desecrated: but the Church will rise again, more pure, more united, and more powerful in its work of saving souls one by one, even though the nations will have ceased to be Christian. Such is the reason why, in this Pontificate of six-and-twenty years, Pius the Ninth has refused all compromise with an anti-social and anti-christian revolution. He is bound to witness for the sacred laws of Christian society. The 'Theocratic Government,' whose epitaph is upon the monument of those that shed their blood for it, was the government of God's laws over the Christian world. If, indeed, it be now at an end, then let all who believe in the Incarnation watch lest they should be deceived. Whatsoever power claims to be sovereign over the Vicar of Jesus Christ is apostate;

and they who aid, or by countenance or acquiescence partake in this rejection of the sovereignty of the Redeemer of the world, will share in the scourges and the judgment, which till they fall upon the nations will be derided, and when they come will be believed too late. I am well aware that these words will be as foolishness not only to infidels and deists, but to the statesmen and diplomatists, the wise and prudent in public affairs. So it always has been. They have always been asking, where is the promise of His coming? And we have always seemed to be dreamers. So be it. We are willing to be derided by the many, if only we may save souls.

The tenth Sermon in this volume is a mere outline of an argument, which, after being despised as mediæval superstition by the apostles of modern progress, must hereafter be treated again by those who will have to reconstruct the Christian society of the world, if, indeed, there be a reconstruction to come in the designs of God. I have there simply sketched the Theocracy of Israel, the commonwealth of the Christian world, the state of the world without Christ and without God. The Italian government, by its epitaph over the martyrs of the Holy See in the cemetery of San Lorenzo, proclaims itself to be the antagonist of the Christian Theocracy of the Vicar of Jesus

Christ. This, like the shadow on the dial, tells us where the world is now, and what its future must be, unless it retrace its progress falsely so called.

At this time there is no civil power, as such, either Catholic or Christian : there is no nation, in its organised and public life and laws, professing Christianity. The tendency of all political and social movements is to the exclusion of Christianity from the public life of nations. We are progressing rapidly in one direction. Let us see whither we are going. I have said that it is to the destruction of the Christian society of the world. Let us briefly run over the signs that are evident. There is at this time no distinction in the public laws of any country between unity and schism, faith and heresy. All fragmentary Christianities are on the same level with the Catholic faith, and all forms of error on the same level with Christianity. The public law of Christendom has ceased to promote or to uphold or even to prefer Christianity. It is one of the religions of the world, not even 'relegated to obscure municipalities,' but to the conscience or the caprice of individuals. In truth, the more earnest men are in religion the more troublesome they become to legislators and governments. The Protestant Reformers did not foresee that 'the religious difficulty,' which they created by heresy and schism, would one day be fatal to Christianity and to themselves. The men of progress have found out that education forms men, and that men form society. They are, therefore, labouring to expel Christianity from education; for men formed without religion will expel it from society. To this end governments are taking education into their own hands; and men of progress are clamoring for education, free, secular, universal, and compulsory. If Christian parents are to have a voice in the formation of their children, the hope of building up a state without God will long be deferred. Therefore, the unrelenting effort to secularise our schools. Thousands of professors in all countries, paid and unpaid, have been preaching for generations that religion must be separated from politics, from philosophy, from science. We are almost wearied into silence. Public opinion is poisoned into believing this falsehood. The youth of these days is being reared upon a literature which is rationalistic and sensuous, if not worse. The period of life in which the mind and the man are to be formed is spent in studies from which Christianity is being more and more excluded every day. The little religion which remains in education is in juxtaposition with science and literature, not in union with it, much less diffused throughout it as its life and governing law. What wonder that so many grow up without God in this world? that the Christianity of many more is shallow, powerless, and, so to speak, not so much as skin-deep? Christianity has been left as a matter of choice to private individuals; but modern education renders it morally impossible for individuals to be formed as Christians. What wonder, then, that society should exclude Christianity from its public acts? that it should cease to look at crime as sin? that it should measure only the offence against society, and ignore the offence against God? To be just, I admit that society as such has no jurisdiction over sin as such. The Church alone has this divine commission. But this proves my thesis, namely, that in rejecting the 'Theocracy' civil society has reduced itself to paganism, that is, to society without God. This is the inevitable consequence of rejecting the Church of God, and of excluding it from the sphere of the civil commonwealth. But this state of simple exclusion is merely for a time. It will soon be followed, as we see, by active persecution of Christianity. A state of indifference cannot long last. Nobody knows this better than our modern Liberals. If Catholics and all honest men are not aware of it, they have only to thank themselves. Our enemies have been shouting and trumpeting their intentions for these ten years. On the 20th of July in 1862 the Italian Deputy Petrucelli della Gattina told the Chamber in Turin that 'the Pontiff of the people would hunt out the Pontiff of Christ.' In Rome and on the Piazza Navona, on the 20th of last July, credible witnesses affirm that the cry was heard of 'Abbasso Cristo!' Another of the Italian Deputies, Fenni, has told us in print, that the way of progress is 'to pull down the Cross.' Another, Civinini, on August 11th, 1863, wrote in the *Diritto* to say, 'Our revolution is tending to destroy the Catholic Church;' and another, on April 19th, 1865, declared, 'It is not only the religious orders that we will abolish, but we will destroy the old trunk which is called Catholicism.' The same Petrucelli della Gattina above quoted with great frankness tells us that the policy of the future consists 'in making war against the preponderance of Catholicism everywhere, against all comers and by all means;' adding, 'We see that this Catholicism is an instrument of dissension and of misfortune, and we ought to destroy it!'[11] The imposture of 'a free Church in a free State' has thrown off its mask. It has already begun to 'destroy Catholi-

[11] *L'Unità Cattolica*, July 26, 1872.

cism,' and 'to pull down the Cross.' It is at work to suppress religious orders, to confiscate their property, to turn them out of their houses, to violate all the immunities of the Church. It has shut up the Vicar of Jesus Christ in a moral imprisonment. It is mere hypocrisy to say that he is free to come out into the streets of Rome. If his life be not in danger—and who could guarantee it in the midst of a population crying incessantly, 'Morte ai preti!' 'Morte al Papa!' 'Abbasso Cristo!'—he is bound not to expose himself to the mockeries of blasphemous litanies, or to processions carrying the heads of murderers, who conspired against him. The taunts and levities of newspapers in this matter are either from simple ignorance or sheer insolence. I have before me at this moment the evidence of scores of assaults, insults, violences, committed against priests, prelates, bishops, even under the windows of the Vatican. And the Pope is free to go out; and is putting on the affectation of imprisonment! The revolutionary papers have not attempted to deny the facts which two Catholic papers, the *Osservatore Romano* and the *Voce della Verità*, in Rome have steadily published with the evidence. But the correspondents of the English newspapers write home their denials, and our journals publish these denials without giving the evidence of the facts. The state of Rome is in this country simply concealed. Our newspapers have never made known to their readers the atrocities of the revolutionary press, the abominable caricatures, the indescribable cartoons with which Rome has been defiled. Since the 20th of September 1870, I have received a constant supply of this garbage. The person of the Holy Father is, of course, the centre of this blasphemous and obscene ribaldry. But on last Good Friday One even greater than he was outraged. Rome was desecrated by a caricature of the crucifixion of the Saviour of the world. Is it into streets where these things are sold, hawked, and placarded, that the Holy Father is invited not only by Garibaldians, and by 'reduci,' and by the Italian government, but by English journalists and by English gentlemen? They counsel him to drive out for air and recreation in the midst of 'expropriated' convents, and to show himself to a respectful populace, who would salute his sovereign person with cries of 'Viva Vittor Emmanuele!' and 'Abbasso Cristo!' If we were not as usual in crass ignorance of facts on the continent of Europe, would not this be hypocrisy?

The theatres in Rome present night after night scandals of so gross a kind that even the journals of the revolution cry out against them. Under the eyes and within earshot of the Holy Father, the Catholic Faith and Church is derided, profaned, and dragged through the mire in its dogmas, in its worship, in its ministers, and in its morality. The foulness of every night on the stage of the theatres has drawn from the *Diritto* the following confession. Speaking of a play called the *Nun of Cracôw*, a mass of obscenity, calumny, and impiety, it says: 'We don't know when we shall come to an end of this rage for plays which brutalise the public taste, and excite every kind of popular foulness.' Night after night cardinals, priests, monks, nuns, are introduced as monsters of every kind of vice. The phrases, 'our holy religion,' 'our holy mother the Church,' uttered with ironical malice, are greeted with hisses and howls. And all this is done under the eyes of the government of the 'Law of Guarantees.' Garibaldi the other day demanded of the government, as a condition of its tolerated existence, that the first article of the statute which declares the Catholic religion to be the religion of the state should be cancelled. It was well answered, that he might save himself the trouble. The state has no religion, whatever the statute may say. Moreover, the Catholic religion serves for farces and burlesques at the Correa, and the Sferisterio.[12] If it were legally abolished, the people would be robbed of their nightly

[12] 'Under one shape or another, the Papal question is the all-engrossing topic of the day. It is discussed in the press, in the political caricatures (the name of which is legion in Rome), in private conversations, and last, not least, upon the stage. We have at this moment three open-air theatres in full work, and drawing crowded audiences every afternoon. And with what do you think? The subject is always the same, namely, the real or pretended misdeeds of the Catholic Church, the horrors of the Inquisition, Torquemada and his 77,000 victims, Peter Arbues the Grand Inquisitor of Aragon, the Massacre of the Huguenots, and other kindred arguments. Nothing else will go down with the Romans at this moment, and those who cater for their amusement take care not to let the occasion slip. The actors are not quite lively enough to suit the tastes of a Shoreditch audience, and a little more cut-and-thrust business would be required to meet the critical demands of a Surrey gallery. Still there is a full feast of horrors notwithstanding, stabbing, poisoning, burning at the stake, beheading, and hanging. And how the people enjoy it all! How they groan and whistle at the recurrence of certain phrases, such as "the Holy Roman Church," "Catholic and Apostolic," "our blessed religion," and so forth; all which the actor is careful to pronounce with a whining unction which serves the purpose of a signal. How the Grand Inquisitor is hissed at and hooted through the three or four acts during which he has it all his own way; and what yells and threats accompany him in his final discomfiture when he meets with his deserts; for the playwrights of the Correa and of the Sferisterio are not scrupulous in the matter of historical fidelity, and when they get to the last act invariably cut the wretch's throat, or string him up, or tie him to the stake in the place of one of his victims. "Monster, thy hour has come!" shouts the avenger in the closing scene. The trembling craven cowers on the ground and sues for mercy. "That's right," cry the people in chorus; "give it him, serve him out, throw him over into the pit!" Sometimes the avenger will not strike just then, as he prefers to wait for a more solemn occasion, and then he is assailed

carrion. And yet there might be more equity of procedure. A correspondent from Rome last week writes as follows: 'As a specimen of the administration of justice, it is well to notice the following fact. One of the illustrated papers last week brought out a caricature of a menagerie, in which the Holy Father, the cardinals, and some religious were represented in cages, with insulting titles on each. The following day a Catholic paper, the *Lima*, brought out a similar caricature, but, in place of the Holy Father and the cardinals, the royal family and ministers were represented. The latter was immediately sequestrated, although the other was allowed free circulation. By the Italian law the person of the Pope

---

with such epithets as "duffer," "ass," and the like, and exhorted to strike while the iron is hot, &c. The clericals are very angry at all this, and would fain have us believe that the three theatres where these popular manifestations take place are filled with *buzzurri* only. The Romans, they say, take no part therein. This I can assert from my own experience to be quite false. Besides, the *buzzurri* had a surfeit of these sensational anti-Catholic pieces years and years ago, and do not care to see them repeated. For the Romans, however, so long kept under restraint, they present all the freshness of novelty and all the flavour of forbidden fruit, and the more staid among them highly condemn the yells, whistling, and other *vassallate* (blackguardisms) which prevent the judicious public from fully enjoying these *belle produzioni*, as they call the infamous trash—infamous, I mean, in a literary sense. Altogether, a visit or two to the popular theatres of Rome at this season will afford the materials for an interesting study of human nature.'—Roman Correspondent of the *Standard*, Sept. 10, 1872.

is sacred, and all acts against him are to be punished in the same manner as those against the king.'

But it would seem that we are in an age when 'the unclean spirits, like frogs,' have gone out of the mouth of the dragon, and of the beast, and of the false prophet, against God and against His Christ. There are nuns of Cracow, nuns at Picpus, scandals at Carcassonne, scandals everywhere: all self-evident, notorious, flagrant, world-wide, to set men on fire against the Catholic Church. After three days all are known to be lies; but they have done their work: the flame is kindled, and cannot be stayed; the matches may be stamped into the mire. And it is into this city of Rome that the Holy Father is invited to take his daily drive! It is not I, but the *Nazione* of August 22d that says, '*Roma è diventata ormai il mare magnum dei birbanti di ogni regione;*' which, being translated, signifies, 'is become the habitation of devils, and the hold of every unclean spirit.' 'Go out from her, My people; that you be not partakers of her sins, and that you receive not of her plagues.'[13]

Such, then, is the aspect of the Christian world. Pius the Ninth, through a pontificate of six-and-twenty years, has vigilantly noted every new step of this modern progress from God to anarchy. By

[13] Apoc. xviii. 2, 4.

a succession of public declarations in encyclical letters, allocutions, and rescripts to Bishops and to others, he has condemned the principles which lead to antichristian and antisocial revolutions. As the witness of faith and truth, he is charged also with the supreme judgment in matters of Christian politics: for politics are a part of morals; they are the morals of society, founded upon the dictates of nature and the doctrines of grace. He is therefore the witness and the guardian of the principles of all authority, order, law, and justice; in a word, of the Christian commonwealth and the foundations on which it rests. The Syllabus is the declaration of those principles, laws, and rights, which modern progress has deliberately violated; and having violated, it invites the Vicar of Christ to reconcile himself to the accomplished facts of impiety and of injustice.

De Tocqueville said that in his day all the currents of human action and thought, all the tide of events, were running fast to democracy. He noted that the influences of men, both of those who laboured for it and those who laboured against it, of all who hoped for democracy and all who feared it, united in forcing it upon the world. So it may be said of the atheism of modern progress. All things are converging to the vanishing point where God will be shut out of His own world. The civil powers have ceased to hold their authority from Him; to acknowledge Him as their sanction; to take His law as the rule of their legislation. The culture of science, of philosophy, of literature, all are independent of His mind. The formation of mankind is carried on as if He did not exist. The society which grows up from such formation is godless; if it be intellectual, by a set theory; if unintellectual, by a sensuous materialism; either way God is not in all its thoughts. Look round the Christian world. The East is in schism; its churches are mosques; the Incarnation has departed from them. Look at the north and north-west of Europe. Protestantism has done its work in beating its fragmentary Christianity as fine as the dust of the summer threshing-floor, and the winds of revolution are carrying it away. Wheresoever Protestantism has been, the old Catholic churches are desolate. The Word made flesh is no longer there. The antisocial and antichristian revolution has descended upon Italy, submerged the whole peninsula, and flooded Rome at last. The Incarnation has no longer a home in the Christian world. The Vicar of Jesus Christ is bid to go forth, because for two sovereignties to co-exist in Rome is impossible. The nations look on and applaud. They are all, either by active co-operation as in Germany, or by tacit connivance as in England, *participes criminis*. One and all alike say, 'We will not have this man to reign over us!' 'We have no king but Cæsar!' It would seem that the 'discessio,' or the falling away foretold by the Apostle, is not far from its accomplishment. We are indeed entering upon perilous times; but we enter them with no fear: 'When these things begin to come to pass, look up and lift up your heads; for your redemption is at hand.' No Catholic doubts of the final and complete overthrow of the powers now in array against the Vicar of our Lord. They are more lordly, imperious, and to human force more irresistible, than ever before. But they have entered the lists not against man but against God. If we have to suffer, so be it. God's holy will be done! May He only make us fit for so high a grace; and hasten the redemption of His Church in His own good time!

Rosary Sunday 1872.

I.

THE TEMPORAL POWER OF THE POPE IN ITS POLITICAL ASPECT:

In the Pro-Cathedral, Moorfields, Rosary Sunday, 1866.

NOTICE.

THE following pages contain the substance of what I said on the day of the general supplication in behalf of the Holy Father. It is confined to the political aspect of the Temporal Power, and deals only with the lowest ground on which it may be argued, namely, that of legal and political justice. I had already at other times claimed for the Temporal Power its higher sanctions, as related to the person and office of the Vicar of Jesus Christ. It was then objected, that this was to remove the question from the tangible region of fact and law, to the impalpable region of faith. Without repeating what I have so often said before, I have here confined myself to the same field of argument on which all legitimate powers repose. If the British Empire can be justified in its sway over the three kingdoms and its dependencies, or the American Union over the Southern States, then far more surely may the right of the Pontiffs be maintained by the same arguments. The only difference I know is, that we and the Americans have bayonets of our own. The Pontiffs are unarmed. Foreign bayonets are a legitimate defence against foreign revolutions. Let the seditious of all nations be withdrawn from Rome, with their acts, conspiracies, and intrigues, and there would be no need for bayonets.

THE TEMPORAL POWER OF THE POPE IN ITS POLITICAL ASPECT.

> Let every soul be subject to higher powers: for there is no power but from God; and those that are, are ordained of God. Therefore he that resisteth the power, resisteth the ordinance of God; and they that resist purchase to themselves damnation. ROM. xii. 1-2.

To-DAY the Catholic Church throughout England and Scotland is united in supplication in behalf of the Sovereign Pontiff. The solemnity of to-day is dear to the heart of every Catholic. It is full of memories of the conflicts and of the victories of the Church. It is the festival of the Holy Rosary of the Immaculate Mother of God, to whose prayers we ascribe these interventions of divine power. No doubt, to the world, the festival and the supplication of to-day is a solemnity of folly. We go out to our warfare not even with a sling and stones out of the brook, but with a string of beads in the hands of little children. The pastors and faithful of Ireland have led the way. England and Scotland close the procession with their united prayers.

I am conscious that I have to speak not only to those who are of the unity of the Catholic Church, but to those who are without; not only to those who believe, but to those who do not believe the Catholic faith. To you who believe it I need say nothing; your faith and fervour anticipate all I can utter, and your instincts of filial love for the Holy Father need no words of mine. But to those who unhappily are not of the unity and faith of the Church I desire to speak frankly, appealing to the truths and principles which they hold in common with us. I trust and believe that the solemnity of to-day, if it does not change the mind of any, will at least clear away much misconception, and mitigate much hostility which springs from error. My confidence of this is founded on the justice of our cause, the force of truth, the honesty of Englishmen, and on the grace of God.

There are here, I conceive, two classes of men: some who believe in the visible Church and its mission to the world; and others who admit only a divine Providence over the world, and the laws of morality.

Now to both of these I offer this declaration of the Apostle, that submission is due to the constituted authority of government, on the principle not of expediency alone, but of conscience: and on this basis I trust to justify the Temporal Power of the Sovereign Pontiff. I affirm then: (1) That the Temporal Power of the Pontiff is a power ordained of God. (2) That it stands at least upon the same basis as all other rightful authority. (3) That it is sacred by every right common to other powers, and by rights and sanctions which transcend those of all other authorities on earth: and lastly (4) That it therefore cannot be resisted, nor can any one excite resistance against it, without sin against not only political justice, but against the ordinance of God. From all these I farther affirm, that the overthrow of that power, if it were possible, would be, in an exceptional and eminent sense, both unjust, and dangerous to the Christian civilisation of the world.

1. First, then, I affirm that the overthrow of the Temporal Power of the Sovereign Pontiff would be unjust, because it is sacred as a power existing *de facto* by the ordinance of God. St. Paul declared that even the heathen empire of Rome was ordained by God, and that every one owed subjection to it. He laid it upon the conscience of Christians to obey it in all things lawful, 'not only for wrath,' that is, for fear of punishment, 'but also for conscience' sake.'

And yet the empire of Rome was not only heathen, but persecuting. It was steeped in Christian blood. Nevertheless he declares it to be a power constituted by God. As such, the Christians obeyed it with an obedience limited only by the divine law of faith. And this law of civil obedience is of universal and perpetual obligation. It is this on which as subjects of the British empire we bear allegiance to our own Sovereign. As Catholics, we obey not for wrath only, but for conscience' sake; it is a part of our religion to be loyal; it is a dictate of our moral sense to be obedient to the law and faithful to the throne. If it were not so, civil obedience would be degraded from its dignity as a moral virtue, and treason would be divested of its highest guilt. There would be no such sin as heresy, if there were not a divine authority teaching among men; nor such a sin as schism, if there were not a divine law of unity. Heresy would be mere error of opinion, and schism a lawful freedom of separation, if it were not for the divine authority of truth and the divine law of unity. So with treason, rebellion, sedition, disaffection: if there were not a divine sanction for authority, they would be offences against society, but not sins against God; breaches of conventional laws, but not of Christian morality towards God. On what other principle is the British empire held together? Like the empire of Rome of old, it is heterogeneous, widespread, made up of elements the most diverse, and even conflicting, and yet bound together by one sovereignty, and by a universal bond of allegiance to the supreme power. Britain was once an anarchy of uncivilised Saxon hordes; then a heptarchy of conflicting kingdoms; then a monarchy of many peoples fused in one; then it became an empire of three kingdoms under one sovereign, with colonies and dependencies stretching into every sea; and all these dominions, in many things so opposite, are held together by one common head, to whom obedience is a duty not only for fear of punishment, but also for the law and will of God. Upon what other law can the duty of obedience be imposed by England upon Scotland and Ireland, upon India and upon Malta?

It is precisely upon this basis, I affirm, that the Pontiffs have claim upon the obedience of their subjects, and that their subjects owe them allegiance for conscience' sake. The Temporal Power of the Popes is as manifestly and as fully ordained of God as the power of Queen Victoria. Neither the one nor the other came by *plebiscite*, or universal suffrage, or votes of inorganic masses; but by the gradual and watchful providence of the Divine Author of human and political society. The British empire succeeds to the Roman empire in Britain by a direct law of Divine Providence. When the last Roman legion left the shores of Britain, it began to gravitate to a centre within itself. The British empire of to-day is formed round that centre, and rests upon it. So, when the Emperor of Constantinople ceased to be able to protect Rome, the Vicar of Jesus Christ became its centre. The Emperor had ceased to rule, and the throne was vacant by the visitation of God. The Pontiffs reigned as pastors and as rulers, and unconsciously and by force of necessity filled the vacant throne. They have reigned in Rome, first with an informal and pastoral sovereignty, and afterwards with a full and explicit sovereignty from that time to this. On what ground, then, can obedience to the sovereignty of Great Britain be claimed, if obedience to the sovereignty of the Pontiff be denied? Every sanction of Divine Providence, and of Christian morals, and of political justice, confirms the Temporal Sovereignty of the Pope.

2. But farther: the temporal power is not only a power *de facto*, but *de jure*. It not only exists, but it exists by a perfect title. It is a rightful authority in its origin, in its formation, and in its claims upon its subjects. The foundation of it is not in the donation of man, but in the ordinance of God.

The donation of Constantine is a fable; but it rudely represents the divine action whereby Rome and its provinces were transferred from the Cæsars to the Pontiffs. In like manner, the alleged donation of Pepin to Stephen II. is equally fabulous. The restoration of Ravenna, and other cities of the patrimony, to the Pontiff, is declared to be a *restitution*.[1] Pepin required of Astolphus the restitution of the cities and territories taken by his predecessors from the Roman Church and commonwealth. He thereby recognises, and recites in the very document by which he made restoration, the antecedent rights which had been violated by the Lombard invaders.

[1] That the Emperors of the East forfeited, in the eighth century at latest, all authority over Rome and its provinces, and that the Pontiffs remained in sole and supreme possession, and that the Emperors of the West never possessed or pretended to sovereignty over Rome and the Pontiffs, are facts as clear as any in history. The heretical and schismatical Emperor Leo made war upon Italy, and sent a fleet to seize the person of Gregory III. He invaded and seized the patrimonies of the Holy See in Sicily and Calabria. At that time the Lombards besieged Rome. The Emperors, so far from defending it, openly declared war against it. Gregory III. wrote to Charles Martel imploring his protection, and in his own name and that of the Roman people offered him the dignity of Consul, on the condition of assuming the office of protector. Charles Martel and Gregory III. died the same year. The Lombards seized Ravenna and the exarchate. Pope Zachary prevailed upon the King of the Lombards to restore Ravenna and the exarchate, which he demanded, not in the name of the Emperor, but in his own and that of the Roman Commonwealth. The King of the Lombards restored them. It is declared to be

He gave back possession of the invaded provinces to their rightful owners, as in our day Rome was restored by the armies of France to its rightful sovereign. When I say that Rome and its provinces were given to the Pontiffs by the donation of Divine Providence, I speak as strictly as when I say that the throne of England was given by Divine Providence to our reigning sovereign. I will not—nor, indeed, in this brief time can I — trace out the

---

a *restitution*. Throughout the history the words *redonavit, reconcessit, restituit,* are everywhere employed. Pope Stephen succeeded to Zachary, and in his time the Lombards, under Astolphus, once more seized the exarchate. Stephen, in A.D. 753, sent into France to Pepin, imploring protection. Pepin and his sons, Charles and Carloman, bound themselves by an engagement to restore to the Holy See the exarchate of Ravenna and the cities seized by the Lombards. The Pope conferred on Pepin and his sons the dignity of Patrician or Protector. Pepin fulfilled his engagement. Anastasius relates the event as follows: 'The most Christian prince Pepin, king of the Franks, as a true defender of the Blessed Peter (the Roman Church), and in obedience to the wholesome counsels of the holy Pontiff, sent his envoys to Astolphus, the wicked King of the Lombards, to obtain treaties of peace, and the *restitution of rights* to the before-named holy Church of God and the commonwealth.' Finally, Pepin was compelled to exact the restitution by force of arms. This is called by French writers the *donation* of Pepin; the word 'donation' being used for *restoration*. Neither Pepin nor any of his predecessors had ever so much as laid claim to Rome. For the full detail of these events, and the quotations of the original documents, see Gosselin's *Power of the Popes, &c.* vol. i. pp. 212-228, and the notes especially at p. 216.

gradual formation of the Temporal Power, from the time of the liberation of the Pontiffs from all civil subjection, through the period of inchoate government, to the formal sovereignty which they have borne for a thousand years. In the five centuries which intervened between the ceasing of persecution and the full sovereignty of the Pontiffs, they held the temporal possession of their three-and-twenty patrimonies in Italy, Sicily, and Gaul; and over those patrimonies they exercised a true temporal power of government. Such was the origin of their sovereignty. Round about these patrimonies kingdoms and commonwealths arose—the first expanding outlines of Christian Europe. Over these also the Pontiffs exercised a supreme spiritual authority in all matters of divine faith and of the moral law. The confederation of Christendom is only the full corn in the ear, the harvest which springs up from the first blade to its ripeness under the hand and eye of the Pontiffs. How could they who had received from the Pontiffs both their Christianity and their civilisation regard them otherwise than as their fathers and guides? The light of faith taught them that the Vicar of Jesus Christ was the supreme interpreter of the truth, and the supreme expositor of the law. How could they regard him in any way as subject to the authority of their princes? The doctrines of faith, the Sacraments of grace, the unity of the Church, the supreme authority descending from one fountain of jurisdiction, bound all Christian nations in one around the patrimonies of the Pontiffs and the person of the Vicar of Jesus Christ. How could they regard him as in any way dependent on human power, and not as superior to them all? As supreme ruler, legislator, and judge, the Pontiffs hold their sovereignty not only by a title equal to all temporal princes, but in a way eminent and singular. If there be on earth a sovereign right complete in every condition of its perfection, it is theirs.

3. And yet it has a higher sacredness: it has the confirmation of the most ancient tradition in the Christian world. While as yet Britain was pagan and barbarous, and France overrun by moving hordes, and Spain hardly counted as a nation, and Germany a forest of the heathen world, the Vicars of Jesus Christ reigned in Rome as pastors and as rulers. It may be said that possession presupposes a rightful title. True; but not always. Possession will confirm an invalid title; nay, it will create a valid one. The titles of usurpation and revolution may by lapse of time be confirmed by long possession against all claims, except that of the Church; for its possessions

are sacred, and cannot be usurped without sacrilege, which no length of possession can consecrate. And if lapse of time confirm a title invalid in the beginning, how much more does it confirm, and, I will say, consecrate, a title rightful in its origin and its history by every condition of justice, both human and divine?

And such is the possession of the Pontiffs over the patrimony of the Church, and such the right of rule as sovereigns over Rome and its provinces. Even the violations of this right by invaders and spoilers have only recorded it again and again in the public law of Christendom. The imperial laws from the eighth century, the laws of all European kingdoms down to the sixteenth, and of all international diplomacy down to this day, have recognised the rights of the Pontiffs to their possessions, and their independent, and therefore sovereign, power. It was reserved for the age of revolutions, and for the inverted political philosophy of this century, to efface the record of these rights from the public conscience of Europe.

Thus far I have argued the Temporal Power upon grounds common to all temporal authorities. It rests upon the same basis, but more securely than all, and has upon it the sanction of a divine Providence, and of a divine protection which no other sovereignty can show.

4. But we must go farther. The right by which the Pontiff holds his Temporal Power is not only sacred by all the sanctions which confirm it in other sovereignties; it has a special and singular sacredness, which makes it exceptional and eminent above them all. The power of temporal rule in him meets and is united with the higher authority of the Vicar of Jesus Christ, which is both divine in its origin and supernatural in its action. I know that I am now passing beyond the bounds of politics, and entering into a region where modern politicians seem to lose their calmness and their clearness of sight. Day by day we are told that we confound together the spiritual and the temporal power; that we make the spiritual to depend upon the possession of a strip of territory; that we proclaim the Temporal Power to be a doctrine of faith, and a part of Christianity which, if the Temporal Power be destroyed, will fall. For my own part, I never yet met any Catholic either so besotted in understanding, or so base in heart, as to fall into any of these monstrous absurdities. Nevertheless, they are repeated day by day, as by the monotonous revolution of a mill-wheel, which perpetually discharges the same noisy flood. It is of no use to

expostulate, to correct, to refute; over and over again, sometimes with a variation of phrase, oftener in the very same words, the same absurdities are poured over us. Of all men, they who believe that the spiritual power of the Vicar of Jesus Christ was derived by a direct commission from our divine Redeemer; that it is contained in the words, 'All power in heaven and in earth is given unto Me; go ye, therefore, and make disciples of all nations,' and 'I dispose unto you a kingdom, as My Father hath disposed unto Me,' and 'Thou art Peter; and upon this rock I will build My Church, and the gates of hell shall not prevail against it;' and that the Church and the Pontiffs for three hundred years, in their spiritual power alone, conquered the world by martyrdom; and that if the powers of the world apostatise from the Church of God, the Pontiffs will once more reign in undiminished spiritual power, though through persecution, and not in peace;—of all men, I say, they who believe these things, and proclaim them as we do, even to provocation, ought to be held guiltless at least of the absurdities of confounding the spiritual and the temporal, or of making strips of territory, or walls of stone, the essence of Christianity, or the necessary condition of spiritual power. I doubt if men really believe these portentous figments. But they fill up space where arguments are not to be had. You who believe that the holy Catholic Church, in its unity and universality, in its supreme legislation and its judicial power over the souls of men, with its perfections and gifts of indefectible life, and infallible knowledge and voice, is the kingdom of Jesus upon earth, and that the Vicars of Christ have reigned, from the hour of His ascension, over both the pastors and the flock, apart from all earthly power, and in spite of all its malice and of all its might, have no need to be told by any one, least of all by me, that we of all men distinguish the imperishable Church of God from all temporal accidents of possession and of power. Nay more, it was the spiritual power of the Church, which, conquering all temporal antagonists, fashioned for itself, by faith, by law, and by beneficence acting upon the reason, the conscience, and the heart of mankind, a new order, a new world, with new temporal laws, and new thrones and new tribunals of temporal sovereignty. It surrounded itself with a new apparatus for the service and welfare of men. The eternal clothed itself in the temporal, that it might mix more intimately and more effectually in the whole corporate and organic life of men and nations, with their public laws, the fountains of their legislation, and the directions of their judges and other rulers. Such is the Temporal Power of the Pontiff: a personal freedom, and a supreme direction over men and nations in all things pertaining to the faith and law of God. And for the peaceful exercise of this supreme office, the providence of God has formed for him a sphere into which no other sovereignty may enter; in which therefore, because sole and supreme, he is invested with sovereign power. And of this too we are confident: that so long as a Christian world exists, so long this providential centre of its unity, the source of its Christian life, will continue to exist. If the civilisation of Europe ever fall back into the mere natural order, and the law and faith of Jesus Christ pass from the reason and conscience of men, then indeed the Temporal Power of His Vicar upon earth might cease. It is therefore transient only, as the Christian world may be thought to pass away. So long as it exists, the laws and relations which fashioned it will remain permanent and changeless; and he who is recognised to be pastor and father, judge and legislator, over all, and Vicar of our divine Redeemer upon earth, will hold the first place in both orders, spiritual and temporal, as Pontiff and as King.

5. And lastly, the Temporal Power of the Sove-

reign Pontiff, sacred as it is by every title which consecrates the right of any ruler upon earth, confirmed by a longer possession and a more ample recognition in the law and conscience of the Christian world, and elevated by the divine commission of the Vicar of Jesus Christ to a singular and exceptional authority, has yet this last title to the obedience of its subjects, to which no other dynasty among men can lay claim. It is a power which has never oppressed its people. In affirming the doctrine of the Apostle, that 'there is no power but from God, and that whosoever resisteth the power, resisteth the ordinance of God,' I am not proclaiming what men are pleased to call the slavish doctrine of blind and immoral obedience. Rulers have their duties as well as their rights, and subjects have rights as well as duties. The ruler has a right to obedience, but he is bound by a duty to rule justly. The subject has a duty to obey, but he has also a right to justice. And the violation of the bond of their reciprocal duties is not only a crime, in both the ruler and the ruled, against society, which is an ordinance of God, but a sin against God, who is the supreme Author of society among men. It is not now the time, nor is it now my duty, to define the limits of this question, or to say when or where a rightful power abdicates its claim to obedience by abuse. Tyranny, as well as rebellion, is a crime and a sin, and both have their just correction. No power can be more absolute than the law 'Thou shalt not kill,' and yet in defence of life both an individual or a nation may take the life of a murderer or of an invading power. I am not here at this time to discuss these limits. They exist; and there are tribunals in every society of men to define them, and to try the facts both of rebellion and oppression. It is enough for me to affirm that no Pontiff in the long line of a thousand, I may say of these fifteen hundred years, has ever abused his power, so as to relax the duty of obedience, or to purge the resistance of his subjects of the sin of rebellion. And this, which may be affirmed of the Pontiffs without fear, can be affirmed of no other line of rulers, of no other dynasty on earth. The Pontiffs have never made wars of aggression; they have never added a square foot of territory to their sacred patrimony by the blood and lives of their people; they have never swept away their homes by forest laws, nor plundered their inheritances, nor desecrated the sanctity of their homes, nor robbed them of the fruits of the earth to keep up a revenue and to live in luxury, nor wrested justice against any man, rich or poor, nor punished with oppressive and sanguinary codes, nor violated any laws of God or man to the hurt of their people. It is notorious as the light, that the sway of the Pontiffs has been mild even to indulgence, and beneficent even to the appearance of laxity. The very charges against it are that it does not drive on with the world, and strain in the race of material inventions. It has prisons because it hardly ever erects a scaffold; and lives that in any other country would have been peremptorily cut off are there benignly spared. Such is the character of the Temporal Power in its government. Its very clemency has emboldened those with whom it has dealt in excess of mercy to despise it. The first amnesty was followed by the first conspiracy, and those who were conspicuous as objects of pardon were conspicuous as the ringleaders of sedition. After a reign of twenty turbulent years, and in the midst of incessant provocations, Pius IX. may ask of his people in his own name, and in the name of the Pontiffs who have reigned before him: 'Whom have I wronged, or on whom has the weight of my authority borne heavily? If any one be aggrieved by me, let him rise up and bear his witness against me.' I will be bold to say that no accuser will be found except they whose witness, as those of old, will not agree together. Men are now acknowledging that the rising against the government of the Pontiff is not because Pius IX. is a bad ruler, nor because his government is a bad government, nor because he has violated the law of mercy and justice, but because his subjects are resolved not to be governed by him. That is to say, 'We will not have this man to reign over us.' If this be not treason, if this be not rebellion, let some man tell me what rebellion and treason are. If people are to be told that they may change their government as they may change their garments, that civil allegiance depends upon their liking, or that dynasties may be overthrown and monarchies dismembered upon such causes as this, let them lay to heart what ears are listening. This is a doctrine which will find a ready faith to believe and practise it among a people not far off. And upon those who preach this gospel of revolution, I, as a pastor, am bound to declare that the sin of instigating rebellion rests, and that all who act upon such doctrine abroad or at home are rebels.

The sum, then, of the matter is this: There is not a title of fact, or right, or possession, by which any crowned head holds authority over its people, which does not unite in the largest and profoundest sense in the person of the Pontiff. But more than this: besides these titles common to all rightful sovereignties, there are two of a higher nature—the sacred character of the person who bears this lesser authority, and the justice, clemency, and mercy, which have marked its administration throughout the course of ages. The subjects of such a power have an inheritance of peace above all people upon earth. It is not disfranchisement to be exempted from the instabilities of the world and from the turbulence of revolution. They have a higher dignity and a nobler freedom than that of parliaments and political contentions; and they who excite them to discontent and to rebellion rob them of a higher inheritance, and fall under the condemnation of those who resist the ordinance of God.

So much for the injustice of this warfare against the Vicar of Jesus Christ. I said also that it is most dangerous to the peace of nations. Injustice must be dangerous: prosper as it may, its end is confusion. But time forbids me to add what I had intended to say. All I can do is to touch the mere outline of what would follow upon the dissolution, if that could be, of the Temporal Power of the Pontiffs. But first let me once for all, or rather once more for the thousandth time, sweep away the absurdity imputed to us, day by day—that we make the Temporal Power a part of Christianity, and that if it were overthrown, Christianity would fall with it. This surpasses even the extravagance of controversy. We do believe, indeed, that the dissolution of the twofold authority of the Pontiff would strike out the keystone of Christendom; that is, of the twofold order of Christianity and civilisation which for a thousand years has sustained the commonwealth of Europe. We believe that then Christianity would stand alone, on its own divine and imperishable basis; and that civilisation without Christianity would return to the natural order, and to the spiritual death out of which Christianity raised it to life.

It is no question of what God could do, or might do, or may do hereafter, for the future of the world. We are as full of faith in the inexhaustible wisdom of divine Providence as our adversaries; but this we affirm, that it is by this twofold contact that the Church acts upon the Christianity and the civilisation of mankind; that so long as Christianity acts alone, it acts upon individuals one by one, as in the ages before Constantine; that so soon as it acts upon races, legislatures, rulers, kingdoms, upon the public law and organic life of nations, the Temporal Power is its legitimate offspring and result. To undo this, is to go backward, not onward. It is to dissolve the work of Christianity upon the world, not to advance it; to pull down, not to build up, the intellectual and

moral perfection of human society. We affirm also
that this retrogression and divorce of the spiritual and
civil societies of the world would desecrate the civil
powers of the world. They would cease to recognise,
as they have already to a great extent, the Christian
law, the unity of faith, worship, communion, or authority, as principles of their public order.

This would speedily bring on a collision between
the two powers always in presence of each other, each
claiming to be supreme, with no arbiter or tribunal,
no third and impartial judge to define the limits of
their jurisdiction or the sphere of their competence.
And this conflict could end only in the worst form
of human government, that is, in despotism, or the
union of temporal and spiritual supremacy in the
civil power, which has ever been the fountain of persecution, of heresy, and of schism. The two powers,
spiritual and temporal, are providentially united in
Rome that they may be separated everywhere else in
the kingdoms of the world. And it is this separation
which has secured the two great conditions of human
happiness—the liberty of the soul from all human
authority, and the limitation of civil authority in its
action upon its subjects. The history of Constantinople, of Russia, of England, and of France, suffices
to prove that the power of monarchs is limited while

the Church is free, and is despotic when it is fettered or opposed. The civil princedom of the Pontiffs therefore is, as Pius IX. has declared, the condition of divine Providence, to insure and perpetuate the freedom of the Church in its Head.

Lastly, nothing is more largely written in history than that despotisms generate revolutions. When civil power becomes oppressive, men are driven to dangerous resolves. Into this I will not enter. I am no prophet; but the history of Europe reads us a lesson in the past, which we shall do well to lay to heart as a warning for the future. Whosoever dissolves the bonds of Christian law and unity brings in the spirit of lawlessness, which is the tendency of all the national currents of this time. Society, to save itself, cowers under military despotisms, which generate reactions; and reactions, unless tempered and restrained by the Christian law, are the forerunners of anarchy. There are signs enough, not only in the sky, but upon every country of the old world and of the new, warning us not to destroy the feeblest bond of our social stability, still less to strike out the keystone of the arch which hangs tremulously over our heads.

Such, then, is the intention of our supplication to-day. God has so ordained that His Church should be always beaten by the water-floods. The red surges of persecution were followed by the inundations of barbarous hordes; then came floods of heresy, and of Cæsarism, and of imperial tyranny, and of corruption; then the hosts of the infidel, which reached to all the shores of Christendom; now the revolutions, which are one and universal, spreading through the nations and rising round the walls of Rome. But wave after wave has swept by, turned by the sea-wall which God, not man, has built—the immovable Rock. For this we pray, and for this we confidently wait. It is but one more of the thousand waves which are spent and gone. The Vicar of our divine Redeemer for these twenty years of his great Pontificate has been sitting all alone upon the hill-top, 'awaiting the events' which God has permitted. The world has passed him by, wagging its head, and men have been 'casting lots upon his garments, what every man should take.' But the words of his Master are sure: *post tres dies resurgam*, 'after three days I will rise again.' Pray, then, to the Eternal Son of God reigning in the midst of us, manifested in the Sacrament of His power. The world is trying its strength with Him: armed in its might, intoxicated with its masteries over the earth which He has made. But there are powers above those of war and of destruction, greater than the laws and agencies of electricity and gravitation, which control this lower world, and of man himself, even when he boasts of his mastery; there is the Word of God and the power of His might; and they are set in motion by the prayer of faith. 'All things whatsoever you shall ask in prayer believing, you shall receive.'² 'Heaven and earth shall pass away, but My words shall not pass away.'³

St. Matt. xxi. 22.   ³ St. Luke xxi. 32.

II.

ROME AND THE REVOLUTION:

In the Pro-Cathedral, Moorfields, Rosary Sunday, 1867.

ROME AND THE REVOLUTION.

> If the world hate you, know ye that it hated Me before you.
> ST. JOHN xv. 18.

IF the first Sunday in October were not set apart by the solemn usage of the Church for the festival of the Holy Rosary, it might be thought that we had appointed it this year for a special design. The ink is hardly dry upon a document, which for its solemnity and its signatures exceeds in public importance any that has ever, perhaps, emanated from the Anglican Communion. It contains a protest against the claim of universal sovereignty for the Vicar of Jesus Christ, and against the intercession of the Blessed Mother of God. We are met to-day to ask her prayers in behalf of the Sovereign Pontiff. What we do protests against this protest; and at first sight, indeed, it would appear as if the act of to-day and that declaration were in irreconcilable contradiction. I would fain hope not; and it is my purpose not to place them in opposition, but, if I can, to bring them into harmony. It may seem scarcely credible, but it is true, that the protest as it stands, and interpreted by the letter, any Catholic might sign. It is indeed a strange result that this authoritative document, so formidable and hostile in expression, should contain, when analysed, nothing which any Catholic would hesitate to affirm. I do not say what was the intention of the framers, nor whether this interpretation be such as the Catholic Church would warrant. But let us hope the best. Certainly it is not the work of charity to exaggerate discrepancies, nor to elevate what can be swept away into mountains of separation. The chief teachers of the Anglican communion have protested against the 'pretension of universal sovereignty over God's heritage asserted for the See of Rome.' But who asserts this universal sovereignty? Primacy of honour and supremacy of jurisdiction over the universal Church, in virtue of the power of the keys given to Peter and his successors, is indeed a truth, for which all Catholics would lay down their lives. Sovereignty over the patrimony of St. Peter; this too we know and understand. But sovereignty over the universal Church, no council, pontiff, or theologian has ever claimed. Here, then, we are in accordance. Next, the protest denounces those who practically exalt 'the Blessed Virgin Mary as mediator in the place of her divine Son.' To this also we say, if any man put the Mother of God in the place of her divine Son, let him be anathema. The protest does not say that the Catholic Church, dogmatically or doctrinally, sets the Blessed Virgin in the place of her Son—thus far, at least, is gain—but that it practically does so. You can best answer this imagination. Is there one of you so unsound in mind, is there any little Catholic child so unintelligent, as to confound the creature with the Creator, and to mistake the Mother of Jesus for the infinite, eternal, incomprehensible, uncreated God? Here again, then, we are in agreement. And, lastly, we are warned against 'addressing prayers to her as the Intercessor between God and man.' But here, once more, we have no difference. 'The Intercessor' here must mean, if it mean anything, 'the Intercessor of redemption.' The Catholic Church does not believe the Blessed Mother of God to be *the* Intercessor between God and man. She did not shed her blood for the redemption of the world. Against such a portent of heresy we protest even more intensely than the protesters. We are therefore in full accordance on this point also; unless it be meant that the Blessed Virgin is not an intercessor at all. If this be meant, these high authorities have need to look to their faith.

d

And how far this denunciation of asking the prayers of the Blessed Mother of God will promote the union which the Anglican Church is so ardently seeking with the Churches of the East, it is not for me to say. I am afraid the Oriental Christians will not stay to analyse the proposition as we have done, hoping to make the best of it; but will take it as it sounds, and treat it promptly, with no favour. But, for ourselves, let us take the benefit of such rules of interpretation as are current in these days; and so interpreted, this solemn protest is altogether an innocent proclamation. I am not sure that I have attained its meaning or the intentions of its framers; but, like a nebula, half luminous, half obscure, it passes harmless over our heads, and the festival of the Holy Rosary will wipe it out of the sky.

Last year, on this day, we made intercession before our divine Lord, in the Blessed Sacrament, through the prayers of His Blessed Mother, in behalf of the person and authority of the Sovereign Pontiff. It was then a moment of great anxiety. On the 12th of the following December the protection of France was to be withdrawn. It was prophesied that when 'the foreign bayonets' were gone, in twenty-four hours the Romans would rise, and the power of the Pontiff would be dissolved. They were withdrawn;

and where are the prophets? Pius IX. reigns calmly still. In the month of June last, half the Bishops of the world were gathered around the throne which ought to have been in dust. And now, again, before Rosary Sunday has returned, the chief antagonist of the Holy Father, the man who has earned his fame by bravado against the Vicar of Jesus Christ, has, by the just authority of his king, been rendered harmless. Such are the events of this twelvemonth past. We are entering on another year. I cannot foretell what it may bring forth. It is full of menace and of peril, and all things seem tending to a crisis. But the events of the year gone by are an encouragement for the year to come.

We may be told that they were but political and human agencies which protected the Holy Father. Be it so. God works through the politics and actions of men. They are instruments in His hands, and over all their powers there is a will and a control which directs and restrains them. God works through the combinations of rulers, whether they will or no; and brings about His ends by the most adverse and unlikely means. There is nothing in the present danger of the Holy See which has not been often before. Its existence in the world is a perpetual miracle: divinely founded, it has been divinely preserved. The power of the Pontiff forms an exception in the history of the world. His spiritual power needs no human aid. Neither kings nor emperors have been able to arrest nor have presumed to patronise it. His temporal power has subsisted for a thousand years by a continuous intervention of divine Providence. It has never possessed a military force able to cope with the weakest temporal prince. It has existed in the midst of mighty antagonists, any one of which might have crushed it; and, by some strange gift of perpetual stability, it has survived all shocks. Always threatened, but always safe— as the Apostle says: 'We suffer persecution, but are not forsaken; we are cast down, but we perish not: always bearing about in our body the mortification of Jesus, that the life also of Jesus may be made manifest in our bodies. For we who live are always delivered unto death for Jesus' sake; that the life also of Jesus may be made manifest in our mortal flesh.'[1] The Pontiffs have thereby represented to the world the union of weakness and power. Five-and-forty times they have been driven out of Rome, or have never entered it. Expulsion, banishment, dethronement, this has been their history. No line of kings has ever survived such vicissitudes;

[1] 2 Cor. iv. 9-11.

their lines have been broken, and their dynasties have passed away. But the line of the Pontiffs is indefectible, and their throne has always been restored. To be protected by the power of Christian nations—first by one, then by another—has always been their providential lot. It could not be otherwise. The divine Founder of the Church has so disposed it that His kingdom should not be numbered among the nations; nor its Head, though supreme over all princes, hold his own by temporal might or military power. Vicissitudes which would have destroyed all other dynasties fall lightly upon the throne of the Pontiffs. Subverted again and again, it is as often restored in undiminished authority. It does not, therefore, make us afraid to see the armed bands of revolution closing around the remnant of the territory, and aiming at the seizure of Rome. What has been often, may be again; but we pray on in confidence, knowing that so long as there is a Christian world, so long the Temporal Power will survive. It is not the might of any nation which sustains it, but the instinct of faith and the dictate of justice which pervade and govern the Christian nations of the world. When these are extinguished or enfeebled, the antichristian revolution may prevail against the Temporal Power of the Vicar of Jesus

Christ; but till then, never. It may be menaced and persecuted, but it will endure. "If it be now again overthrown, we believe that it will be again set up. Such is our confidence, and for this we pray. As I said last year, we go out to battle with not so much as a sling and a stone, but with a string of beads, a superstitious multitude.

But there are still other thoughts which press upon me to-day. Our Lord has prepared us for the hostility which is everywhere about us. 'If the world hate you, know ye that it hated Me before you;' and that in proportion to our separation from the world. 'If you had been of the world, the world would love its own; but because you are not of the world, but I have chosen you out of the world, therefore the world hateth you.' Now, of this we have a signal example. There are two persons whose names are in almost daily contrast. Is there any one on whom such a continuous stream of contempt and bitterness is poured as Pius IX.? There seems to be a delight in recounting his dangers and humiliations, in predicting his downfall, in encouraging his enemies, in justifying their actions, in bidding God-speed to their conspiracies, and glorying over their violence. If things turn in his favour, there is disappointment and irritation; if they go against him, there is exultation and joy. Why? Not for any known reason, but because he is Pope; and, as such, most like his Master. Such, for the most part, is the tone of our journals.[2] Nevertheless, I must here openly bear witness that my words do not apply to certain public writers who in the last year have shown much restraint and justice in their language. On the other hand, there is a man whose name I will not utter, whose antecedents and impieties I will not recite. He has made himself conspicuous by enmity against the Church and the Vicar of Jesus Christ. Within the last three weeks, this man has been twice described by those who guide the public opinion of this country in the words which follow: as a man of 'almost godlike self-denial;' and again, 'of a boundless goodness.' I had thought that there was but One Infinite, 'that none is good but God alone.' What comes next is still more portentous: his 'goodness passeth all understanding,' which would appear to be an attribute of our divine Redeemer borrowed

[2] The Florence Correspondent of the *Times*, dating October 12, writes: 'As matters now stand, we may hold the danger to be averted. A complete change has occurred, within a few days, in the tone of certain parties and journals here. Some who recently were wishing success to the Papal Zouaves are now hot in the contrary sense. The manner in which the situation has been appreciated by the English press has had a powerful effect in Italy.'— *Times*, October 17, 1867.

from the language of St. Paul. We have here the two standing face to face before us. The one the object of the world's enmity; the other the object of the world's admiration, or rather of the world's apotheosis or deification. Now, these two persons represent two systems, two principles, two spirits. They are the legitimate heads of 'the mystery of piety' and 'the mystery of impiety,' as the Apostle describes them. On the one side is the Vicar of Christ, and all that are united to Him by the laws of supernatural justice. On the other, the antagonist of Christ, and all who are banded together against His Church on earth. Between these there can be no reconciliation, no compromise. There is an intrinsic enmity, an essential variance, derived from their very nature. We have not far to seek for the reasons of this enmity.

First, this enmity is directed against the revelation of Christianity as such, which, by making known the truth, has limited the license of the human reason. The truth that there is one God has narrowed the field of human error. No man is at liberty to think that there are many gods, or that there is no God. Polytheism and atheism are not only follies, but sins. In like manner, by revealing the Incarnation of His Son, God has imposed another limit on the freedom of the human reason. No man is at liberty to say that God is not incarnate. And so of every revealed truth—of the Church, of the seven Sacraments, as also of every known truth of every kind. The liberty of the human reason to dispute at will is restrained by being elevated to the light of knowledge. Nevertheless men resent this as a bondage.

This, if possible, is still more true of the revealed law of God. The divine commandments which require obedience, justice, truth, and purity, are so far limitations of human freedom. Men are not at liberty to violate these laws. They have no right to be disobedient, unjust, untruthful, impure. The will has no right of liberty to infringe these laws at choice. It is this yoke of faith and law, imposed upon the intelligence and the will, that galls and irritates the world.

So, again, the Church is a more explicit object of their enmity, because it is to the Church that God has committed the custody and the execution of His truth and law. The Church—as witness, teacher, and judge—contradicts and offends the spirit of license to the quick. It will not compromise, it will not be silent, it will not connive, it will not accommodate its doctrines to modern progress, or to the new developments of religious or secular thought. Immutably, inflexibly, it witnesses and teaches, judges and condemns. And this variance is rendered still more intense by its moral teaching. It assumes to pronounce upon the right and the wrong of public legislation, of domestic authority, of personal conduct. It will not indulge either tyranny or rebellion, oppression or sedition. It will not sanction the despotism of parents nor the disobedience of children. It will not suffer unrebuked the scandals of public immorality or the license of private vice. It is a censor of our lives, and an inexorable judge, not only of what we do, but even of what we are. And this is all the more galling, because of the standard of morals it holds up before the world. It is not content to teach the bare letter of the ten commandments. It requires of men obedience to a discipline and to precepts which exact interior conformity of the heart and will. And even more than this. It holds up as a standard to be honoured, if not to be imitated, by all, a life of counsels, and a state of perfection, most contrary and mortifying to the world and to the flesh; obedience, poverty, and chastity —'extinct virtues,' which are still so vigorous in the members of the Church and in religious Orders throughout the Christian world, that they must needs be cut down and rooted out by spoliation, prohibition, dissolution, and endless contempt.

But there is yet another object of the world's enmity, more visible and more within its reach. The faith is impalpable; the Church is too vast to be controlled; its morality can only be derided; but the priesthood may be grasped. It is a tangible enemy, and men may lay hands upon it. Moreover, to the priesthood is committed the office of making the revelation of God an authoritative reality among men. Priests are teachers, guides, and judges; they are in constant contact and in perpetual conflict with the world. The more like they are to their Master, the more hated they must be; the more faithfully they bear witness against the world which crucified Him, the more they inherit the scandal and the enmity of the Cross. It is inevitable. A holy priesthood must be hated by the world. It is false to say that the priesthood is hated for the sins of priests. The world would not hate them if they were like itself. It hates them because they are unlike it, and because they remind it of their Master.

But last of all, and above all, there is one on whose sole head all those enmities descend at once. They are concentrated upon the Vicar of Jesus Christ, who most nearly represents Him to the world. All the enmities against the divine truth and the divine law, against the Church and its morality, against religious orders and the priesthood, fall at once upon the chief witness for the revelation of Christianity, the head of the Church, the guardian of morality, and the protector of the priesthood. All these things meet eminently in his person, and all the hatred of the world against these things he bears in an eminent degree, and that in our behalf. There is an instinct in the world which tells it, that if the shepherd be smitten, the sheep of the flock might be scattered; that if the head of the Christian superstition could be overthrown, the battle would be half won. Therefore it is that all the conspiracies of men are attracted to one point. The whole array of heresy and schism, of infidelity and impiety, of sedition and revolution, is directed against the person who in himself sums up and represents to the world the rights of God and of His Church. You see, then, before you the two persons and the two systems. The conflict is perpetual, and their enmity is irreconcilable. They may be called two Churches and two Gospels. On the one side is the Church of 'men of good will,' one, holy, visible, and universal; on the other, the *ecclesia malignantium*, as the Scriptures call it, the

Church of men of evil will; one in enmity against the Church of God, though manifold as the multiplicity of evil; unholy in thought, word, deed, intention, and will; invisible, because secret, stealthy, subterraneous, working out of sight, and in darkness undermining the private purities of home, the public order of States, the thrones of princes, and above all, the throne of the Sovereign Pontiff, in whom both spiritual and civil powers unite. It is not more certain that the Catholic Church spreads visibly over the earth than that an antichristian conspiracy of infidelity and revolution spreads in secret under the Christian world. These two systems are in presence of each other. Hitherto the Christian order has maintained its supremacy. How long it shall endure, God only knows. So long as there is a Christian world, the Temporal Power of the Pontiffs will be sustained by its conscience and its instincts; when the Temporal Power is dissolved, the Christian world will have been dissolved before it. Therefore, all the storm is pointed at the Vicar of Christ. He holds the key of the position; or rather, his own sacred person is its strength. And these two Churches have their two Gospels. The one is contained in the Encyclical and Syllabus of Pius IX., in which are condemned the chief errors that are now menacing the Christian society of the world. The other was preached in the Congress at Geneva. In the former are promulgated the great truths and laws on which the Church, the State, and the family repose. It declares the obligations and authority of reason and revelation, of the Christian and the civil law, of the Church and of the State. It confirms the lawful authority of rulers, and the duty of obedience in subjects. It is the gospel of order, peace, and purity to all mankind. The other was proclaimed by the 'goodness which passeth all understanding;' incomprehensible indeed, but happily not divine. Its chief dogmas are: 'That the Papacy must be destroyed,' and 'that the religion of God must be propagated throughout the world.' At the sound of a religion to be propagated, the indevout and indocile disciples cried 'No, no!' But the religion of God was soon so explained as to allay their fears. It is the religion of science, of reason, and of genius, the apostles of which I will not name. I had thought that the religion of reason had hardly survived its last great festival, when that deity was worshipped on the high altar in Notre Dame, impersonated in a form I will not describe. The religion of science is at this day somewhat capricious. It traces mankind to a progenitor among the least graceful and most grotesque of creatures, and affirms that thought is phosphorus, the soul a name for the complex of nerves, and, if I rightly understand its mysteries, that our moral sense is a secretion of sugar. From want of light my exposition may be heterodox; but of one thing I am certain, that this religion of God is founded in the denial and destruction of Christianity and of the Vicar of Christ. But in all this there is nothing new. It is the same stupidity of unbelief, the same persecuting bigotry of the infidel revolution, which from age to age has periodically tormented the Christian world. This same delirious impiety was preached more than half a century ago, only it was then not by an Italian, but by a Frenchman. France was then the 'first of nations,' which was to send forth its spirit and to renew the face of the earth. Now it is Italy. Only the other day I read a rhapsody on the mission of Italy among the nations. It was the utterance of the prophet of the Italian revolution. Italy is to teach the nations how to live, by abolishing Christianity. Let us hear, then, how this gospel was preached some seventy years ago. In the *Moniteur* of June 1793 appeared certain letters of ghostly counsel to the Pope. The admonitions begin as follows: 'You, Holy Father, who trample under foot the ashes of the Camilluses and the Cincinnatuses; you who gravely play your ridiculous farces on the superb theatre where the Scipios and the Paulus Æmiliuses dragged in triumph kings bound to their chariots; do you really think that liberty is so easily snatched from a people ardent to preserve it? The Declaration of the Rights of Man contains in itself a force absolutely invincible, because it is the force of nature. Never did Zoroaster and Confucius, Solon and Lycurgus, Numa or Jesus; never did any sage of antiquity present a code of morals more simple, more natural, more attractive. What a majestic spectacle to see the first nation of Europe rise up altogether, and, with one only voice, say, *I am free, and I will that the whole human race be free together with me!* People of all climes, arise! shake off the chains of credulity, of error, of superstition, and of despotism! Let us no longer suffer a barbarous caste to lead us astray in *seeking a chimerical salvation. Perish the priesthood!* It is with our earthly happiness that we ought to occupy ourselves. Assemble your people, Holy Father; arise in the midst of them, and say, Descendants of the grandest people of the world, too long imposture has desecrated your country; the day of truth is come. Cast off all ridiculous fables. Enter again into the enjoyment of your natural rights. Be free and sovereign. Be you the only legislators. Restore the republic of Rome! But to save you from the vices and the abuses which destroyed the ancient republic, do not suffer among you patricians, nor knights, nor cardinals, nor prelates, nor bishops, nor priests, nor monks, nor vestals. Be you all citizens. I place my tiara in your hands; I hope my clergy will follow my example.'³ On the 13th Ventose, be it when and what it may, the President Merlin announced to the Council of Ancients the great news (of the fall of the Temporal Power, and restoration of the Roman Republic) in a message as follows: 'Citizen representatives, after 1400 years humanity demands the destruction of an anti-social power; the cradle of which seems to have been placed under the reign of Tiberius, only to appropriate to itself the

---

³ Since the above was written, General Garibaldi has completed the parallel for us. The Italian paper, *Il Diritto*, gives a letter addressed to the Italians, as written by his own hand. It is more than enough to quote the three first sentences.

'Italians!—To-morrow we shall have set the seal to our beautiful Revolution with the last shake of the tabernacle of idolatry, of imposture, and of Italian disgrace.

'The pedestal of all tyrannies, the Papacy, has received the anathema of the whole world: and the nations are now gazing upon Italy as upon a redemptress.

'And shall Italy, because of the arrest of a man, withdraw affrighted from this glorious mission?'

duplicity, the ferocious tyranny, the gloomy policy, the thirst for blood of the father of Nero.'[4] Where now is this fabric of impiety? And where in a little while will be the stolid blasphemies of this hour? The Christian world must perish before this godless anarchy can destroy the source of its peace and order.

And here I would fain break off. But there are thoughts nearer home which compel me to go on. The influence of this country for good or for evil, for order or for disorder, is great. As a Christian and an Englishman, I deplore the license of nameless writing and irresponsible speech, which, for the last twenty years, throughout the whole Pontificate of Pius IX., has encouraged and stimulated the anti-christian revolutions of the Continent. We have among us public voices which make themselves heard far and wide. And they, too, have preached the gospel of sedition. They would not have proclaimed the same maxims for the guidance of our own colonies, or for the three kingdoms of our own country. But against the Pope anything is lawful. I will not quote chapter and verse, nor name the evangelists of these fatal doctrines. It is enough to recite a few axioms of their political morality. We are told that

---

[4] *Moniteur*, tom. xxxix. p. 165. Gaume, *La Révolution*, vol. i. première livraison, p. 149-152.

a people may lawfully, at any time and for any cause, overthrow its government; that the will of the people is a sufficient, justifying reason; that national aspirations are legitimate and supreme motives for the dissolution of a government, even though confirmed by possession, prescription, and immemorial right; that a discontented minority may lawfully call in the aid of foreign sedition and foreign arms to overthrow its government; that the principle of non-intervention binds governments but not individuals; that even governments bound not to interfere openly may do so secretly; that they may do by 'moral countenance' and encouragement in words, what they may not do by arms; that they may look on approvingly when their subjects sow sedition in the peaceful provinces of neighbouring states, organise conspiracies in their capitals, and send arms and money to the conspirators. All these things have been publicly preached among us; and these evil seeds, wafted all over the three kingdoms, all over the empire, have already fallen on a prepared soil, and are bearing bitter fruit. We designed them only for our neighbours, or only for the Pope; but they have struck root in our own land, and we shall reap as we have sown. As a Christian and an Englishman, I protest against this gospel of sedition; and I pray God that my country may not, by the remotest influence or by a passing word, be partaker in its diffusion; that its public opinion and loud public voice, and the power of its Legislature, may be restrained by Christian order and by international justice, and that we may not be guilty before God of abetting, by the lightest act, the infidel revolution which now threatens the Vicar of Jesus Christ.

If, through our pride or blindness we do so, God will not be mocked. We have been sowing the wind, and we shall reap the whirlwind. When we have preached the gospel of sedition to all nations, then shall the end come. Already the warnings are upon us. There are forerunners on the horizon, and storms below it. There are agencies which elude control and discovery; secret and sudden combinations which threaten us where we seem strongest and safest. We have dallied with the evils which only threatened others, and they have now recoiled upon ourselves. I trust in God that, in the day when we shall be visited for this sin, they at least, who have protested against it, may be held guiltless of the great offence.

III.

CHRIST AND ANTICHRIST:

At the Requiem of those who fell in defence of Rome, in the Pro-Cathedral, Moorfields, 1867.

CHRIST AND ANTICHRIST.

We fools counted their life madness, and their end without honour. Behold, they are numbered among the children of God, and their lot is among the Saints. WISDOM v. 4-5.

THERE is a day to come which will reverse the confident judgments of men. In that day 'the first shall be last, and the last first.' The wise in this world will be fools, and the fools in this world wise. The mad in this life will be the heirs of a better inheritance. It is no wonder to us that, day after day, base, craven, hireling names should be showered upon the noble-hearted men who have joyfully laid down their lives for the Vicar of Jesus Christ. I should break the peace of this hour if I were to repeat the heartless and bitter railings which have been pelted at them. They would taint the fragrance of this sanctuary. I will therefore examine the cause for which they fell; and I will appeal from their nameless accusers to a tribunal which is seldom unjust—to the broad, calm, common sense of Englishmen, and to the nobler and higher instincts of Christians.

The dead for whose repose we offer the Holy Sacrifice to-day were slain in battle for the defence of the sacred person of the Vicar of Jesus Christ, of his lawful authority over the city which, under the providence of God, he and his predecessors have held, by martyrdom, suffering, and sovereignty, for 1800 years; for the liberty of his person and office as Head of the Universal Church; for his supreme guardianship of the faith and law of Jesus Christ, in which all Christendom has its vital interest; and finally, for the rights and spiritual liberties of the whole Catholic world.

If it be madness or baseness to die for such a cause, tell me what cause is holy, what cause is glorious? If the world call such men hirelings, the whole Christian world will honour them as martyrs; and we will abide the sentence of the Judge from Whom is no appeal.

There was a time when the whole of Western Christendom held it to be noble and glorious to volunteer in arms to defend the Holy Sepulchre from the powers of Mahometanism. Why is it not in like manner noble and glorious to defend from an antichristian revolution the Vicar of Jesus Christ, the liberty, the purity of the Church itself? If it was an act of Christian chivalry to defend the frontiers of Christendom, why is it not both Christian and chivalrous to defend its head and centre? If it was a noble courage to fight and to fall for the Christian liberty and purity of souls and of homes threatened by Mahometanism, how is it ignoble and hireling to defend the Christian Church at the centre of its liberty, purity, and life, against the violence of men who have blasphemously trumpeted their hatred of Christianity, and stained the cities of Italy with impurity and blood? If a war for justice be sacred, and if all Christians may lawfully and with dignity help their brethren of every nation, and die in such a cause, how can a Christian hand write names of infamy upon them? I appeal from such wresting of judgment to the Christian conscience and Christian justice of Englishmen. I say, of Englishmen, because the hearts and consciences of Irishmen are already wounded and burning at this violation of every instinct of their faith.

But perhaps we shall be told that Rome is the capital of Italy.

We deny it. Rome is not the capital of Italy; it is the capital of Christendom. God has so made it, and man cannot unmake it. All Christian nations have a right in it. Italy has its share in Rome as France has, and every other Catholic people; and neither less nor more. But Rome is in Italy, and Italians speak one tongue. Geography and language create no rights. If it were so, Canada would justly be annexed to the United States. North America, 'one and united,' would not be 'made' till it had incorporated Canada in its national unity of language and geography. Spain may say the same of Gibraltar, Italy of Malta, and the races of India in their several limits of territory and language. To this portentous theory of nationalism we answer, that it is a denial of all true national and international justice, the source of schism in religion, and of revolution in politics. Until the schism of the sixteenth century shattered the unity of Christian Europe, this theory of confusion was never known. A higher unity and a higher law bound together the nations of the Christian world, and consecrated the authority of States, while it protected the liberties and rights of the people. As Christians, and as Catholics, we refuse to break up the unity of Christendom for the unity of Italy, and to sacrifice the Christian and supernatural order of the world to the 'national aspirations' of any particular race.

For the last thirty years the doctrine of nationalities and non-intervention has been preached with a subtilty and a confidence which has seduced many, and stunned more. Men have been afraid of raising their heads against the claim of a nation's right to make revolutions. The doctrine which the Protestant Reformation used as a wedge to split off nations from the unity of the Church has been since applied as the lever to overturn thrones, and to destroy international rights. It is now wielded to overturn the Holy See. We are told that the highest and ultimate unity on earth is the unity of a nation; that each nation may isolate itself both in religion and politics at will; and that non-intervention is a reciprocal and universal duty of all nations to each other. Against this system of national supremacy, antichristian and immoral, we protest in the name of Christendom. There is a unity higher than the unity of any nation, in which the welfare of all nations is bound up: the unity of the Christian world. The maintenance of this unity, in its head and centre, in its order and laws of national justice and co-operation, is the highest interest of all nations, and the guarantee of their reciprocal duties and rights. England isolated itself from the Christian world in religion three hundred years ago, and its present attitude of political isolation is the inevitable result. Russia in like manner is cut off from Europe by its schism, and its schism dictates its policy. Prussia is still half united to the Catholic world. The other nations of Europe are for the most part, or altogether, members of the Catholic unity. It is not possible for any one of them to claim the Russian or English exemption from national responsibility to a higher unity, without renouncing their Catholic character. This, in an evil hour, Italy has been lured, taunted, tempted to do. And in an evil hour it has listened. It has claimed the capital of Christendom by a vote of its parliament as the capital of Italy. But the Catholic world will not submit to this usurpation; and France, not as France, but as the mandatary of the Catholic Powers, has defeated, and will defeat, the usurpation, and protect the centre of Catholic unity and the Head of the Catholic world. This is our answer. The unity of Christendom will not make way for the unity of Italy.

It was for this cause these brave men fell.

And yet it was not against the monarchy of Italy they fought. They were face to face with an antichristian horde, which the King of Italy disowned. Some ten thousand men of all parts of Italy, and of many other countries, armed and organised, without authority of public law, and in direct violation of the same, invaded the States of the Church. They made a private war in the name of the Red Revolution. This horde was led by the man who in 1848 stained Rome with innocent blood, and the other day demanded the overthrow of the Christian religion as essential to the welfare of the world. They were on their way to Rome to dethrone, not the 'Pontiff only, but Jesus Christ. God has not permitted the outrage to be perpetrated. While we were praying, day by day, in the holy Mass, and before the most holy Sacrament; while in Rome households were saying, at the first hour of night, the Litany of our Blessed Mother, with an invocation of St. Peter and St. Paul for the protection of the city—the head of the revolution, with its leader in all his prestige, was crushed and swept off the patrimony of the Church by a blow so sudden and so complete, that not a vestige, except the dead, wounded, and arms of the invaders, remained on the field. Men will read this event differently. Some will see in it no more than a battle and a victory. We see in it also an answer to prayer, and an act of the power of God. It has once more saved the head and centre of Christianity from outrage and sacrilege; and they who gave their lives in the defence of Christianity may be numbered with the martyrs. But over that field of slaughter and of flight there hangs a gloom as of a funeral pall. The unhappy men who fell with weapons in their hands raised against the Vicar of Jesus Christ were regenerate in baptism, and once illuminated with faith, and members of the holy Catholic Church. In boyhood they had made their first confession and first communion as you did. But some terrible illusion of Satan, and the snares of secret societies, blinded and entangled them. I would fain say, 'Father, forgive them; they know not what they do!' But how could they be ignorant of their sin? There is mourning for them in many homes, and we mourn over their misery; but our tongues are tied, and our thoughts suspended. Our hearts can only ascend in secret to the infinite perfection of the divine mercy.

I have said, that those for whom we pray did not fall before the Italian monarchy. But there are depths in these events which we cannot fathom. The armies of the King of Italy did not disarm or hinder the invaders. They were bound to do it, but did it not. They entered the Roman State in the rear of the revolution, and stood awaiting its success. I know not how to interpret this conduct; but I know how it would have been interpreted in England, if the armies of the United States had not repressed the armed bands which a year ago, from their frontier, threatened Canada; still more, if they had advanced in the rear of the marauders to hold for the American Union what might be successfully seized by force. Such a course would not be ignoble because Great Britain is strong, nor is it noble because the Pope is weak. Neither are the 'national aspirations' of Italy for Rome more legitimate than the national aspirations of the Union for Quebec. Italy has no more claim on Rome than on Dresden or Paris. Rome is protected by as sacred a right of sovereignty against the usurpation and ambition of Italy as Vienna or Madrid. Sovereigns do not lose their rights because they are in the neighbourhood of stronger powers. If proximity and geography and the unity of language constitute a right for the greater powers to absorb the weaker, then Brussels may be lawfully annexed by France, and Amsterdam by Germany. We have loudly aided and encouraged Italy in this usurping policy. We have lavished upon it the 'moral support' of leading articles; and we shall reap the fruit of our labours.

It is a strange simplicity which pretends to wonder why France should ever have made a Convention when it withdrew its protection from the Holy See; and why it should have surrounded it with 'a moral cordon,' reserving to itself the right of intervention.

It did so because the Holy See is to France and to the Catholic world a centre in which they have supreme and vital rights; and it placed the security of the Holy See within the same defence which protects our persons and properties from burglars and murderers: the justice and conscience of Christian men, the public law of Christendom, backed by a supreme power which 'bears not the sword in vain.'

I have no doubt that they who counsel to Italy moderation 'for the present,' and hold out the hope of Rome in reversion when Pius IX. goes to his rest, sincerely believe themselves to be wise and equitable men. We are told also that the signs of the times are enough to show that Pius IX. is the last Pontiff who will hold a temporal sceptre. Some men will read even holy Scripture backwards. They can also reverse the signs of the times. Those signs rather indicate, that so long as there is a Christian world, so long the Pontiff will be Sovereign. If the world should apostatise from Christianity, it then may be that God will scourge it by the fulfilment of its heart's desire.

But it is well for them to know that the Catholic world neither now nor hereafter—neither at the decease of Pius IX. nor yet at any time—will yield one shadow of the inalienable right of the Sovereign Pontiffs to the capital of Christendom; nor will it for a moment suffer the denial of its own supreme right and duty to intervene for the protection of the Holy See. The moral cordon of justice and order will be always drawn around it; and the right of execution will never depart from the Catholic world. In the days of Pius IX., it is France alone which has executed the will of Christendom; in the days of his successor, it may be a league of Catholic Powers, or the force of two hundred millions, concentrated and brought to bear by some future organisation, which shall give expression and effect to their will.

For twenty years the antichristian seditions of all the world have aimed at the overthrow of Rome, at the destruction of the Temporal Power first, of the Spiritual Power afterwards. They hate the Temporal Power much, but they hate the Spiritual Power more. They think that, if it were possible to destroy the Temporal Power, the Pontiffs would be either persecuted or subject. A Pope subject to a Royal Supremacy would reduce the Spiritual Supremacy to absurdity; and derision would be a keener and more deadly weapon against Christianity than persecution. For this end, therefore, all the spirits of antichristian

f

revolution have united against Rome. They have poisoned the public opinion of Europe against it by lying, or by truths perverted, which are the worst of lies. They have misled and influenced governments, stirred up popular bigotry, painted the government of Rome in the darkest and falsest colours, organised in secret a propaganda of sedition to disgust, alienate, and goad on the subjects of the Holy See to discontent and to rebellion. Finally, when the people of Rome would not rebel, nor accept them as deliverers, nor take the baits of sedition, the revolutionary hordes of all countries entered the Roman State in arms. It was at once proclaimed as the rising and insurrection of the Roman State. Foreign invasion played the part of domestic insurrection. Every art to seduce or to compel the peaceful population to rise has been used. Provisional governments, revolutionary committees, petitions signed by imaginary thousands, plebiscites, proclamations, conspiracies in Rome, shells thrown among the loyal inhabitants, gunpowder-plots, mines under the walls — all has been tried; but all in vain. In the end, moved by a just indignation, delayed, through Christian endurance, only too long, the soldiers and protectors of the Holy See crushed and scattered the lawless bands of the revolution. It was a just and noble act for the

Catholics of all countries to sweep the seditions, conspiracies, and armed outrages of foreign invaders[1] out of the Patrimony of the Church. If the unbelievers of other countries, banded in secret societies, have a right to plot the overthrow of the Sovereign Pontiff, the faithful of other nations have likewise a just and perfect right, in open and lawful array, to defend his person and his throne. If the revolution invade his State, the Catholic world has a right to turn it out. Foreign aggressors may justly be destroyed by foreign troops. And yet no Catholic power is foreign in Rome. Every Catholic has a right in the Holy See, and in the city where God has placed it. The theory of non-intervention has no application in this case. Non-intervention may be a policy of the natural order; but it must be confined to the sphere of politics, and to the mutual respect of civil governments. When applied to Rome, it is a mere deceit, in order to mask the question. No Catholic power can proclaim the policy of non-intervention when the Vicar of Christ and the Head of the Catholic Church is threatened. To do so, would be to renounce the Ca-

---

[1] A private letter from one who is in attendance on the prisoners in Rome says that there are ten Englishmen among them. The foreign correspondent of one of our newspapers states that four Spaniards fought under Garibaldi in the uniform of General Prim's army.

tholic character and name. Protestant or schismatical governments may perhaps proclaim non-intervention as their policy, because they have forfeited their rights in Rome. They may also in their theories divide the Temporal from the Spiritual Power of the Pontiffs. But all Catholics know these things to be providentially united for the free and peaceful exercise of the mission of the Church among the nations of the world. The intervention of the French people to defend the person and authority of Pius IX. against external violence, from whatsoever nation, race, or government it may come, would be, by all the prescriptions of Christian international law, an honourable, just, and noble act. How much more, when France has intervened against a lawless and immoral band of invaders, rebels to their own government, and disturbers of the peace of the Christian world. By this act, which is only one more in the traditional office of France in protecting the centre and head of Christendom, she has placed herself in the lead of the Christian order, the Christian justice, the Christian chivalry of the world. May God maintain her firm and inflexible in this noblest mission upon earth. The Catholic world will confirm her acts by the sympathy and assent of its heart and conscience. France has thereby invoked upon herself the enmity, scorn, and railing of anticatholic and antichristian factions. But she has won to herself the confidence and the sympathy of every man among the two hundred millions in all lands, who refuses to offer up the supernatural unity, order, and purity of the Christian world as a homage to the tyranny of modern nationalism, the deification of the civil power, the antichristian hatred against the Church of God. Let France stand firm, and she may stay the plague which is devouring Christian Europe. The prayers of all good men will ascend for her. These things bring to my mind others of a sadder cast, and nearer to ourselves. But I forbear to speak of my own country.

There are, however, happier thoughts, to which I gladly turn.

The late events have detected and exposed, with a terrible but just retribution, the hollowness, the imposture, the falsehood, the vainglory, the impotence of the Revolution. Grandiloquence, mystery, pretended ubiquity, for a long time terrified or distracted the friends of order. But the veil is rent, and the idol is broken. On the 1st of November the ringleader of this godless anarchy proclaimed to the world from Monte Rotondo: 'I here, alone a Roman general, with full powers from the only lawful government—that is, of the Roman Republic, and elected by universal suffrage—have the right to maintain myself in arms on this territory of my jurisdiction."[2] Before the moon was up on the night of the 3d, he and his hordes were swept away, not by the soldiers of Christendom, nor by the armies of France, but by the just judgment of God, Whom, in the Vicar of His Incarnate Son, he had outraged and defied.

Thus, then, is one vast scandal and danger swept out of Italy. Year by year there have been arising in Italy the harbingers of a better day. It has suffered much; and the shadow of a greater suffering, which may still come, is cast before upon it. But there is yet time, and there is yet hope. Italy is both Christian and Catholic. Infidelity and revolution have tormented and tainted Italy; but Italy is neither revolutionary nor infidel. Factions have risen, from time to time, to the surface; and the traditional mind and will of Italy is for a while confused and paralysed. But it is evidently rising again in vigour and control; and if only wise and Christian counsels prevail, the Christian mind of Italy will be once more in the ascendent. Then, and then only, can the reconciliation of Italy and Rome be accomplished. No worse enemy ever came between

[2] *Unità Cattolica*, Nov. 7, 1867.

them than the infidel revolution. When Italy returns upon the path of its old Catholic glories, the heart of the Catholic world will return to it. We love and venerate it, as the soil on which the greatest glories of the Catholic Church are inscribed, and the Head of the Christian world is divinely placed. Apart from these prerogatives, Italy has no claim on our goodwill beyond other nations; against these supreme laws of Providence, Italy has no rights. We pray that all temporal prosperity may be upon her; but on condition of her fidelity to the order and unity of the Christian world.

There remains but one more thought; an image which rises in our minds high above all in calmness, dignity, and grandeur—the Vicar of Jesus Christ, immovable in confidence, inflexible in justice, the father of his people. Against him can be found no accusation. Many have borne witness against him, but their testimonies do not agree together. No man can convict him of injustice, of cruelty, of oppression, of even lawful severity. He has been conspired against and betrayed; but he has pardoned the conspirators and betrayers, to be conspired against and betrayed again. He has taken no man's goods, not so much as a shoe's latchet; he has never harassed the poor of his people, nor driven them from the humble homes of their fathers, nor wounded their conscience in that which is dearest to a Catholic people. The line of Pontiffs stands alone for justice and mercy in the history and the assembly of kings. One accusation against him can alone be proved. He is a Priest of Jesus Christ. Some men are to be found who think this enough to justify his dethronement. The Christian world is not yet of their opinion. Neither were these noble hearts who gave their life-blood, as millions in all nations are likewise willing at this hour to do, to beat back this great sacrilege. In that little band were men of noble blood, of time-honoured names, of high culture, fighting side by side with simple, hard-handed, broad-hearted peasants, who, full of devotion, left their hamlets and their homes to defend the Vicar of our Lord, and with striplings of seventeen, eighteen, and nineteen years of age, mature in faith, and the manhood of Christian chivalry. These were the men who, forsaking home and all that life holds best and dearest, went to bear arms as private soldiers, without hire and without hope, except that of defending the person and authority of the Vicar of Christ, and of shedding their blood, if need be, in the justest warfare and for the holiest cause. God has accepted this offering only from a few; but there will be fathers, mothers, sisters, wives, who will mourn over this bier. You will pray for the dead, though the sanctity of their cause almost forbids it, that they may enter into the joy of those who, face to face, see Him for whom they died. And we may trust that their places here will be filled up tenfold—a hundredfold —that the manhood and chivalry of Catholics in all nations will spring forward with a new energy of devotion, and close around the person of Pius IX. and of those who shall come after him, as an impenetrable wall of living strength, against which, if revolutionary violence or ambitious nationalism shall hereafter dash itself again, it may be for ever broken.

This outrage and its chastisement warn all nations of the Christian and civilised world to provide for their own safety. It is but one more of the outbursts of antichristian and antisocial revolution which have in time past struck at the head and centre of Christendom. It will soon renew its assault. It has been utterly and bitterly foiled; but we do not deceive ourselves with the hope that it is crushed or extinct. It will return again. Its hordes are driven out of view, but they lie under the horizon. They will re-form their array, and return hereafter. We have need therefore to prepare more solidly and resolutely than ever.

Three things, we may trust, will come of this offence against the Christian order of nations, which has all but plunged Europe into war.

First, that France declare to all comers, and to all who may affect to doubt it, that the traditional mission of a thousand years as the protector of the Holy See will not be relaxed; that it will execute it hereafter, as it has now, with inflexible decision; that in all diplomatic calculations this must be taken into account; that, while others talk, France will do.

Secondly, that all European nations take security against the renewal of these dangers to both their external and internal peace. The Catholic nations have a vital and all-pervading interest in the safety and independence of the Head of their religion. The nations not Catholic have among them so many millions of Catholic brethren and fellow-subjects, that their own internal welfare, as well as their external peace, is perpetually threatened by these outrages and scandals. It is the highest interest of all to protect, by international law and reciprocal engagements, the neutrality and exemption of Rome from all political conspiracies and conflicts, and to secure the independence and dignity of the Head of the Catholic world.

Lastly, the example of this noble blood from

Rome, from France, from Switzerland, from Belgium, from Holland, from Ireland, from England, and from other lands, which has been generously shed, calls with the voice of a trumpet upon the youth of all Catholic people to form a circle around the Vicar of Jesus Christ. Let the world count their Christian chivalry to be madness, and their end to be without honour. There is One reigning in the realms of light above this dark world Who will accept their reproach, and, if so be, their life-blood, as an offering to Himself.

IV.

THE SYLLABUS:

In the Pro-Cathedral, Kensington, Rosary Sunday, 1868.

THE SYLLABUS.

Many of His disciples, when they heard this, said: This is a hard saying; who can hear it? ST. JOHN vi. 60.

OUR Lord is here speaking of the great mystery o His Body and His Blood, which He would give for the life of the world. Some who stood by did not understand His words. They counted it a hard saying, and went their way. So it ever has been. The enunciation of the truth has always had two effects: those who believe are strengthened, and those who will not believe stumble at the truth.

To-day we keep once more the festival of the holy Rosary; a day marked in the annals of the Church by one of the most momentous events in Christian history—the overthrow of the antichristian hosts of Mahometanism in the great battle of Lepanto. The world was then so threatened by the power of that vast infidel empire, that Christendom must have been ravaged in all its provinces, had not its fleets been utterly destroyed. We commemorate also to-day another great victory by land over the same persecuting empire. These two great blows, dealt by the Christian world against the Mahometan Antichrist, for ever broke its dominion and its strength; and to this day the Christian nations, so far from being menaced by its existence, are themselves propping it lest it should fall. These two great contests were waged under the direct sanction and guidance of the Roman Pontiffs, who, as the heads of the Christian world—the most illuminated to know its dangers, and the most powerful to avert them—combined, organised, and directed those heroic defences of Christendom, calling together the princes and chivalry of Christian Europe to fight for its very existence. The Church, therefore, year by year, on this day, ascribes these two great events to the infinite mercy and providence of our Heavenly Father, and to the prayers of our Immaculate Mother; for it was while the holy Rosary was being recited in the streets of thousands of cities, and in ten thousand sanctuaries, that those two great victories were won.

But there is another Antichrist and another menacing array which is now pressing upon the Christian world, in the face of which the Church and the Pontiff stand inflexible. For three hundred years, a power, sleepless, stealthy, organised, and malicious, has hung round about the unity of the Church, and at times has found an entrance within it, in the subtil form of intellectual error, against which Pius IX. stands now, as Pius V. stood then. These intellectual errors reach to the very basis of Christian society; they undermine the foundations of Christian civilisation; and against them the Sovereign Pontiff at this hour has dealt a blow which has been felt throughout the whole Christian world, both by those who believe, for their strength and consolation, and by those who will not believe, for their confusion and defeat — I mean the Syllabus. To be clearly intelligible, I will explain the meaning of the word and the source from which it came. In the year 1864, and on the 8th day of December, the feast of the Immaculate Conception, the Holy Father published two documents, the one called an Encyclical, or circular letter, addressed to all patriarchs, primates, archbishops, and bishops throughout the whole Christian world; the other called the Syllabus. Now, the word Syllabus simply means a collection or gathering together of certain propositions, which, in the eighteen years of his Pontificate, he had already published. During the preceding eighteen years, he had in numerous documents and manifold acts condemned a multi-

g

tude of the intellectual errors of the day; and the Syllabus is nothing more than a collection, from all the documents and acts of those eighteen preceding years, of the chief errors which he had already condemned. That Syllabus contained eighty such errors, with their censures affixed, together with a reference to the former acts and documents in which the same condemnations had been already published. Now these eighty errors are partly in matters of faith, partly in matters of morals; in both of which, as you know, the Catholic Church, and the Head of the Catholic Church also, by Divine assistance, are infallible; that is, they are the ultimate interpreters of the faith, and the ultimate expositors of the law of God, and that not by the light of human learning only, but by the light of Divine assistance, which secures from error. Under morals are also included a number of errors relating to the political state of the world, the Church, and its Head. I believe, if the Holy Father had confined himself simply to faith and to morality, in the ordinary and inadequate sense of the word, very little would have been heard of the Syllabus. But under the head of morals, he had—for his duty demanded it of him, as the universal teacher of the Christian world, as the pastor of the universal flock —pointed out and condemned certain errors in political philosophy which strike at the root of morals. Therefore the world has risen in uproar. Governments have declared that the Syllabus lays the axe to the root of their political society: but if it does so, it is so much the worse for those nations; for they must be constituted on an antichristian basis. Now I may be asked, Why should the Holy Father touch on any matter of politics at all? For this plain reason: because politics are a part of morals. What the moral law of the Ten Commandments is to the individual, politics are to society. Politics are nothing more than the morals of society—the collective morality of Christian men united together under social law. Men might as well say that they will permit us to instruct or censure a penitent in the confessional, but blame us for correcting and condemning the error of a congregation, as censure the Holy Father for extending those condemnations from the errors which affect the private lives of men to those which affect the public life of Christian society. Politics are morals on the widest scale.

Now, to make still more clear what is the subject-matter of the Syllabus, I will farther say that it contains ten chapters. The first four chapters are on Atheism, Pantheism, Rationalism, Socialism, and Communism. These are uncouth terms; but they describe uncouth things. Of the next three chapters the first is on the errors affecting the constitution of the Christian Church; the next on the errors affecting the relations of the Christian Church to the Christian state; the third on morals. The eighth chapter relates to the Sacrament of Matrimony, and to divorce; the ninth to the Roman Pontiff and his jurisdiction; and the tenth to liberalism, progress, and modern civilisation. I will take only one error thus condemned, and that because it will contain in itself a complete and perfect outline of all that goes before. The last error condemned is this: it had been asserted that the Roman Pontiff can, if he will, and ought therefore, to reconcile himself and to conform himself to liberalism, progress, and modern civilisation. He condemned this assertion as false; which is, therefore, to say that the Roman Pontiff ought not, and cannot, reconcile or conform himself to liberalism, progress, and modern civilisation. A bold error, and a bold condemnation.

Like the two fleets drawn up on the waters of Lepanto front to front, we have here a long array of falsehoods, and their condemnations direct and authoritative by the Head of the Christian Church. He declares that he cannot, ought not, and will not conform himself to this world in its mutabilities and changes.

This shall be our subject. And to make the matter plain, I will recite what is contained in the Encyclical to which the Syllabus is attached, describing the nature of the modern civilisation, to the progress of which the Roman Pontiff is invited to conform himself.

The Encyclical describes the claims of modern civilisation in the following propositions. First, the political society of men ought to be constituted entirely on the foundation of nature, without any regard to religion, or, at least, in perfect indifference to all religions. Secondly, that an unlimited freedom is possessed by every man, not only to believe as he likes, but to speak as he likes, and to write as he likes; and that, because he has the liberty to think as he likes. He may therefore publish, by writing or printing, anything he chooses on any subject, and on all subjects, and in every sense. Thirdly, that the family or the domestic life belongs to the order of nature, and therefore belongs to the state; that households and families are under the authority of the civil government in this sense—that the civil government has a right to determine the question of marriage and divorce, and also to control and to decide on the nature of the education of children.

Now, in order to show clearly why the Roman Pontiff—that is, the whole Church of God; for it is all contained in him, and where the Head acts, all act with him—ought not to conform himself to this liberalism and progress and modern civilisation, it will be necessary to describe in outline what are the two societies that now stand face to face—the civil society, and the Christian society of the world.

1. The civil society, or civil power, is a thing sacred in itself. It comes from God; it has God for its Author; and it must be treated as of divine origin. It is sustained by authority, obedience, and equality—the three laws of the human family—which began with the first creation of man, namely, the authority of parents, the obedience of sons, the equality of brethren. These three laws bind human society together. God is the Author of them. When families multiplied, and expanded into races, nations, and states, these three laws, which were domestic and private in the beginning, assumed the public and recog-. nised character of what are called constitutions and commonwealths, from which arise monarchies, empires, and civil order throughout the world. The sovereign authority, therefore, which governs mankind, is derived not from the consent of men, bargaining and bartering, and compromising and chaffering together, as it were in a market-place; it is derived from God Himself, and is given immediately to hu-

man society. But the particular form in which society may be cast, and the particular person or prince, be it one or many, who bears the sovereign power, come not immediately from God, but mediately from society. It was of this that St. Paul spoke when he said: 'Let every soul be subject to the higher powers,' though he was then speaking of a heathen emperor; 'for every power is of God. The powers that be, are ordained of God. He that resisteth the power, resisteth the ordinance of God; and he that resisteth shall receive to himself damnation.' St. Paul says this of the civil society or political order of the world; of the Roman empire, persecuting and pagan as it then was. Within the sphere, therefore, of political society, there are human authorities competent to make human laws; but, as water cannot rise above its source, the natural society of the world cannot rise so high as to make laws to bind the conscience in matters of faith or religion. These things belong to God; they do not belong to man; they do not belong to human society, but to one which is neither of man nor by man, but directly from God Himself.

2. The other society is the Christian society of the world, and the beginning of that Christian society is the person of our Lord Jesus Christ Himself, who, when He came into the world, assembled His apos-

tles and disciples around Him, instructed them, conformed them to His own mind and will, and gave them authority and laws. He gave them that one faith by which alone men can be united—that one supreme jurisdiction by which His Church on earth was founded and is held together. He constituted in the world His own kingdom. He ascended to His invisible throne in heaven; but He left on earth His Vicar and representative—one who should be the depository and the executor of His supreme power over the Christian society which He founded: who should be for ever the supreme and final interpreter of the faith, the supreme and final expositor of His law; and that society, one in its origin, one in its faith, one in its jurisdiction, one in its identity throughout the world, uniting all nations in one family, is the Holy Catholic Church. There will be those two great societies to the end of the world —the one natural, the other supernatural; the one human, the other divine; the human and the natural society perfect and complete within its own sphere and limit, but imperfect and incomplete, and that in a high degree, as regards the true perfection of man and his destiny hereafter. For this it must depend upon the Church and the laws of Jesus Christ.

3. And such was the will of God. He ordained that these two societies should be so united as in their action to become one. Just as man is perfect in his own nature, though fallen by original sin, and needs to be elevated to a supernatural order by regeneration and grace, remaining the same individual, but receiving a perfection above his nature; so it is with the natural society of the world; and when the Church of God, like the heavenly city coming down from heaven, perfect in its beauty, symmetry, splendour, and unity, descended on the face of the world, it took up into itself all the elements of human society that were pure and true, and incorporated them with itself. But before this work was done, the Roman Empire, which was spread over the nations of the world at the coming of our divine Saviour, was destroyed off the face of the earth. The races it had subdued and held in its iron hand revolted against it. They came up with their legions and their hordes; they tore from it province after province. First they devastated and desolated Italy; last of all, they sacked and ruined Rome. The whole material structure and fabric of that great empire, the greatest and most perfect human society the world had ever seen, was utterly crushed, crumbled to dust, and swept away before the winds of heaven. Then the Chris-

tian world that now is rose into existence. It was the Christian Church which created the Christian world. It had a double mission; for the Christian Church has a mission first to individuals, and then to society—first to convert and save the soul, and next to consecrate and elevate the political society of the world. As Christianity spread from household to household, each family became germs and patterns of Christian society. As cities became Christian, they were combined together under Christian laws. As kingdoms arose from age to age, they were bound together under the supreme unity of jurisdiction and in the light of the one faith. The Christian world, as we know it now, appeared. What, then, was the foundation of this Christian world? The one faith, the one baptism, the Christian Sacrament of matrimony, the supreme jurisdiction of the Head of the Christian Church: these four elements created and have sustained the Christian world.

The Roman Empire, which fell and was swept away, fell not more by the external violence which came upon it from without than from the internal corruption, intellectual and moral, which ate away its vitality within, and turned it from end to end into a heap of intellectual and moral ruin. It would be out of place, and I have not now time, to dwell on what

I say farther than this: I would ask you to take any history of Rome, and read the domestic life of the Romans in the Augustan, the golden period, as it is called. The state of personal and domestic morals presents a picture of incredible and unimaginable horrors under the roof of every family. And if such was the private life of men, if such was the state of their homes, what was the state of the Commonwealth —of the empire at large, in its public morality? The human imagination cannot conceive, without the facts before it, to what a depth of utter moral corruption that natural society of the world had fallen. The Christian society of the world came as the purifier and the corrective of the evils of personal and domestic immorality; and purifying the personal and domestic morality, it purified the public morality and public life of nations. And this was brought about by the faith and knowledge of God; by the laws of God; by the Sacrament of matrimony; by the union of the husband and the wife restored to its primitive unity and its indissoluble contract; by the supreme authority of the Christian Church; by that pastoral authority whereby men are retained in obedience and order: these things slowly elevated the natural society of men into the Christian world.

Then began a great conflict; the natural society

of the world strove to sweep the Church of Christ out of the earth. Three hundred years of persecution followed, and the Christian society gained, little by little, its ascendent over the minds and wills of men, until the world was weary of persecution, and the Church entered into peace. From that time onwards the natural and supernatural societies of the world have been at least in a state of amity, down to a time we will hereafter mark. Then Christendom or Christian Europe began to arise. The spiritual and civil powers stood side by side — with many jars and contentions indeed, but nevertheless with public laws and mutual relations and duties, acting in co-operation together, so that the natural society of the world, which had taught the unlimited lawfulness of divorce, learned the absolute indissolubility of Christian marriage; the natural society, which held that fathers had power of life and death over their children, was taught that their children were the children of God—theirs in the order of nature, but not theirs in the order of grace, heirs of the kingdom of Heaven, wards committed to their guardianship, whom they were bound to bring up in the nurture of God and the knowledge of His Son Jesus Christ. They were taught also the duty of mutual charity one to another. The laws of authority and equality, as taught in the Christian Church under the supreme authority of one Head, were transcribed into the public law of nations. Such was the state of the Christian world when these two societies were in amity together—when every member of the State was a member of the Church; when the laws of the State were in conformity with the laws of the Church; when the laws of Christianity were part of the laws of the land; when men believed that human society had not its perfection in the order of nature only, to the exclusion of religion and of God, but then only when it is founded on the one only truth revealed by God, the one only way of life eternal.

4. Such was Christendom once. Such it is no longer. The amity of the natural and supernatural societies has turned into discord, and their union is dissolved. Three hundred years ago, Germany and England and the north of Europe separated themselves from the Christian Church. They broke the bands of unity, and renounced its supreme authority; they constituted themselves independent upon the basis of their own natural authority, and they went their way. And what that way was, we will endeavour to trace. There were three things in that separation. The first was schism; the second was a rejection of the divine authority of the Church; and

the third was the setting in motion of that which men now call progress, the unlimited and licentious action of the human intellect and of the human will without law and without guide. Look at the condition of Germany now. We were told the other day that it is a question whether four-fifths or three-fourths any longer believe in Christianity. I will not determine the proportion. Look next at England, divided, subdivided, parcelled out into I know not how many sects and denominations, each man interpreting the Bible for himself, because the supreme authority of the Church had been cast off. In every country that separated itself from the unity of the Church three hundred years ago, Christian matrimony as a Sacrament was rejected by the public laws. The indissolubility of Christian marriage has been destroyed, and the law of divorce has been introduced. The foundation of the natural order of the family itself has been broken up. Wheresoever divorce enters, the authority of parents, the obedience of children, and the foundations of the family, are shaken, if not destroyed. What the effect of that change has been, I will leave those to say who have the daily reports of the tribunal, where such cases are adjudicated, before their eyes. It has also been announced as a principle, that national education must be without religion — that the education of children belongs to the State. Within the last few months we have seen it, again and again, declared in the newspapers, which are believed to represent public opinion to a great, but I hope not to the full extent, that it was not for fathers and mothers to determine how their children should be educated; that the nature of education must be determined by the supreme authority of the State. We have been told that in the matter of religion, it is indifferent whether men agree *or not:* it may be good if they can; but the State has nothing to do with it, and that every man has a perfect, unfettered, unlimited freedom, not only to think as he likes — for the State has no right over his thoughts — but to speak as he likes, and to sow broadcast with both hands errors, heresies, impieties, and blasphemies, where he will; that there is no authority on earth to restrain the sowing of that seed of universal desolation, immorality, and unbelief, which robs posterity, children unborn, of their inheritance of truth and of salvation, to gratify the licentious liberty and the noxious freedom of each individual man. If ever there was a spirit of revolt against God, it is this; and yet this is inscribed in the public laws of what is called modern civilisation.

Here then we have the meaning of liberalism, progress, and modern civilisation. Liberality means the giving to every man his due, and giving of our own freely for his good; liberalism means giving to another that which does not belong to ourselves. The truth of God, and the laws of God, and the rights of parents—these belong to no government, and to give them away is an impiety.

What, then, is the meaning of progress? A departure from that union of the natural order and of the natural laws of States with the supernatural order and law which the providence of God has ordained for the perfection of mankind.

And what is the meaning of modern civilisation? The state of political society which lays down as principles of rational liberty and social perfection, divorce, secular education, contradictions in matters of religion, and the absolute renunciation of the supreme authority of the Christian Church.

Can it, then, be matter of wonder, that when the Roman Pontiff published the Syllabus, all those who were in love with modern civilisation should have risen in uproar against it? Or can it be wondered at, that when the world, with great courtesy sometimes, with great superciliousness at other times, and great menace always, invites the Pontiff to reconcile himself to liberalism, progress, and modern civilisation, he should say, 'No, I will not, and I cannot. Your progress means secular education: I maintain that education is intrinsically and necessarily Christian. You maintain that it is a good thing that men should think as they like, talk as they like, preach as they like, and propagate what errors they please: I say that it is sowing error broadcast over the world. You say, I have no authority over the Christian world; that I am not the Vicar of the Good Shepherd; that I am not the supreme interpreter of the Christian faith: I am all these. You ask me to abdicate, to renounce my supreme authority. You tell me I ought to submit to the civil power; that I am the subject of the King of Italy, and from him I am to receive instructions as to the way I should exercise my supreme power. I say I am liberated from all civil subjection; that my Lord made me the subject of no one on earth, king or otherwise; that in His right I am sovereign. I acknowledge no civil superior; I am the subject of no prince; and I claim more than this: I claim to be the supreme judge on earth, and director of the consciences of men—of the peasant that tills the field, and the prince that sits on the throne—of the household that lives in the shade of privacy, and the legislature that makes laws for king-

h

doms. I am the sole last supreme judge on earth of what is right and wrong. Your progress is departure from Christian civilisation; in that path you may have many companions, but me you will not find.'

The Sovereign Pontiff, even in that Syllabus, has invited those who are wandering from Christian civilisation to what they call modern civilisation to return again; to come back to Christian marriage, Christian education, Christian unity of faith and worship, and Christian submission to Him who is the Pastor of pastors. This is the meaning of the Syllabus. I know you who are my own flock respond with your hearts to what I have said; but I am speaking to many who are not members of my own flock, and I put it to them to judge, with that integrity, uprightness, honour, strong vigorous good sense, clear conscience, and desire to do right, which I know Englishmen to possess, longing to know the truth, and willing to follow it, whether I have indulged to-day in words of asperity or of unreason, and whether I have not pleaded calmly for the laws of the Christian world. Do you not yourselves long for the reconciling of divisions, so that we may once more be one together, and make an end of contentions and of conflicts? The Syllabus, then, is no offence; it is the word of truth and of charity — the word of the chief Christian Pastor, speaking to the Christian world, and calling it back to the one Name under heaven given among men whereby we can be saved: to the one faith, the one baptism for the remission of sins, the one fold under one Shepherd, and to the one chief Pastor, the Vicar of Jesus Christ, whose voice of supreme authority you have heard to-day.

V.

POPULAR OBJECTIONS TO THE VATICAN COUNCIL:

At the Church of St. Mary, Bayswater, on the Feast of
St. Charles, 1869.

POPULAR OBJECTIONS TO THE VATICAN COUNCIL.

It has seemed good to the Holy Ghost, and to us, to lay no farther burden upon you than these necessary things. ACTS xv. 28.

You were told this morning that St. Charles was the guide and the life of the Council of Trent. That great Council lingered on for eighteen years, and might have lingered longer, had it not been for the vigorous will and the indomitable perseverance with which he pressed it onwards to its close. The name of St. Charles is indissolubly united to the Council of Trent. It may be said that no Saint of the Church so represents its authority. He was the nephew of the reigning Pontiff, Pius IV.; and being always at his side, he had influence with him so to urge onward the work of that Council as to bring it to its completion. Between him and the Fathers at Trent there was constant intercourse. He gave strict orders, that when the couriers came from Trent, bringing as they did, day after day, the results

of their deliberations, at any hour whatsoever, by day
or by night, whether waking or sleeping, he should
be immediately informed. He had divided a room
into three parts; the two first of which he called his
sanctum, and the third or innermost part the *sanctum
sanctorum*. In the two first he placed all matters of
discipline, and such as related to civil society; in
the last he placed the decrees relating to doctrine and
sacraments. He studied the decrees of that Council
with a pious reverence; and when its sessions were
concluded, it was at his suggestion that the *Catechismus ad Parochos*, which explains to the faithful,
through the mouth of their pastors, the decrees of
the Council of Trent, was drawn up. After the Council was over, St. Charles returned to his diocese in
Milan, and was the first to carry into execution its
decrees. In the diocese of Milan was seen the Council of Trent in life and activity; and the administration of St. Charles became the model and example
for the whole Church; and is so to this day.

These facts would alone suggest to me the subject on which to speak; and if this motive were
wanting, the time itself, the last night before I am
compelled by duty to leave my flock, in obedience to
the summons of the Sovereign Pontiff, to attend the
Council at the Vatican, would point out to me, al-

most impose upon me, the subject of which I ought to speak. I have therefore taken these words from the book of Acts: words of the Holy Ghost, describing the first General Council, I may say, of the Church of Jesus Christ.

It was held in Jerusalem. The cause of its meeting was this. Certain men, not as yet fully illuminated in the faith, went down to Antioch, where the Gentiles had begun to receive the doctrines of Christ, and troubled their consciences by teaching that, unless they were circumcised, and kept the law of Moses, they could not be saved. They therefore sent up men to Jerusalem to receive from the Apostles a decision on this point. A decree was framed, and sent to Antioch. In that decree are the words I have taken: 'It hath seemed good to the Holy Ghost, and to us, to lay no farther burden upon you than these necessary things.' They then go on to describe those necessary things: 'That you abstain from fornication, from meats offered to idols, from things strangled, and from blood.'

Now I wish to call your attention to two points in this decree, and then I will pass on to our main subject. First of all, observe here the great forbearance with which this Council made its decree. It considered the weakness of those for whom it was legislating. From a delicate instinct of supernatural charity it would not lay upon them any burden beyond that which was absolutely necessary. It proportioned the weight to the strength that was to bear it. Secondly, what were these 'necessary things'? To refrain from certain obvious violations of the moral law; and also to abstain from things strangled, and from blood. These last were prohibitions of the old law. We are not now bound to abstain from things strangled, and from blood. They are lawful matters of our food; and we are not forbidden to use them. If we are not forbidden, I ask by what authority were we set free? That decree was an act of the supreme authority of the Church of God; and the Apostles spoke by the Holy Ghost. No authority less than theirs could undo what they then decreed. The decree they then made, if not lawfully rescinded, would be binding still on all members of the Church. Why, then, are members of the Church not bound by it now? The Apostles did not rescind it. Whosoever has intervened to release us must have acted by an authority equal to that of the Apostles speaking by the Holy Ghost. There is therefore on the earth an authority equal to the authority of the Apostles. And the Council which is now assembling will meet with the same authority to say, 'It hath seemed good to the Holy Ghost, and to us;' and that Council will bind or loose the consciences of men with the same force of obligation as that of Jerusalem.

These are no new truths to you. They are the teachings of our Catechism, wherein we learn that the Church of God has always the same divine assistance, the same divine Person as its head, the same divine Teacher as its guide; and that its decrees are therefore made now in the same Name and power of the Holy Ghost.

Let us now turn from this obvious truth to some of those strange sayings with which the whole atmosphere has been full during the last months. Before I go from you, I wish to say a few words of encouragement, and also of forewarning; to put you on your guard, lest you be misled and troubled by the confident talk of those who are without faith.

1. We are told every day that this Council is ignored by the whole world; that it is a matter of curiosity perhaps, but of nothing more; and that the nations, both Catholic and Protestant, treat it with a supreme indifference. It is wonderful, then, that, being so utterly powerless and insignificant, not a week should pass—I might say, not a day—without all kinds of manifestos, in every country of Europe and in every language, all for the purpose of repre-

senting this General Council as utterly contemptible. If so, it seems to be very wonderful that they should have need to tell us this every day. We do not occupy ourselves every day with that which is utterly contemptible. That which is contemptible dies of itself. Men do not waste their time upon it. But why are their minds so full of the Council, why so preoccupied by it, that they can talk of little else? Great political events may turn their attention away for a moment; but still they always return to the General Council. It is not enough to call this curiosity. Is it not an evident fear lest the Council should make some decree contrary to their will— something condemnatory of their cherished theories or opinions? There is about this an anxiety, a fear, a restlessness, which they cannot conceal. A shadow has fallen upon them. But why should they fear it? The shadow is the shadow of Peter, which heals where it falls.

There is in this fear a consciousness of a presence, a recognition of an authority and of a voice, which will be heard throughout the world; of a power which will be obeyed by Catholic nations, and felt even by Protestant nations, through evil and through good report. By assent or by contradiction the Council will make itself felt throughout the Christian world.

It is in vain for men to say that nobody cares about it. More than a shadow is upon them. There is the finger as of a man's hand writing on the wall—a sign and a warning that there is here a presence and a voice greater than man, which will in a little time make itself heard and felt.

2. And again: we are told—and this is even yet more strange—that the Council will not be Œcumenical, that it will not be a General Council, after all. It will be a packed meeting of Bishops gathered from here and there; but not a Council of the Universal Church. Many reasons are given for this; and the first is so passing strange that I cannot help repeating it. I saw the other day, in the writings of a man certainly of learning, and undoubtedly of vigour, that the Œcumenical Councils of antiquity were Councils of the Roman Empire; that the word 'œcumenical' signified the universal civilised world, then under the sway of Rome. He then asserted that, the Roman Empire being now dissolved, it is impossible to assemble an Œcumenical Council. How any man evidently of learning could have been so blind in the light of Church history, I cannot understand. Before a Christian empire yet existed in the world, the Church was three hundred years old; and in those three hundred years it had its perfect organisation,

its perfect unity, its supreme authority, its universal jurisdiction, its expansion, not only throughout the empire, but even beyond the bounds of the empire; for we know that Christianity had already spread farther than the eagles of Rome had ever flown. The Church therefore was the empire of God — a kingdom not of this world, not dependent on the empire of Rome, but reaching beyond it and enveloping it. The Church was not in the empire; but the empire was in the Church; and that Church had its organisation, its unity, its authority, its episcopate, and its government, perfect in itself, and capable of all acts necessary for its own direction. Why then did not the Church in that age, before a Christian empire existed, convene a Council? For this self-evident reason: those three hundred years were years of persecution unto death. The Bishops of the Church had enough to do to maintain their flocks at home. All they could do was to correspond with each other. It would have been morally impossible for them, without drawing down a persecution, to meet in an Œcumenical Council. They were in catacombs, hid out of the light of the sun. To manifest themselves openly would have been to concentrate upon themselves the enmity and cruelty of the whole heathen world. Nevertheless, before the Roman Empire was Christian, the Church did hold local and partial Councils, and legislated for the faithful: and now that the empire has been dissolved and swept off the face of the earth, the Church still stands as it stood before. It survives the ruin and desolation of the empire, and stands now, as it was, complete from the beginning. An Œcumenical Council, then, does not signify a Council of any empire of man's creation; it signifies the gathering together of the pastors of the Universal Church dispersed throughout the world. That which in the beginning was impossible to the Church by reason of persecution, became possible in the time of its peace, and is possible at this hour. The same authority which convened the early Councils convened the last and convenes the present; not the authority of any empire, but of its own head. The Christian emperors did indeed use their authority in co-operation with that of the Roman Pontiff, but only as in the middle age they acted in union with the Church. Such is not our state. Now all civil powers in the world have with one consent gone their own way. They have left the Christian Church standing in its supernatural isolation, its spiritual independence, its universality, its unity, and its authority, as in the beginning. Now therefore its supreme authority alone convenes the Councils of the Vatican. This then is the first objection: that Councils are summoned by princes, and that to be Catholic is not to be Œcumenical. Strange, as I have said, and utterly at variance with both truth and with fact.

3. But there is another still stranger objection, that the Council will not be Œcumenical, because the Greek separation in the East, and the Protestant separation in the West, will have no place in it. What would be thought of the man who should say that the Imperial Parliament of Great Britain is no longer competent to legislate because the United States are not represented in it? The Imperial Parliament no longer contains the representatives of those who have set up for themselves. Those who set up for themselves absolutely refuse thereby to recognise the supreme authority of the imperial government. So is it with the Church of God. They who have separated themselves from its unity have forfeited all right to be present at its Councils. They claim to be independent, and they eat the bread of their independence, which is twofold—forfeiture of Catholic rights, and subjection to the civil power. The reason, then, why neither the Eastern schismatics nor the Western nations, which have been separated from the Holy See for the last three hundred years,

are represented in the Council now about to assemble, is this—that they, by their own act of separation, have forfeited and renounced their claim. They must renounce either their claim or their schism.

4. Once more: it is objected 'that the Council will not be free; or, in other words, that some superior power or authority, some constraint or influence, will overbear the freedom of its deliberations and decrees. A Council which is not free cannot be a true General Council, but an instrument in the hands of some superior and usurping power.' I would ask the objector, What is there on the face of the earth that can coerce a General Council? Common sense would tell us that a local synod, like a convocation, can indeed be coerced; or synods, as at Constantinople, under the authority of the Byzantine Empire, or of the Porte. Such assemblies might be compelled to make decrees according to the will of the civil power. But what power can coerce a Council made up of the Bishops of all nations? What power, I would ask, could coerce the Catholic Bishops of England? What power, civil or otherwise, is there on the face of the earth that could coerce us sitting in the Council? What power is there that could coerce the hundred Bishops of America and of the British colonies? If Bishops under governments which meddle with reli-

i

gion can in any way be swayed, we at least cannot.
There will be a large element in that Council on
which not even the shadow of human authority can
fall. I should do dishonour to the Bishops of France,
of Austria, and of Spain, if I were to conceive, or
allow you to imagine, that any power—any civil authority, or any human influence—could turn them
a hair's-breadth aside in the free deliberations of the
future Council. But perhaps it may be meant, that
the influence of the supreme Head of the Church
may be too strong. It was well said the other day,
that all the influence of the Holy Father could not
coerce one poor Carmelite friar. It was then well
asked, how should it prevail to coerce a thousand
Bishops? But these are mere insinuations, in contumely or contempt. Nobody believes them. Even
they who make them know them to be absurd. They
are not the reasonings of men. They do not come
from the intellect nor from the conscience: they come
from the will and from temper; from the irritation
of temper with a secret ill-will in the heart. The
coercion of a General Council would be a serious undertaking. Whence could come the power sufficient
for this task? Not from its own Head. Its own
Head is the protector of its freedom. He stands as
the tower of its strength, free from all human au-

thority. Through a stormy pontificate of three-and-twenty years he has borne the brunt of revolutions, refusing to lay down his own independence, because it would betray the independence of the Church. They who talk of coercion imply that the Church is not free. I answer in two words, which are not mine; they are the words of the Holy Ghost: *Ubi Spiritus Domini, ibi libertas*—' Where the Spirit of the Lord is, there is liberty.' Where the Holy Ghost is, there is a freedom, not of men, but of God. The other word is : *Verbum Dei non est alligatum*— 'The Word of God is not bound.' You may bind man, you may put his limbs in fetters; but you cannot bind even his intelligence. Who, then, can bind the Word of God? You may as well try to bind the wind, or the rays of the sun, or the tides of the sea. The light of the Holy Ghost in the Universal Church of God no man can coerce—no power can bind it; and when the Church meets in council, no authority whatever can prevent or constrain its decrees, which flow from the light and the liberty of the Spirit of God. But what they who so speak really fear is this : they fear lest those decrees should bind them by the obligation to submit their private criticisms and theories to the consent of the faithful and the mind of the Church, which is the mind of the Spirit. They fear to lose the freedom of the private spirit in the necessity of submission. Therefore they prophesy that the Council will not be free.

5. But there is yet another objection. It is said that the Council will condemn all progress and civilisation, and put itself in opposition to the culture of human nature and the advance of the human intellect. Surely, the powers of darkness have never been so active or so bold during the past three hundred years as now. There is at this time on every side a rising of the birds of night. The bats and the owls are abroad, to obscure, if possible, the intellects of Christian men. Who was it, then, that civilised the Christian world? Was it kings or princes? Or was it pontiffs and pastors? Who laid the foundations of the Christian civilisation? Who ripened it to maturity? Who, under God, sowed the seed of the progress of the nations? What was it but the light of faith and the grace of the holy Sacraments that compacted the organisation of Christian society? Was this the work of a human power? Was it the work of human magistrates and lawgivers? It was the work of Christianity, that is, of the Christian Church. The mission of the Church is both to convert and to civilise the world. And its mission it has fulfilled. I am almost afraid to begin again about progress, on

which I have spoken already, and, it seems, to the displeasure of some. If progress means the cultivation of science, as it is commonly understood, the Church has ever fostered it. If it means the development of the arts of life, I ask who developed the arts of life in the middle ages? If it means the advancing civilisation of the Christian world, who took the lead in it? All progress in the material arts the Church has always sanctioned and promoted. The other day I pointed out that what is called 'progress' was really 'departure;' that progress in the true Christian sense would be the ripeness, the maturity of Christian homes, the Christian education of children, the unity of religious faith and worship, the obedience of all to the one supreme authority of the Christian Church; that all this should grow to perfection, as the acorn rises into the oak. It is the steady unfolding of the same principles of life into a perfect symmetry and stature. But the progress which begins by dissolving the foundation of domestic life, by separating the education of children from Christianity, by breaking up the unity of faith and worship, by withdrawing obedience from the authority of the Christian Church —I deny this to be 'progress.' When, the other day, I said these words, some did, what many always do; they took half of what was said: they would not take the whole. I do say that the Church opposes and condemns this inverted progress, because this 'progress' is not 'progress' but 'retrogression;' a departure from the 'progress' of the Christian world, and a return to the society or state of nature. Men might as well say that the decay of a limb of a tree is growth, as to say that the violation of the laws of the Christian Church is 'progress.' I gave then, and I give now, a description of what 'progress' is. Modern 'progress' signifies the state of the world which has rejected the control of the Christian faith and of the Christian Church. This is not to advance, but to go back. I say again, that when the bond of Christian marriage is declared to be dissoluble by human law; when children grow up without religious education; when men are divided in religious contests which end in indifference or unbelief; when the spiritual authority derived from God is cast off,—I deny that that is 'progress;' I deny that these are the principles from which the progress of civilisation springs. If men expect that the Church or the Council will sanction these disorders, this 'retrogression' to the state of nature, they are greatly mistaken. But the Church is not for that cause an obstacle to the progress of human society. They are the obstacle who, by destroying the foundations of society, are turning it back again to the disorders of the world without faith. Be sure the Council will condemn nothing which is for the advancement of science or of human society; nothing which tends to its moral and material perfection. What may be decreed will, on the other hand, powerfully promote the progress and growth of civil society along those same true and unswerving lines from which it originally sprung.

6. There is still one farther objection on which I will touch, and then conclude. It is said that the Council is about to define doctrines which were never revealed. I am not now going to enter into what doctrines the Council may or may not be going to define. That is a secret with God. I do not know what they may be; but of this I am sure, that the General Council will not, because it cannot, define any doctrine which has not been revealed. If you ask me, on the authority of what theologian I make this assertion; I answer, the first little Catholic child from the school will be theologian enough for this. Every Catholic child would make its act of faith in words like these: 'I believe, O God, all that Thou hast revealed, and all that Thy Church, guided by Thy Spirit, proposes to me to believe.' That is to say, the revelation of God is the only object of our faith; and the Church alone has the custody of that

revelation. The Church, therefore, alone knows the limits of its trust; and alone knows what has or has not been revealed. According to the words of the Apostle—'What man knoweth the things of a man but the spirit of a man which is in him? even so the things of God no man knoweth but the Spirit of God.' The Spirit of God inhabiting the Church knows what He has revealed; and the Church, having the illumination of the Spirit within, knows likewise the contents and limits of that revelation. Be assured, then, that whatever is defined by the Council will have its root in the day of Pentecost; and no authority can tell what is contained in revelation but only the Church itself. Who, then, are they that tell us that the Council is going to define doctrines not contained in revelation? They are three classes of men. First, unbelievers, who reject all revelation. They, I think, may leave the court. Their testimony is not the testimony of credible witnesses. Next there are those who are in separation from the Catholic Church; who therefore do not know its faith, and cannot understand its mind. I think they also may leave the court, as witnesses to whom we need not listen. There are lastly those whom, I am sorry to say, I must call false brethren; Catholics in name and by the grace they have received, and by the account they will have to give; who, by contact with unbelievers, and rationalists, and men of little faith, have learned to speak their language, if not to think their thoughts. They, too, add themselves to this medley of witnesses, who say that the Council is going to define new doctrines not contained in revelation. I ask, why should men be in such alarm, if they were not conscious in their hearts that by its decrees the Council will in some way condemn themselves? In the history of the Church there never was a Council free, in the judgment of those whom it condemned. Councils are always General until they condemn the error of somebody, who thenceforward denies their authority. Pontiffs are always infallible until their censure falls upon the head of somebody who has erred from the faith. Be assured that those who use this language thereby betray a soreness in their heart. They fear that the authority of the Council, guided by the assistance of the Holy Spirit, may detect and condemn the opinions they hold or the doctrines they teach.

I have now gone over six of the objections which are rife at this moment. I feel confident that, before I see you again, you will abundantly hear them. I foresee that after the Council has concluded, we shall hear the incessant repetition of these things, because those who are smitten by its authority can find no other way of avoiding their condemnation. Read the history of the Council of Trent. Before it was opened, whilst it was being carried on, and after it was concluded, these same things were said of it. 'It was not free.' 'It was not general.' 'It interfered with the authority of this king and of that prince. Its doctrines were Tridentine, not revealed.' Every kind of objection was made to it without ceasing, in every country in Europe: and with what result? The Council of Trent has governed the whole Christian world for three hundred years. It has created a new discipline and a new order; it has infused a new vigour, and given a new expansion to the Catholic Church. When the Council of Trent assembled, it was made up almost altogether of the Bishops of the Catholic countries of Europe. The Council which is to assemble next month will be made up not only of the Bishops of Europe, but also of the Bishops of America, of Asia, and of Australia,—an Episcopate which spreads throughout the world. Never since the beginning of time was there a Council so vast in its representation, never was there an Episcopate so wide-spread, as that which is now meeting around the See of Peter. Do not, then, allow the talk of the day, the pretentious criticism of adversaries, for a moment to affect your mind. All inventions are in motion to misrepresent the Council before it meets; they will be redoubled at its close: but knowing beforehand the devices of the enemy, we are prepared for the assault.

Of this be sure, the Council will make manifest the unity, the universality, and the authority of the one only Church of God throughout the world with such a luminous evidence, that even those who refuse to submit to it will not be able to deny its presence. No man, knowing what passes round about the throne of the successor of Peter in the next six months, and seeing gathered together the pastors of the universal flock from east to west, from sunrise to sunset, can fail to see that the Christian, Catholic, and Roman Church not only transcends in dignity, in vastness, and in authority, all Christian communions or Christian churches (if I am so to speak), but that it has alone the notes which mark the imperishable Church of God. Remember how it was that those three names by which we are called arose in succession. Cherish them; for they are a precious birthright. 'The disciples were called Christians first at Antioch,' to distinguish them from those who did not believe in Jesus Christ. When among Christians local errors or false doctrines arose, Christians that were true to the universal faith were called Catholics; not Catholic in the modern sense of latitudinarian comprehension in which all errors meet, but in the true and divine sense of absolute exclusion of all and everything contrary to the one faith. That faith alone is Catholic which is identical in every place, without change or variation of jot or tittle throughout the world. And thirdly, when among Catholics heresies arose, as especially in the time of Arius, the faithful Catholic Christian was distinguished by this, that he was also Roman: that he was under the jurisdiction and in the communion of the successors of Peter. To be called 'Christian,' 'Catholic,' and 'Roman,' are three degrees of test and of assurance that we are legitimate descendants of the first disciples of Jesus Christ; that we are under the pastoral care of the Apostles, and within the unity of the one only fold of the one Shepherd. I recall to you these truths of your childhood, because we have read lately, in a melancholy document, of doctrines which are Roman, but not Christian. There are no doctrines which are Roman which are not Christian. They are Christian because they are Roman; the test of their Christianity is that they have the stamp and authority of Rome: for the faith of Rome is infallible. The Council will bring before the world with surpassing light this great truth; and the countersign of this supernatural fact will be the universal crumbling and dissolution, the passing and vanishing away, of all forms of fragmentary Christianity, which within the last three hundred years have sprung up round the unity of the Catholic Church.

And now, I would rather have bid you farewell by speaking of truths more personal to us all, more simple, more near to our hearts; but, as I said before, the time chooses for us that on which I should speak. I bid you therefore to stand steadfast in your faith. We live in a country in which we are compelled to breathe an intellectual atmosphere which is not Catholic. The bright mirror of steel exposed to the damp of evening contracts a rust which will eat away its perfection. Day by day you read or you hear confident assertions which come from those who have not faith. It is not possible, except by special grace, that your faith should not suffer somewhat in its instincts. We are more than ever brought into contact with the outer world. So long as the Church was under penal laws, in this at least it was safe—it was hidden out of sight; it did not penetrate society. Now it has entered into the public and private life of England. It is in contact with every body and with every thing. Contact brings and propagates contagious evils. There are intellectual and moral diseases which are propagated by contact; for the errors of the mind are contagious. Be, then, on your guard. If you ask me how to be safe in these dangers, I will not tell you to study theology, or to read learned books. I will not lay on your pastors the heavy and intolerable burden of perpetually answering controversial mis-statements. I will give you that which will preserve you safe through every peril — that by means of which you may go through the most pestilential atmosphere unhurt. Every day, and often in the day, make the act of faith: 'My God, I believe in all Thou hast revealed, for Thou art the Truth, who canst neither deceive nor be deceived; and I believe all that Thou teachest me through Thy Church, because it is guided by Thy Holy Spirit.' And what are these words but an act of confidence in the promise of God to His Church which cannot fail? 'My Spirit that is in thee, and My words that I have put in thy mouth, shall not depart out of thy mouth, nor out of the mouth of thy seed, nor out of the mouth of thy seed's seed, saith the Lord, from henceforth and for ever.'[1]

[1] Is. lix. 21.

VI.

ROME THE CAPITAL OF CHRISTENDOM:

At the Pro-Cathedral, Kensington, Rosary Sunday, 1870.

ROME THE CAPITAL OF CHRISTENDOM.

Pilate, seeing that he prevailed nothing, but that rather a tumult was made, taking water, washed his hands before the people, saying: I am innocent. ST. MATT. xxvii. 24.

I DO not intend to draw any historical parallels of persons, nor to affix any names; but to make a parallel of certain motives and actions, with their inevitable results.

It is evident that Pilate was not willing to condemn our divine Lord to death. Again and again he sought to let Him go. But the clamorous multitude would not. The more he sought to save Him, the more they clamoured. And when Pilate saw 'that he prevailed nothing, but that rather a tumult was made,' to clear himself he took water and washed his hands before the people, and said: 'I am innocent.' But neither God nor man holds him guiltless.

The other day we read a letter of a Catholic King to the Vicar of Jesus Christ. It stated, not that he

k

was impelled by duty or by justice, but that he was unable to resist the aspirations of the people; and that he had, therefore, no choice but to enter Rome, and to seize its sovereignty. 'The state of feeling,' he says, 'among the populations governed by your Holiness,' constitutes 'evident dangers for all.'

I do not doubt that this King is a brave man in battle, generous to the poor, and that he has still the faith of his ancestors, whatsoever be his acts. But the multitude clamours, and their aspirations he cannot resist. How far his filial protestations will clear his innocence, is for the judgment of God.

Such were the motives; what were the acts? An army of sixty thousand men and a hundred and fifty guns encompassed the city of Rome.

On this the Sovereign Pontiff issued to the commander of his small but heroic army a letter in these words:

At this moment, when a great sacrilege and an injustice of the greatest enormity are about to be consummated, and the troops of a Catholic King, without provocation, nay, without so much as the least appearance of any motive, surround and besiege the capital of the Catholic world, I feel in the first place the necessity of thanking you and our entire army for your noble conduct up to the present time, for the affection which you have shown to the Holy See, and for your willingness to consecrate yourselves entirely to the defence of this metropolis. May these words be a solemn document, to certify to the discipline, the loyalty, and the valour of the army in the service of this Holy See.

As far as regards the duration of the defence, I feel it my duty to command that this shall only consist in such a protest as shall testify to the violence that is done to us, and nothing more: in other words, that negotiation for surrender shall be opened as soon as a breach shall have been made.

At a moment in which the whole of Europe is mourning over the numerous victims of the war now in progress between two great nations, never let it be said that the Vicar of Jesus Christ, however unjustly assailed, had to give his consent to a great shedding of blood. Our cause is the cause of God, and we put our whole defence into His hands. From my heart I bless you and your whole army.

Pope Pius the Ninth.

From the Vatican, Sept. 19.

The rest is soon told. On the 20th of September the fire of five hours made a breach in the old crumbling walls. The Italian army entered in, followed by thousands of exiles and fugitives, who, for offences of many kinds, had fled or been banished from Rome; with them troops of women. The legitimate Sovereign was deposed, and a provisional government was then named by the invader. Such are the facts. Now for the fictions with which the unsuspecting English people are misled.

It has been sedulously propagated that the Sovereign Pontiff was not free; that he was under the dominion of a 'foreign soldiery,' 'ruthless hirelings,' 'mercenary cut-throats,' 'fanatics,' and 'legitimists.' So are described some of the noblest and purest blood of Europe — men who for the Vicar of Jesus Christ offered their wealth and their lives; and others who, if poor, and therefore, like our brave British soldiers, receiving their food from the Sovereign whom they volunteered to serve, were not behind the nobles who led them in chivalry and devotion. The letter I have read proves this base accusation to be a falsehood.

Again, it was said that the Roman people received the invaders as deliverers, and hailed their entrance with acclamations of joy. The rejoicing and applause entered ready-made through the breach with the invader, duly prepared beforehand.

Lastly, it was said that the Pope was compelled to call for the protection of the Italian army against his own subjects: that is to say, an invading host had overthrown all order; a mob gathered from all parts had burst into Rome, and crowded the Piazza of St. Peter's under the eyes of the Holy Father. Every form of tumult followed, and insult with violence. Murder was committed in open day. The invaders had driven all police away, and had taken captive the army of the Sovereign Pontiff. They had brought a flood of turbulence into Rome, and they alone had power to control it.[1]

Such are the lies with which the public mind of England has been poisoned. And such are the facts which refute them, known to me not only through public but private channels. I am glad also to know that it was by no English hand that these things were written: but I am ashamed to know that English journals lend themselves to spread these falsehoods wheresoever the English tongue is read.[2]

Rome, then, has been seized by violence; and the

[1] A hostile hand proves this:

'The Pope appears disposed to wait and see how this program will be carried out. General de Courten having informed him that his disarmed soldiers solicited his benediction before leaving Rome, the Holy Father looked out on the assembled corps from a window, exclaiming, "You are going, my children; and may God bless you! I remain. I shall see what they will make of me." Soon afterwards a mob of Roman roughs swarmed into the Piazza of St. Peter's, and made a rush at the entrance to the Vatican, shouting, "Death to Antonelli! Death to the Pope!" Fortunately the Holy Father retained a guard of about thirty gendarmes, who, firing from the passage, kept the ruffians at bay till the bersaglieri came up at the charge. The mob was then driven out of the piazza, but not till the bersaglieri fired a volley, which killed and wounded about a dozen of their number. Since this affair the Holy Father has spoken quite affectionately of the bersaglieri. By the capitulation he is empowered to retain the Noble Guard, Swiss and Palatine, and 150 gendarmes.' *Pall Mall Gazette*, Oct. 3, 1870. The 'roughs' were in Rome; but not of Rome alone, but of all Italy.

[2] I add the following as specimens. I need not remind the reader of the 'charred bones' which were found in the dungeons of the Inquisition in 1848; nor need I say that every statement here

Head of Christendom, and Christendom itself, has been robbed. The capital of the Christian world is reduced to the capital of a nation; and to-day, the Festival of the holy Rosary, is fixed for the Plebiscite. This day, hitherto sacred in memory of the deliverance of Christendom in the battle of Lepanto, by the Christian powers animated and sustained by the spirit and energy of a Pontiff, will hereafter be memorable

---

bears falsehood on its face. I had hoped that Miss Ratcliffe's novels, and *Maria Monk*, had exhausted this kind of calumnious nonsense. 'There are, however, some tribunals which are now, and will probably for ever henceforth remain, closed. First among these is the Tribunal of the Holy Inquisition, directed by the Dominicans. These worthy disciples of Guzman have not yet made their appearance in the streets of the city; for, like the Jesuits, they are anything but popular in Rome. People still remember here that hundreds of poor wretches were shut up in the prison of the Holy Inquisition for the great crime of eating a sausage on a Friday, or because they had forgotten to kneel down when the miraculous 'Bambino' of 'Ara Cœli' made his appearance in the streets. At the Café de Rome a man was shown to me this morning who was kept in a dark prison of the Holy Office for three months because he had ventured to state publicly that the *Misérables* of Victor Hugo was the best of books. A poor woman reduced to poverty stopped a cardinal at the promenade, asking him to give her some money. His eminence having refused, in her indignation she said that princes of the Church had no heart, and were hypocrites. The poor woman was sent to the Holy Office, and was condemned to a month's imprisonment. I could quote a hundred facts of the same kind; but the two above mentioned are enough to explain how it is that the tribunal of the Holy Inquisition is not popular in Rome.' *Daily Telegraph*, Oct. 4, 1870.

I cannot refrain from adding another sample of the absurdities cooked for English credulity, with which the keen Italian intellect

for the mockery of a Plebiscite, taken with all the freedom of a siege, and helped by the presence of an invading army. Such are the events. Now for the results, of which some are immediate, some future, but all inevitable.

Let us estimate the moral character of the deed which has been done.

1. First, it is a sin. In an old book there still is

---

amuses itself at our expense. I need hardly say that 'the little window of St. Peter's in the Vatican' physically cannot exist, and that 'in the Vatican' the interior of St. Peter's can only be seen by clairvoyance; nor that the Pope's 'head at the crack of the door' is fabulous and foolish. Any one who knows the locality will know that such a tale must be a fabrication. But the aim of it is as evident as its malice. The whole is intended to make mischief between the Holy Father and the noble men who the other day exposed their lives in his defence. But neither will this succeed: they know him, and he knows them, too well. 'The Pope in the mean time amuses himself by watching, himself unseen, through a little window of St. Peter's in the Vatican, the Italian soldiers, who visit the great temple with much devotion, and, passing before the statue of St. Peter, bow and kiss its toe, and make the sign of the cross. On the evening of the 26th he said to Cardinal Patrizzi: "Does your Eminence know that these Italian soldiers seem much better Christians than those who were in my service a week ago? Good fellows! good fellows!" A few days since, two Italian officers of artillery entered the Vatican to visit the museum, and on entering ascended by mistake the grand staircase to the right instead of the one in front. The gendarmes and halberdiers made way for them with every sign of respect. In the same respectful manner they were saluted by prelates and abbés. Passing from hall to hall, they arrived at a spot where were dignitaries of the highest rank, cardinals, bishops, &c., in great numbers, one of whom asked what they desired. "To visit read a law, now obsolete, which runs: 'Thou shalt not steal;' and in the same statute, another forgotten precept may be read: 'Thou shalt not covet.' Now, he that 'aspires by force' after his neighbour's house, or his neighbour's goods, both covets and steals. Again, in the same book is recorded the sin and the judgment of one who 'shed the blood of war in peace.'[3] This deed, then, has these three stains upon it.

2. Farther, this deed is a manifold injustice, even against the laws of nature. It is a war of offence; and all offensive wars are murders. It is also contrary to the laws of warfare, for it was perpetrated, as the doer professed, by a 'son' against a 'father,' in time of peace, and without even a declaration of war. As such, it was also contrary to the laws of natural justice which bind nations together. More-

---

the museum," answered the officers. "You have mistaken your way," said Cardinal Pacca; "these are the apartments of his Holiness, and this is his ante-chamber." Pius IX., at the unexpected clank of sabres, putting his head at the crack of the door, saw the officers bowing themselves out backwards with all manner of reverences before the clerical dignitaries. Upon being told the cause of their appearance, he exclaimed, opening the door, "Fine fellows! brave youths!" Pius IX., who was himself an officer of hussars in his youth, is decidedly pleased by the Italian soldiers. These are trifles which I tell you; but they may have more influence than any one imagines upon the *modus vivendi*.' *Pall Mall*, Oct. 3, 1870.

[3] 3 Kings ii. 5.

ever, it was a violation of sovereign rights, the oldest and most sacred in the world. For more than a thousand years, the Vicars of Jesus Christ have reigned as sovereigns over Rome. They are the most ancient of Christian kings. Compared with them, all European sovereignties are but of yesterday. The crown rights of all existing dynasties are less sacred by antiquity, prescription, and possession than the rights of Pius the Ninth.

3. And this sin, which would be injustice against any sovereign, is also sacrilege against the Vicar of Jesus Christ. It is a violence against a person who is sacred, and a violation of sacred things. The sovereignty of Rome is a sacred trust in behalf of the whole Christian world. The freedom of the Church and the liberty of the truth are contained in it. Pius IX. received it from his predecessors as a trust, and is bound, before God, to hand it on intact to those who shall come after. His throne is not that of earthly right alone, but of the Vicar of Christ; a power not won by conquest, nor sought by ambition, nor bought by gold, nor filched by intrigue, but forced upon the Pontiffs by a moral and political necessity. When the people of Rome and of Italy had no other protectors, they made the Pontiff to be their king. Christian Rome became afterwards the germ of Chris-

tian civilisation and of the political order of the Christian world. But the Christian order of the world is a creature of divine Providence, and has a sacred character, of which the Sovereign Pontiff is the centre and head. The attempt to depose him is therefore a sacrilege against the Christian order of the whole world. Such, then, is the moral character of the deed that has been accomplished.

And now, to show what are its results, I would ask two questions:

First, what will be the consequence of this act upon the Church?

St. Hilary says that the wounds of the Passion pierced the Manhood of Jesus, but the Godhead they could not reach. Like as the keenest weapon cutting a flame of fire passes harmless, and the flame is impassible, so with the Church; this outrage and sacrilege cannot reach the life and powers of the Church. It remains intact and inviolable; its faith, its divine authority, its indefectible life, its indissoluble unity, its infallible Head and Voice, all alike undiminished in purity, energy, and freedom. It was not Temporal Power that sustained the Œcumenical Council the other day, when all the influences and menaces of the world were concentrated against it. It was by the supernatural power of its own Divine authority that it held on in its majestic course, without swerving a hair's-breadth from its duty. Temporal power is of use to the Church only for the peaceful exercise of its prerogatives. Its spiritual power cannot be wrested from it, nor suspended, by any hand below God.

If the Church be spoiled, even the spoiling will, in one way, work for good. When the world persecutes, persecution purifies. While the Church is in peace, morbid humours gather. One thing is certain: we shall have among us fewer bad Catholics, worldly Catholics, lax Catholics, and liberal Catholics. When the world turns upon the Church, such men are either reclaimed or fall off. When trial comes, it does not pay to be a Catholic; to be firm costs something. Only those who hold faith dearer than life stand the test. We are not afraid of this sifting. Nominal Catholics are our weakness and vexation, our scandal and our shame; sometimes they are our greatest danger. When there is nothing left for the ambitious or the covetous, the Church will have more health and peace; and so long as this usurpation lasts, it will have at least this wholesome effect. For three hundred years, not only without temporal power, or the friendship of the world, but even in persecution and perpetual conflict, the Church rooted itself, and rose and ripened to its perfection. We have no fears, then, for the Church, if its destiny be to return into its first state of isolation. We have seen it already in Ireland, not only separate from the world, but in endless war with it. The Church in Ireland has subsisted as by miracle, not only without temporal power, but against all temporal power, in the face of it, and in spite of it. The faith of pastors and people has been and is inextinguishable; the alms of the faithful inexhaustible. No royal supremacy could ever establish itself over the faith of Ireland. And what is true of Ireland is true of America. In the freest people under the sun the Church wields its authority, and spreads daily. So, come what may, the Catholic and Roman Church will thrive of its own intrinsic life and vigour. And if its future relations be not with dynasties, which seem to be passing away, they will be with the peoples, who cannot pass away. The constitution of the Church is indeed immutable, because it is ordained of God. The constitution of political societies may be changed, because God has not ordained any particular form of civil power. In the principles and order of the Church we can yield neither jot nor tittle, and the world therefore counts us fanatical and obstinate; but in the political order we are bound to no theories of government, no special kind of constitution. What is it, then, to the Church, if dynasties commit suicide? It can renew its relations with every form of civil order. And it would seem to be in the future that the government of the world will descend into the hands of the people; and with the people the Church is always at home. The people hear it gladly, as they heard its divine Master. Let no man, then, deceive himself, by thinking that the Pontiffs need emperors or kings. They are never stronger than when they are the guides of the people, walking to and fro in the midst of them. Let no one imagine that the Temporal Power is over, because a king has invaded Rome and spoiled the Pontiff of his rights. There is a future also for Italy; and the people of Italy have few dynastic reminiscences, but the memory of their Catholic freedom, and of their Pontiffs, is vivid and fresh. Rome will see many changes yet; but there is one thing which will never change: the See of Peter and the voice of the Vicar of Jesus Christ.

The other question I have to ask is this: What will be the consequence of this act upon the world? In a word, it will reduce it to the order of nature, from which it was elevated by Christianity. The Church has a twofold mission: the one, to convert individuals, one by one, to faith, and to bind them into a spiritual society; the other, to civilise and to elevate the political order of mankind. It was this latter office of the Church which, when nations were converted to the faith, united them under public Christian laws, and bound them together by international compacts under one supreme judge of all. Of the former part of its mission, nothing under God can deprive the Church. Of the second it may easily be discharged. If the political order of the world separates itself from the unity of faith and from the authority of the Church, then the Church can no longer fulfil its mission as the guide of the civil society of men. For three hundred years the separation has been accomplishing itself. In every country of Europe the Church and the civil powers have ceased to act in unison, or to be united by common laws. In Rome alone the civil order remained Christian. And this deed has dissolved this last union of public law with Christianity. The King who did it may not have intended it. But the Revolution did; and he has done its work.

The effect of this is inevitable. Throughout the whole of Europe, the political order is now parted from the authority of Christ. Christian faith and Christian law are left to individuals, one by one.

States and nations are Christian no longer, when their public life and law and conduct are withdrawn from Christianity. If they legislate in conformity with Christianity, it is not because they recognise Christianity as a rule, but because the popular will may happen to fall in with it. If it happen to fall out with Christianity, they will legislate against it.

Christendom, then—that is, the family of Christian peoples united in one body, one spirit, one Lord, one faith, one baptism, under one common law and one common Father—is dissolved. This deed has dethroned the representative of Jesus Christ among men, and the nations of the world look on without moving a finger to restore him to his right. The international law of justice and mutual respect is gone. Diplomacy is a name without authority; talk, without force to do; and, by this act of disintegration, Christendom returns into the order of natural morality and natural sanctions. What it retains of Christianity, it retains not as such, but as expedient, or politic, or of mere custom. In its public order it has no worship, and is therefore without God in the world. In its morality, it has no higher sanction than the awards of penal retribution; in its education, nothing higher than the service of this world. Therefore this disintegration reproduces itself in every civil state throughout the world. One by one, they are dissolving by the same law and force which has dissolved the unity of Christendom at large. Wheresoever the plague of revolution enters, its effects are antichristian and antisocial. Two things surely follow in its train: the dissolution of Christian marriage by divorce, and the abolition of Christian education. Where these things are, society is smitten at its root, and the offspring of society grow up without faith, and therefore without God. Woe to the people among whom the young are rising to manhood without Christianity. And how shall they be Christian, if Christianity be expelled from education? And what dissolves states, dissolves also homes, and in the end the canker eats into men and their very nature. The intellect, developed without faith, is the prey of all error and perversion. The will, grown strong without Christian law, is the source of all rebellion. And to such a state of nature the public apostasy of nations from Christianity is reconducting society, homes, and man. All this may seem far-fetched. But so is the early calculation by which the shoals and reefs and sands are foreknown and avoided.

You may ask, What has all this to do with the Temporal Power of the Pope?

The Temporal Power of the Pope is the providential guardian of the public order of Christian law in Europe, from which our ripe Christian civilisation sprang; and the dissolution of the Temporal Power leads straightway to the dissolution of that public, domestic, and personal commonwealth.

Men will not believe that under temporal forms and accidents lie concealed and guarded the highest moral laws. They denounce St. Thomas of Canterbury because he resisted King Henry II. in matters of church lands and manors, and tribunals, and appeals. They accuse him of pride, worldliness, and avarice. But St. Thomas saw by an intuition that under these things lay faith, morals, and the divine authority of the Church; and that in these all was at stake. He won his contest by the shedding of his blood, and he saved these things to the English people for more than three hundred years. The usurpations of Henry II. triumphed in Henry VIII., whom Thomas Cranmer served and flattered, when he ought to have withstood. The instincts of St. Thomas are proved to be unerring by the spiritual and moral state of England now. The poor have been disinherited of their spiritual patrimony; and the civil power, with its laws, has departed century by century farther from the unity of the Christian

Church and faith. But these things men will not hear from our lips. They have been spoken lately by one from whom I am sorry to be widely parted, but for whose fearless zeal I have a true respect. He has described the state of London as he sees it, and as we know it to be.[4] And London of to-day is the legitimate fruit of civilisation without Christianity. This is the work of the same antisocial, antichristian spirit, which is now exulting over what it believes to be the downfall of the Temporal Power of the Vicar of Jesus Christ.

But, to be brief, I will put in a proof above suspicion. A book has lately appeared which tells the

[4] Lord Shaftesbury, speaking at Ryde on Friday on behalf of the London City Mission, said that 'he believed that the next census would show a population in London of nearly 4,000,000, a serious proportion of whom were in a state of moral and social degradation so great, that, in his opinion, unless something were done to improve them, the British Constitution would not be worth a quarter of a century's purchase. His lordship thought that most of the evil was attributable to the fact, that all who could afford it lived out of town, away from their poorer neighbours. The ignorance and poverty of the large masses of the people of the metropolis exceeded anything that could be described. When times of trouble came—and they would come—the lawless classes would emerge from their doors by thousands; and they might depend upon it, that unless the mass of people were brought under the influence of the Gospel, the great city of London would some day present a spectacle of conflagration, plunder, and bloodshed, that would astonish the civilised world.' *Pall Mall Gazette*, Aug. 29, 1870.

truth, but yet not a thousandth part of the truth. It bears for its title, the *Seven Curses of London*. If men will not hear our testimony, let them at least listen to their own.

And now I have but two other words to add.

The one is this: that the Roman question, which men say is now ended, is only now beginning. Do not think me fanatical, or blind, or senseless, if I affirm that the Temporal Power is not ended yet, and that the Roman question is only now once more begun. We have had to repeat, even to weariness, that some five-and-forty Popes before now have either never set foot in Rome, or have been driven out of it. Nine times they have been driven out by Roman factions; times without number by invaders. Why not, then, a forty-sixth time? Pius VI., Pius VII. were prisoners; why not Pius IX.? Pius IX. has been already once in exile; why not a second time? Nine times the city of Rome has been held by usurpers; why not a tenth? Seven times Rome has been besieged; why not an eighth? Twice it has been nearly destroyed; and once so utterly desolate, that for forty days, we are told, nothing human breathed in it, and no cry was heard but of the foxes on the Aventine. Warfare, suffering, wandering, weakness, with imperishable vitality and invincible power, is the lot and the history of the Pontiffs; and Rome shares their destiny. There has nothing happened now that has not happened, and that often, before; the end that has often been predicted has not come: why should it now? Men are always saying, 'Now at last is the end.' But the end is not yet.

I say that the Roman question is only beginning, because the statesmen, and the diplomatists, and the princes of Europe have undertaken to solve a question which has only one solution, and that solution they have rejected. For more than a thousand years the providence of God has clothed the Head of the Christian Church with a temporal sovereignty, in order that he may exercise his supreme spiritual power in peace. His supreme spiritual power is not of man or by man, but from God alone. He has exercised it in persecution and in peace. In the one state or the other, exercise it he will, until the end. In pagan days he exercised it in persecution; in Christian times in peace. Therefore it is not for its exercise, but for its peaceful exercise among Christian men, that the Temporal Power is needed. Between persecution and peace there is no third state. When the world became Christian, its instincts proclaimed that the Vicar of Jesus Christ could be the subject of no mortal sovereignty; therefore he became sovereign. Between subject and sovereign there is no middle state. Men saw that the Head of the religion of all nations could not be national—that is, the subject of any nation—lest national jealousies in politics and religion should set the world on fire at all its corners. But if not national, or the subject of any nation, then he must be extra-national, or independent of all nations; and then he must be sovereign: for between independence and sovereignty there may be a difference of sound, there can be no difference in reality. Such is the solution of divine Providence. Therefore the Vicar of Christ and Head of the Universal Church has reigned independent as sovereign for more than a thousand years. But now men will not accept this solution of the Providence of God. They must find another. They must revise His solution, and find a better. But they will find neither a better nor another; and while they are seeking to solve this riddle, time will run, and the Roman question will not be ended. It will entangle itself more and more, and be farther from its end the longer it is unsolved. Nay, I will be bold to say they will end it in one of two ways. They will either find, after all, that Providence is wiser than they, and they will put back the Head of Christendom into the throne and possession of his rights; or they will keep him out of them, and the whole of Christian Europe will be torn by political and religious conflicts. The Roman question will then last longer, and will cost all nations something more stern and solid than the illuminations and *vivas* of the Italian monarchy.

The other word I have to say is this: the principles of the Roman question are applicable to all kingdoms in the world.

The Jews had a proverb, that 'tithes are the fence of property.' God's freehold is the defence of man's freehold. The respect paid to sacred property is the guardian of all human rights. If so, the violation of Divine rights is the violation of all.

Now what is the first principle of this Italian deed? The deposition of kings; and that by invasion; without declaration of war; and without a cause. 'A monarchy of more than eleven hundred years,' we read the other day, 'has fallen.' I say, No, it has not fallen; it has been violently broken down. What crowns are safe when this is possible? Let no man say, crowns are safe when people are contented. People are not contented when systematic intrigue and bribery buy them for seditious uses. There are in every country, even in the best governed, masses whom no government will content. They are the ready material for sedition and conspiracy. Englishmen believe England to be well governed; let them look to the classes below those who have anything to lose. For twenty years a revolution, the most systematic and the most stealthy, has surrounded and pervaded Rome. If countries not far from us were treated in like manner, if Belgium had been so treated by France, how long would contentment last? In all this long conspiracy there has never been a charge of cruelty, of injustice, or of oppression, which would bear the touch of examination. The government of the Holy Father has been a government of clemency and of forbearance, even to excess. No secular government in the world would have spared the lives of criminals whom Pius IX. has spared, to lead the outrage and sacrilege of the 20th of September.

What, then, is the cause of discontent? 'We will not have this man to reign over us'—*Nolumus hunc regnare*. No crime of violated rights or of unendurable oppression can be proved. These things might lend a colour to a popular judicial process against a hard or unjust ruler. Nothing of this kind is so much as alleged by the hundred tongues and pens always going against the Holy Father. It is *Nolumus*, 'we will not.' His only crime is one which cannot be purged. The government of the Vicar of Christ is the government of a priest.

And this the world hates, and the Revolution hates still more. It has an instinctive hatred against a priest at the altar; what, then, against a priest upon the throne? But there is a Priest upon a throne who in this enmity against His Vicar reads the true motive, which is enmity against Himself. I know that I shall be thought a babbler, to utter these things in the nineteenth century and in England. But they are truths which are not affected by time or nation, and will outlast both.

Another principle, then, of the Roman question is, the deposition of a king without cause or crime, because the people will not that he should reign.

Again, possession of immemorial rights, which among men and nations has until now consecrated the just title of the holder—this has been violated with such signal audacity and such ostentatious contempt, that no right, no prescription, no possession, can give title against those who can back their aspirations by sufficient violence.

Lastly, a principle of profound deception has been sanctioned in a Plebiscite freely exercised, forsooth, in the midst of an invading army. This is pregnant with a future. The principle that a discontented minority, encouraged by sedition acting secretly from without, and supported by a foreign invasion, may renounce its allegiance, and depose its legitimate sovereign, has been installed among the axioms of political justice and of public morality. I will not pursue this subject. On the head of the public writers who, day by day, have glorified these principles, because they were of use to pull down the Pope, shall rest the undivided responsibility of this gospel of rebellion. They have preached it loudly, confidently, and scornfully; and wherever the English tongue is known, these words have gone out to the uttermost ends of the earth. But there are ears listening, and eyes reading, not far off, to whom this gospel is glad tidings indeed. They are learning it well; and the teachers of these things must answer, and, I fear, pay for it. Had I spoken a tithe of what they have written, I should be accused of sowing sedition with both my hands.

Here, then, ends one period of the Roman question. But a far wider, darker, and more lasting period is, I fear, before us. The year 1796 raised a question which was not solved till Europe had suffered for twenty years. The future of the world is dark indeed. The blood already shed between two great nations may be little, compared with the streams which will flow, if these principles gain a head. No washing of hands before the people will cleanse any man, be he preacher or demagogue, prince or statesman, who shall teach men this gospel of anarchy.

St. Paul has foretold the coming of one whom he calls *the* lawless. No word more truly describes the state of the modern world. All ages have, indeed, been lawless, in the sense of violence which breaks the law. But the modern world is lawless in that it rejects the *idea* of law, and destroys the *basis* of law, by resolving all authority into the will of numbers. The idea of right as limiting popular aspirations is extinct. Facts are taken to be just, because accomplished; as if robbery could become lawful by completion. The logic of facts is the series of wrongs which, once begun, necessitate each other. And the logic of facts is now one of the supreme reasons of state. The popular will may aspire after its neighbour's house and goods, all right and justice notwithstanding; for the popular will is a law to itself, and makes law by its aspirations. What it desires it wills, and what it wills is right. What is this but the reign of license, the corruption of liberty, the extinction of morality, the negation of justice, which is the negation of God? And yet such is the substitute in the modern world for the even law of nations and of God, which, at least by public recognition, ruled and sustained Christendom.

And with this lawlessness comes the supremacy of might. Once, right and might met together, sanctioning and confirming each other's acts. Now, might without right tramples down right without might. The weaker perish, and the stronger reign, till by mutual destruction men and nations execute on each other the just judgment of God. That this is in store for Europe, if these principles prevail, who can doubt? That this will be the solution of the Roman question, if this sacrilege be not repaired, is sure as the sun to-morrow.

The future of the Church may now be cloudy, but 'in the time of the evening there shall be light.'[5] The Church may have to suffer, and in all probability it will; but all the more surely will it do its work. There is to-day a kindling of indignation throughout the Catholic world wheresoever the tidings of this great wrong have spread; and where the indignation is, reaction will follow, and the nations of the Christian world will pronounce whether they consent to the spoliation of Christendom to gratify the aspirations of a revolution. If there be yet life in the Christian world, the Temporal Power of its Head is

[5] Zacharias xiv. 7.

not dissolved. If it be dissolved, then it will be known that there is no public religious life left in nations and states which once were Christian. But the undying Church will still remain—the living among the dead. Be, then, of good courage! To-day in ten thousand homes, and in ten thousand sanctuaries, millions of hearts are lifted up in prayer, through the intercession of the Mother of God, to her divine Son. You will to-day adore His divine Presence in the most holy Sacrament, and pray to Him that He may put forth His power upon earth, and still reign. Keep yourselves innocent of this great offence. Protest, not only before Him, but before men, that you abhor this sin and sacrilege. Do not share, even by silence, with those who consent in this deed. Speak out boldly and plainly, that all men may know your fidelity; and fear not. No man has laid hand on the Vicar of Christ and prospered. For a time they may seem to be in great power, and to be lifted up as the cedar in Libanus; but in a little they will be gone, and their place shall know them no more.

So it has been from the beginning. The emperors of heathen Rome laid hands upon the Pontiffs, and perished. The Greeks of Constantinople, barbarian hordes, Lombards of the north of Italy, Normans of the south, counts of the Marches, nobles of Rome, emperors of Germany, emperors of France— the first Napoleon, I mean; for of the third, in profound compassion, I say nothing;—all these strove with the Pontiffs, and have passed away. Now, last of all, Italy lays its hand upon the Vicar of Jesus Christ; and they who wish well to Italy are full of fear in its behalf: for he whom it has dethroned is the Vicar of One who shall judge the world.

VII.

THE PONTIFICATE OF PIUS IX. AND THE YEARS OF PETER:

At the Opening of the Triduum, in the Pro-Cathedral, Kensington, June 16, 1871.

THE PONTIFICATE OF PIUS IX. AND THE YEARS OF PETER.

Let Thy hand be upon the Man of Thy right hand, and upon the Son of Man Whom Thou hast confirmed for Thyself.
PSALM lxxix. 18.

WHOSE hand is this but the hand of the Almighty God? And who is the Man of His right hand but His Incarnate Son, whom He made strong for Himself, that is, to manifest His wisdom and His power in the world? These words which apply, first, to the Son of God at the right hand of His eternal Father, apply likewise to His Vicar, who is His representative on earth. The hand of the Almighty is upon the head of him who, in this world, represents the Son of God; and the strength of the Vicar of Jesus Christ is not the strength of man, nor of the sons of man, nor of the powers of man, but of God, who has confirmed him for Himself, for His own kingdom, and for the fulfilment of His own will. The words of prophecy, which are spoken to the Incarnate Son of God, belong also to the person of His Vicar. 'I have set My King upon My holy hill of Sion;' and 'He must reign until He hath put all enemies under His feet.' These words, which apply first and directly to the Son of God, at the right hand of His Father, apply also, by direct consequence, to him whom He has chosen to be the witness of His presence and of His sovereignty among men. And the sovereignty of Jesus Christ reigning over the nations is the fulfilment of prophecies and of parables, and the manifestation of the presence and of the omnipotence of God in the world. The prophecy of Isaias, 'A King shall reign in justice, and princes shall rule in judgment,' has been fulfilled in the Christian world under the sovereignty of Jesus Christ.

In appreciating the signs of the times, we are liable to fall into two contradictory errors. Sometimes we are tempted to believe that the times in which we live are exceptionally great and momentous; that to the magnitude of the events which have happened in these days the past history of the world bears no proportion. This is a common error of exaggeration. On the other side, we are tempted to think that the days in which we live are as nothing in comparison with the days which are past; that they are commonplace and unemphatic, because by use they are familiar to us. We to-day, perhaps, stand in danger of falling into one or the other or both of these errors. We have to-day to appreciate the just value and the true importance of a providential fact, which even the world cannot deny, cynically and unwisely as it attempts to explain away its moral import. The facts of chronology, at least, are beyond the jurisdiction of the men of this world.

To-day we celebrate the fulfilment of the twenty-fifth year of the Pontificate of the Vicar of Jesus Christ; a fact since the martyrdom of Peter without example in the line of the Pontiffs. The years of Peter have been supposed to be a bound beyond which no successor would pass. Pius IX. passes them this day. Let us consider, then, whether, in the times in which we live, there be anything exceptional; whether in the event we commemorate there be anything singular, and what is its moral purpose.

That these days are exceptional in the history of Christianity, I think no man with common knowledge of history and common candour of mind can doubt. We are, at this moment, in the midst of what may be called the century of revolution, the century of the upheaving, the shaking and dissolving of the foundations of Christian society. We are, at this time, in the presence of the most formidable anti-christian powers the world has yet unfolded. This, then, is a time which certainly has upon it a character of its own; and, as I think we shall hereafter see, so exceptional as to mark the Pontificate of Pius IX. with a peculiar greatness. What, then, I purpose to draw out is this: that whereas in the twenty-five years that are past, the reigning Pontiff has exercised and fulfilled in himself all those prerogatives and acts which are common to his predecessors, there are some singular and exceptional acts and events which belong to him alone. No man of candid mind, meditating upon what I shall lay before you, can, I believe, fail to see that there is about the Pontificate of the last five-and-twenty years a peculiar character and significance, which manifests to the world in a more luminous and surpassing degree the sovereignty of Jesus Christ.

1. First of all, I may repeat the words which I have heard again and again from the lips of Pius IX.: 'We are in conflict with an anti-social and anti-christian revolution.' The principles which threaten the Christian society of the world, which deny the sovereignty of Jesus Christ, have indeed been working for centuries, but there was never a moment when they had reached what I may call high-water mark so visibly as now; the powers of disorder were

never so organised and widespread, so menacing, or so confident. I will not attempt, for time forbids me, to draw out the working of this anti-social and anti-christian revolution in other countries : I confine what I have to say to Italy alone. Since the beginning of this century the principles of impiety, immorality, and anarchy, which had scourged and overturned the ancient monarchy of France, burst through the Alps like torrents of fire, with the invasion of the French armies. The whole length of Italy was devastated. The seeds and sparks of poison and conflagration were scattered broadcast. The Voltairian philosophy, with its mocking spirit, took possession of a multitude of the upper classes; secret infidelity spread among many who had not the courage to avow it; but what they had not the courage openly to avow, they had the malice secretly to propagate. With this came also an overthrow of the civil order of Italy. The old municipal institutions, which had grown for centuries, and which had adapted themselves to the genius of the people who lived under them, were swept away. New codes, new forms of government, for which they had no adaptation, were forced upon them. The new institutions in Italy planted seeds of disorder, with wide-spread discontent, and caused a constant chafing of the subjects against their rulers. For the last fifty years there has been a system, a subtil seditious organisation of political conspiracy, such as, for refinement and perversion, never existed in the world before. The autobiography of its chief master testifies that it has covered the whole of Italy, entering into all its cities, and spreading through every rank with its organised unity, and that it waits only the moment when it shall at once rise everywhere. This, during the past twenty-five years, has been culminating to its height. You remember its first outbreak in the year 1848, when the reigning Pontiff was driven from the city of Rome into exile. You remember the faithless and sanguinary invasion of the patrimony of the Church, which at Castelfidardo wrung from the Holy See two-thirds of the patrimony of St. Peter. And finally, you remember the 20th of September in last year, of which I feel confident you would rather that I should not add a word. At this moment, the Vicar of Jesus Christ is stripped of the last semblance of that power with which, providentially, he has been invested; of those possessions which God Himself in the order of His divine dispensation has bestowed upon the Vicar of His Son. When I say he is divested of the last semblance, I must correct myself. We have heard of guarantees.

which invest him with the inviolability of a sovereign person. This is not a new device. We have read of a crown of thorns, and a purple robe, and a reed that was put into the hands of a Sovereign when He was hailed 'King of the Jews.' I think any one may see that the century of the anti-christian revolution, of which Pius IX. has been the object, has reached, as I said, the mark of inundation beyond which it cannot go. This, then, is exceptional in his Pontificate.

2. I will take another point; it is a brighter and a happier one. In the whole of the line of Pontiffs there is not one that has ever drawn and bound to himself, by love and by confidence, the heart—I will not say the hearts, but the heart—of the whole Christian world with bonds more close, more intimate, and more fast, than Pius IX. Three times in the last twenty-five years, if not the whole Episcopate mathematically numbered, at least the whole Episcopate morally represented, obedient to the voice of his invitation, has come from the ends of the world, over land, over sea, from the four winds of heaven, to gather round his throne. The first time was when, in 1854, he did an act which alone would have made his Pontificate exceptional in history; that is, when, with the infallible voice of the Vicar of Jesus Christ,

he defined the truth of the Immaculate Conception, which the whole world had already believed, and, when defined, received with joy from his unerring lips. The next time was when, in 1862, surrounded by the Bishops of the Church, he canonised a host of martyrs. Lastly, when, in 1867, on the eighteenth centenary of the martyrdom of Peter, a larger concourse of Bishops than was ever known in Rome, save only the great Œcumenical Council of the Vatican, came again with the speed of gladness from the whole world to celebrate the martyrdom of the Prince of the Apostles. Do not think that these assemblies were mere ceremonies, festivals, or pageants. They were deep moral facts, and they had the effect of awakening the hearts of the pastors, if indeed they needed to be awakened, to a deeper attachment to the Catholic unity; they bound them to their Head with the intimacy of personal knowledge and personal converse, with the love and the attachment of sons who had spoken face to face with the Father of the Faithful. But when the pastors of the Church are united together, the people of the Church cannot be divided. The pastors of the Church are the bond of unity among the people. As every diocese centres in its bishop, so, when the pastor is united to his Head, the whole flock is united through him. Of this England is an example. The

pastors of England are united with the Vicar of Jesus
Christ with so intimate a bond of conformity in will
and heart, that their people likewise have but one
heart and will. That which we do here to-day is
done in every church throughout this diocese; and
in every church throughout England the pastors
and flocks are united together in an acclamation of
thanksgiving for the singular providence manifest in
this anniversary.

3. But it was not only to the unity of the pastors
and of the people to the Head of the Church on
earth that the Bishops gathered in Rome bore witness.
They recognised in Pius IX. the Head of the visible
Church, the successor of the Prince of the Apostles,
the Vicar of Jesus Christ, invested with plenitude of
jurisdiction, and with plenitude of the faith, bearing
the two keys of Authority and of Doctrine. It was
a profession of faith as well as of love. I well remember when, in one of the Consistories, I saw before
me some five hundred Bishops assembled together
over the portico of St. Peter's, the thought came to
my mind, 'This is the noblest senate that the world
has ever seen. These five hundred men represent
thirty nations, of divers tongues and races. They speak
in the name of two hundred millions of men, and of
the Universal Church of God.' And from that senate

there came forth an acclamation, 'The words of Pius are the words of Peter: what thou teachest we teach; what thou condemnest we condemn.' From the hearts and from the lips of these five hundred men came forth a testimony which affirmed the Divine guidance whereby the Head of the Christian Church cannot err. But, because it was only an acclamation, and not a definition, those who knew how error winds its way, knew well that it was not enough. Nevertheless, in the history of the faith, I believe there has never been, save only in the Council of the Vatican, an act more majestic than this profession of faith in the name of the Universal Church amid the solemnities of St. Peter's martyrdom. And that which was begun on that day received its perfect accomplishment in a higher and more authoritative form. You have heard, even to weariness, of definitions by acclamation; you have heard the servants of this world endeavouring to cast suspicion upon those who desired to define the Infallibility of the Roman Pontiff, by accusing them of schemes to define it by acclamation, to take men by surprise. Let me assure those who so speak, that they who had part and lot in that work knew too well that the whole history of the Church is full of acclamations, from the Councils of Chalcedon and of Constantinople down to the centenary of St. Peter's martyrdom; they knew, too, that acclamations are not definitions of faith, and that the perverse and the unbelieving can evade an acclamation, but a definition they cannot escape. They well knew that the time was come, that the work must be done; and they resolved by God's help to do it. The Council met, and the work was done; and will stand to the end of the world. There is no need of my telling you, that on the day in which our divine Lord and Master on the coasts of Decapolis said, 'Thou art Peter; and upon this Rock I will build My Church, and the gates of hell shall not prevail against it,'—that on that day He created the Church and the Head of the Church, both indivisible, not only in His power, but in His truth. The infallibility of the Church and of its Head is contained in these words. The living and universal tradition of divine faith in all ages from the beginning of Christianity has taught, without wavering, that the dogmatic teaching of faith and morals by the Vicar of Jesus Christ is, by Divine assistance, preserved from error. There never was any man professing to be Catholic—and I was about to say, professing to be Christian, save only heretics and schismatics, who, in the fact of their heresy and schism, denied that Divine prerogative—there never was any man within the unity of the Church who ever dared to deny this special privilege of the Head of the Church, until the proud, worldly spirit of nationality, with the growth of modern languages and modern kingdoms, before the Council of Constance, arose to threaten the unity and authority of the Church of God. Then first sprang up this perverse error. From and after the Council of Constance—indeed, for some four hundred years and more—the Catholic Church was tormented by this subtil mischief; an error in those who knew no better; a heresy in those who, with eyes open, departed from the divine tradition of the faith. The spirit of nationality, which began to divide the Church in the Council of Constance, consolidated itself chiefly in France. And there, in the seventeenth century, was first shaped into form a specific denial of this divine truth. You know well, and I will therefore not dwell upon it, what have been the bitter fruits of the so-called Gallican liberties. They were the bondage of the Church, and the cause of its corruption, of the secularising of pastors, and of the neglect of the people. The salt lost its savour; and why? Because national pride and the power of kings paralysed the spiritual action of the Church by usurping upon the supreme prerogatives of the Vicar of Christ. In more than one country of Europe this spirit of insubordination, and of intellectual error, perverted many; and for two centuries error by tradition grew strong. Pius IX. therefore, in the Vatican Council, extinguished for ever all such national religions. The Divine command to go and make disciples of all nations, baptising them in the name of the Father and of the Son and of the Holy Ghost, brought in a higher unity, in which all nations are taken up and assimilated. Nationality in religion then passed away; and in Christ Jesus 'there is neither Jew nor Greek, there is neither bond nor free;' all nations are elevated by the grace of faith in the supernatural unity of the mystical Body, in the light of which the nations walk, but within which they have no national jurisdiction. I say, that national religions are extinct for this reason. The national Gallicanism of France has passed away. England has national Christianity, indeed, but no national religion. The Catholic religion is not the national religion of England; neither is any other. National religions have passed away. Christianity remains, and I rejoice to know that the people of England cherish, as they cherish their life-blood, the tradition of their national Christianity. It is shattered, indeed. And may the Spirit of God in His power and love build up the breaches of its walls.

In the Council of the Vatican, then, the only two remaining subjects on which there was divergence of mind among some within the unity of the Church were closed. Those subjects were the constitution of the Church under the supreme jurisdiction of its Head, and the Divine guidance and preservation of its Head from error in faith and morals. In the Council of the Vatican, these points, which had been the matter of intellectual divergence in the mode of treatment, and in the manner of explanation, were closed for ever. It is the genius of the Church of God to close all open questions; it is the policy of human systems to leave disputed questions open. Such is the contrast between truth and error. Truth is intolerant of open questions. In all such there is an 'ay' and a 'no;' there is a truth and a falsehood; there is light and darkness. Between these there is no fellowship. The divine Teacher and Witness of the truth is therefore intolerant of an open question; for an open question is doubt at best, and in faith doubt cannot be. In every doubt, on one side there is inevitably falsehood; and in the doctrines of faith there can therefore be no open question. We stand, then, in conflict with the world, face to face. The divine authority of Christ in His Vicar has closed the last divergence among the faithful, in the face of a world which is disintegrating every day by throwing open its religious opinions as insoluble. The world doubts, and the Church defines. This, then, once more, gives an exceptional character to the Pontificate of Pius IX. Other Pontiffs have, indeed, held General Councils, and defined doctrines in detail; but no other Pontiff has so excluded the principle of error by defining the supreme doctrinal authority of the Church.

4.. There is, again, another subject, so large, so various, and so vital, that I hardly dare to touch it, because I must only touch it in passing; and cannot, therefore, treat it as I would. In all the line of Pontiffs, there is not one who, in the face of kings and lawgivers and peoples, has proclaimed the sovereignty of Jesus Christ in terms more full, more luminous, or more inflexible. The document conveying that message, in condemnation of the gospel of anarchy, which for the last century has tormented the Christian world, is the Syllabus; a word in the mouth of multitudes who never saw it; a word used for ridicule and contempt by those who have never read, and perhaps, if they had read, could not or would not understand it. And yet, to those who have the will to understand, the Syllabus is as clear as the light of day. What, then, is the Syllabus? The condemnation of atheism, of the abuse of reason, of the anarchical and rationalistic principles which are undermining the civil society of the world; the condemnation of the heretical and schismatical errors which are assailing the authority of the Church; the condemnation, in detail most profuse and most explicit, of the errors which are assailing Christian society, Christian and even natural morality, the domestic life, the indissoluble bond of marriage, the true progress and civilisation of mankind. If there can be found a document which reflects the Gospel of Jesus Christ and the legislation of the Sermon on the Mount, it is the Syllabus. And how was that Syllabus formed? It was not written in a day. It was not a composition drawn up by a commission charged with its preparation. It is nothing more than a collection of the vigilant and successive condemnations of errors which, in a Pontificate of seventeen years, from time to time, in particular nations, schools, and men, have arisen to threaten the faith and morals of the Christian world. Pius IX., as the chief Pastor, Guardian, and Witness of the faith, sitting in the seat of Peter, and, as St. Leo says, on the watch-tower, casting his gaze over the whole Christian world, wheresoever he has discerned the rise of an error, has at once condemned it; and the collection of these condemnations, eighty in number, is what is called the Syllabus. We all remember, when that document was published, the storm and tempest with which it was received. It reminds us of a passage in our own history twenty years ago—which, I believe, many Englishmen would blot out of the records of England—when unreasoning violence took possession of the minds of calm and reasonable men, and carried them to unjust and unreasonable actions. The uproar twenty years ago published the founding of the Catholic Hierarchy in England. Men, women, and children, were thereby made aware with a living consciousness of the supreme act of the Vicar of Jesus Christ. That storm and tempest served the purpose against which it raved. The storm and tempest against the Syllabus has done likewise. It is a rule of canon law, that the acts of the Pontiffs need nothing but promulgation to bind the conscience. The Pontiff issues an act, and the world, by its opposition, gives it promulgation. We have now reached a time when that Syllabus has its justification.

There are two diseases which have been paralysing the life of Christian society; the one calling itself Liberalism, and the other lately named Communism. They are elder and younger brothers; their relation is of intimate consanguinity; and those who begin with the principles of what is called Liberalism, if they were logical (as happily most men are not), would not stop short of the principles of Communism. We hear men calling themselves Liberal Catholics; that is, Catholics under reserve. It is not we who fix the name upon them; they attach it to themselves. It is a name and a title of which they are proud, and for which we are thankful; for they write upon themselves the words, 'Beware of these men.' If there can be found a justification of the Syllabus in any event or in any one place rather than in another, it is in the terrible and visible scourges of the Divine hand, which have fallen upon the city in which the publication of the Syllabus was forbidden, and a Bishop of the Church was reprimanded because he published it, for an abuse of power. I will not enter farther into this, which would be a painful, and perhaps a wounding subject. But it may well be said, that no Pontiff, from the beginning, has done more to save the foundations of the Christian world from anarchy, to forewarn kings, princes, and legislators, to arouse people to be on their guard, lest the creeping cancer of revolution, drawing atheism and the ruin of Christian morality in its train, should undermine their homes and their national welfare.

I have but one more point to add. Those of which I have spoken are clearly exceptional in the Pontificate of Pius IX.; but I can conceive that some men might contradict or might try to evade what I have said. No one can deny or evade what I am going to add. Pius IX. to-day exceeds the period that any other Pontiff has attained since the martyrdom of Peter, and by to-morrow will exceed the years of Peter. This is not without a purpose. It is not in man to prolong life. God alone, the Giver of life, can sustain and prolong it. And He has prolonged it; and I may use of Pius IX. the words of holy Scripture: 'The sun has not hasted to go down,' but stands 'still in the midst of heaven;' 'As the sun when he shineth, so he shines in the temple of God.'[1]

The splendour of his life and his example, unclouded and clear, stands out in the eyes of the Christian world. These twenty-five years have been the unfolding and manifestation of the character of Pius IX. I enter into no details, but I will affirm that the whole of his Pontificate is an exhibition of three things so luminously, and I may say so articulately, that they have spoken to the intellect and to the heart of the Christian world. He has been emi-

[1] 1 Ecclus. i. 7.

nently a Pontiff of justice, standing for justice against injustice; a Pontiff of inflexibility, standing in the midst of a yielding and compromising world; a Pontiff of charity, full of tender and generous love, not only for his children, but for his enemies, in the midst of a world in which charity has grown cold. The manifestation of that character has won to him not only his own children, to whom his pastoral tenderness is best known. Every one who has been brought into contact with him—and many who hear me, no doubt, have knelt at his feet—can bear witness of his paternal love. I know, from the lips of those who are not in the unity of the Church, that they never entered into the presence of any man who has made upon them so profound an impression of true sovereignty and fatherly goodness as Pius IX. I have heard this from old statesmen and old diplomatists, whose experience had brought them in contact with the sovereigns of their time in all the nations of Europe. There goes forth from him a benign influence which has touched even his enemies. Throughout the Christian world the name of Pius IX. is venerated for justice, inflexibility, and charity.

Now, is all this without purpose? Is this without any design? A Pontiff who, for twenty-five years, has stood immovable against the flood of anti-social and antichristian revolutions, standing alone without fear; a Pontiff who has gathered round about him the pastors of the Church, and bound them to his person, and, through them, their people in one worldwide flock, over which he is the one supreme Shepherd upon earth; a Pontiff who has extinguished the intellectual divergences which before marred the perfect unity, not of Catholic faith indeed, but of Catholic thought; a Pontiff who has defined, by the supreme authority of the Church, those prerogatives with which the Son of God invested His successor; a Pontiff who has preached to the kings and the peoples of the world the gospel of order, the limitation of authority, the duty of obedience, for the conservation of Christian society, as no other ever has; and lastly, who has outlived the years and the time of all, save only the Prince of Apostles,—I ask you, is all this without purpose? No, assuredly; in the history of the Pontiffs there is not one who has so made the world to feel the sovereignty of Jesus Christ, who has so made men to acknowledge whether they will obey or no, that there is a power greater than man on earth, an authority higher than all human authority among men; ruling still, though disobeyed, striven against, but reigning on, and with a power which shall last for ever.

All that I would at present deduce from this is, that God has permitted the Vicar of His Son upon earth, who in the words of the Psalmist may be called 'the man of His right hand, whom He has confirmed,' or made strong, ' for Himself,' to be stripped of all earthly things—of possessions, of power, and of protection. He literally stands alone, without protector, without defence. There was never any Pontiff since his Master stood alone in Jerusalem, who has been more completely abandoned by the powers of this world. In past ages, if one sovereign forsook the Vicar of Christ, another was faithful; if one people rose against him, another stood up in his defence. But now, there is not a sovereign in the world that utters a single word in behalf of the rights of the Vicar of Jesus Christ; of that sovereign who was before them all; under whose shadow they have grown up as it were but yesterday. Who was it that consecrated their ancestors, and confirmed the laws of their kingdoms? They once regarded him as the keystone of the sovereignty of the whole civilised world. And yet there is not now a sovereign or a prince who at this moment speaks one word for the Vicar of Jesus Christ. God has so permitted it. But alas for them! The peoples of the world still recognise him as the Vicar of Jesus Christ, the successor of Peter, the Head of the Church of God, for which they would give their lives. The day is coming when the peoples of the Christian world will do what the princes will not. God, when He means to work with His own hand, pushes aside the hands of all men; and when He begins to work, He works with the least exercise of His power. The touch of His almighty finger is enough to create a world. He is preparing for the manifestation of His will. He is dissolving one by one the antagonists who have disobeyed Him. Empires have crumbled, kingdoms will; emperors have fallen, and kings may not long stand. All antagonistic powers are passing, the winds of confusion will sweep them away; and then will be God's time, when the faith of the Christian world shall move men to do the justice of God.

If there be one thing more than another for which Pius IX. has inflexibly stood these twenty-five years, it has been the liberty of the Church of God. He cares nothing for provinces, or for cities, or for revenues, or for royal state. 'Temporal Power,' as it is called, is the providential order, the clothing, whereby the liberty of the Church has been protected. The Head of His Church on earth has been liberated from all civil superiors, that he might stand in the freedom and power of God alone. That conflict for which the great St. Gregory VII. (whom we commemorate to-morrow) stood through all his stormy Pontificate; that great warfare for which our glorious martyr St. Thomas of Canterbury gladly shed his blood, was for the liberty of the Church of God, the liberty of its spiritual power, of its judicial authority, of its guiding voice, and of its supernatural law. In these its liberty is contained; in its liberty also its purity of faith and morals, and its power to sanctify the nations of the world. For this through the twenty-five years of his Pontificate Pius IX. has stood. The cause is God's. The world has thrown down the gauntlet, and the Son of God has taken it up, and that defiance is now in the Hand that was pierced on Calvary, but can be no longer nailed. The Christian world seems sick unto death, but it will not die yet; this sickness is that the Son of Man may be glorified thereby. The time is not far off when the prophecies and promises of God will have their sure fulfilment. He said, by the prophet Jeremias, speaking to His Church of old, and through it to the Church of Jesus Christ, and to the Head of the Church both in heaven and earth: 'I will make thee to this people as a strong wall of brass, and they shall fight against thee and shall not prevail; for I am with thee to save thee and to deliver thee

... out of the hand of the wicked, and I will redeem thee out of the hands of the mighty.'[2] And again He said, by the prophet Isaias: 'And the multitude of all nations that have fought against Ariel shall be as the dream of a vision by night, and all that have fought and besieged and prevailed against it. And as he that is hungry dreameth and eateth, but when he is awake his soul is empty; and as he that is thirsty dreameth and drinketh, and after he is awake is yet faint with thirst and his soul is empty; so shall be the multitude of all the gentiles that have fought against Mount Sion.'[3] And lastly, God says to the Vicar at His side: 'Fear not, thou worm of Jacob, you that are dead of Israel; I have helped thee, saith the Lord and thy Redeemer, the Holy One of Israel. I have made thee as a new threshing wain with teeth like a saw: thou shalt thresh the mountains and break them in pieces, and shalt make the hills as chaff; thou shalt fan them, and the wind shall carry them away ... and thou shalt rejoice in the Lord, in the Holy One of Israel thou shalt be joyful.'[4] For the Vicar of Jesus Christ is the servant and the witness in this world of Him to Whom the words were said: ' Sit thou on My right hand until I make Thine enemies Thy footstool.'

[2] Jeremias xv. 20, 21. [3] Isaias xxix. 7, 8. [4] Ib. xli. 14-16.

VIII.

THE DIVINE COMMONWEALTH:

At the Pro-Cathedral, Kensington, Rosary Sunday, 1871.

THE DIVINE COMMONWEALTH.

I have compassion on the multitude, because they continue with me now three days, and know not what to eat; and I will not send them away fasting, lest they faint in the way. MATT. xv. 32.

IT is always with reluctance that I turn to any other matter than those divine and interior truths, which are necessary to our salvation; but the times in which we live, and the errors that are rife, together with the ever-growing audacity of those who contradict the faith of our Lord Jesus Christ, and lift up their heel against the divine authority of His Church, compel us to lay aside the simple work of evangelists, and to bear witness for the truth on the great laws and facts which affect the course and conduct of this world.

Rosary Sunday, the great festival of our Blessed Immaculate Mother, which we celebrate to-day, the commemoration of great victories which her Divine Son has accomplished, through her intercession, for His Church, reminds us, every year, of the deadly warfare of the world against the Vicar of Jesus Christ. It has also fallen out of late, year after year, that this time and this festival have been marked by some great event in the hostility of Italy against the Holy See; and as each year came round it has fallen to my lot to speak to you upon those events. To-day it will be impossible to be silent.

Those who have watched the course of revolution in the last twenty years have not been surprised and have not been discouraged to see that the adversaries of the Holy See have become more and more audacious, and to the eyes of the world more and more triumphant. We well knew, that false principles, once put in motion, would inevitably pursue their whole career and complete their circle. As the storms at sea, which, we are told, revolve upon an axis, and do not disperse until they have completed their revolution, so is it with the risings of men against the Church of God. Therefore it is, that the event of the 20th of September in last year, which accomplished and filled up the whole measure of the antichristian revolution of Italy, was to us no surprise, and is no cause of alarm. We look upon it as nothing more than the last act of an insolent usurpation against the Church of God.

Now it is because every day you are assailed by

the voices of men, who rejoice over what they believe to be the downfall of the temporal and spiritual power of the Vicar of Jesus Christ, it is because every day your ears are filled with exultings of this kind, and because you may be in some degree not shaken, but saddened, and perhaps amazed and out of heart at the apparent failure of all you revere as sacred, that it is our duty to encourage you by bidding you not to fear, and to point out how what has now befallen Rome is only one more in the series of unrelenting storms against the Holy See, which will pass as all have passed before.

Rosary Sunday is, as you remember, the feast on which we commemorate the great battle of Lepanto. The Mahometan power, then threatening to encompass Christendom, was suddenly struck down, and so entirely scattered that from that day to this it has ceased to be a cause of fear. It so falls out that this year 1871 is the third centenary of that great victory; for it was in 1571, in the pontificate of Pius V., that this great victory was won.

But there is, as I have said before, at this day another antichristian power which has arisen, and one more formidable to us for many reasons.

The Mahometan Antichrist was external to Christendom, and the Christian nations of the world were united; but there is now an Antichrist which is within the circuit of the Christian world; and unhappily the Christian nations of the world are so miserably torn asunder, that they cannot unite for common action. It has been well said, that, so great was once the power of that Mahometan Antichrist, that all the chivalry of the Christian world united could not overthrow it; and now it is so feeble, that any one Christian power might overthrow it if the jealousy of the other Christian nations did not intervene. What, then, is that new Antichrist which has risen in this day? It is the Antichrist of apostate Christians—the Antichrist of anti-social revolution—the Antichrist of men without God. The next conflict will be between God and society on the one hand, and atheism and anarchy on the other. The Antichrist of this hour is the Antichrist of infidelity, and the Antichrist of disorder.

Now I have taken those words of our divine Lord to guide me in what I shall say, because they are not political. But these divine words contain the very life and spirit of all true Christian politics: 'I have compassion on the multitude.' The divine King thought for the multitude of His people. His compassion was not upon classes or distinctions of men, but upon the whole multitude. It was for mankind that He became incarnate, and with mankind He was closely bound in the most tender and loving human sympathy. He had compassion upon their faintness and thirst and hunger. They had been with Him three days, and had nothing to eat. He would not send them away fasting, lest they should faint by the way. He wrought a divine miracle, that they might be filled.

Here, then, we have the true example of a Christian king; we have the true laws that ought to govern Christian nations—charity, compassion, sympathy, fellow-feeling, and along with these, equity, justice, and mercy. I have lately endeavoured, according to my power, to explain to you the foundations of the Christian world, and the distinction of the two societies which God has founded. I shall therefore assume that those principles are present in your mind. I will now add only one farther point: God, who is the Author of the civil or political society of the world, has given to it no fixed constitution of any sort. It may be an empire, a monarchy, a republic, a democracy,—it may be what you will, if only it is founded upon His natural law. But to the supernatural society of the world—that is, to His Church—He has given a constitution so precise, so definite, so inflexible, that no man without sin can

o

depart one jot or tittle from it. He has enthroned His Vicar upon earth, invested with the plenitude of His communicable authority; and under him He has instituted the Episcopate to watch over and to govern His whole flock on earth. This His constitution is so precise and inflexible, that no man can depart from it without ceasing to be a Catholic Christian.

Therefore the Church of God, in its dealings with the civil state of this world, can unite itself in amity and peace with any form of government whatsoever. The Holy See recognises, at once and freely, in all parts of the world, any true and legitimate government, of whatsoever form or constitution it may be. Once for all, then, cast out of your mind the idea that the Church is committed or entangled with any form of political government or constitution on the face of the earth. If I were now to enter farther upon such a question as this, the matter would become political, and I should break my word. I will therefore set it aside, and treat chiefly of religion, industry, education, and morals; that is to say, of those social elements without which states cannot exist. In order to make this matter clear, we will take three pictures. The one shall be the Jewish commonwealth, the second shall be the Christian commonwealth, and the third shall be the commonwealth without Christianity.

I. In the Jewish commonwealth the constitution of Israel was given by God Himself. This is the singular and only instance in the history of the world in which the Divine will directly gave what may be called a form of political government. God called one man to be the lawgiver of that people. To Moses He joined a council, who should assist him in the government of the tribes. He guided him by His inspiration in the framing of laws. He instituted tribunals of justice. Let us now see what were the statutes of this divine commonwealth.

The first law of Israel was : 'Hear, O Israel, the Lord thy God is one Lord.' The first law of the Jewish commonwealth was piety towards God. Impiety was a capital crime, and the offender was stoned with stones. Next, crimes committed against the people, or against the rulers of the people, were punished not only as offences against society, but as sins against God. Not only the danger, but the sinfulness of crime was the motive of punishment. Bear these two principles in mind, and we shall see hereafter how the civil order of the world has apostatised from God.

Next, in matters of justice, the legislation of God

was minute, equitable, and merciful. It was ordained that any man who found a robber breaking into his house in the darkness of night might kill him in self-defence; but if the robber entered after sunrise, no man could take his life without committing homicide: so fine were the distinctions of justice. Again, any man guilty of man-stealing, that is, who by violence reduced another to slavery, was capitally punished. Once more, the sin of adultery, which Christian nations do not punish as a crime against God, was punished capitally. Again, a son who cursed his father or mother was to be put to death. The laws of domestic morals were thus protected by Divine sanctions and punishments of the last severity.

Then as to property: every fiftieth year all the land in Israel which by sale had exchanged owners returned to the original possessor. No land could be alienated from any man, family, or tribe, except for the period of fifty years, whereby the state of permanent poverty became almost impossible. Once more: usury, or the exacting interest for money which the possessor did not need for his own uses, thereby taking advantage of the poverty of those who needed help, was rigorously forbidden: and farther, if any man should ask a loan of a neighbour, the lender was forbidden to take as pledge of repayment the stones with which the borrower ground his corn, or the raiment with which he covered himself from the cold; or if the garment were taken during the hours of the day, the law required that it should be restored by sunset, that the poor man might sleep in his own raiment. More than this: in every seventh or sabbatical year all debts were cancelled; every debtor went free; and there was an express prohibition lest any rich man, when a poor man asked of him a loan of money, should say to himself, 'I will not lend, for the seventh year is near at hand;' that is, they were forbidden to consider the nearness of the year of restitution, so as to shut up their hand from their poorer brethren in need. Running through the whole law of Israel there is this tender and Divine compassion for the poor.

It was expressly forbidden for any man in reaping his harvest to reap it down to the ground, in order that much might be left for the widow, the orphan, and the stranger; and if, in carrying the harvest, a sheaf was left in the field, he was forbidden to go back and take it away, because it had become the right of the poor. In gathering the grapes of the vineyard, or the olives in the oliveyard, the Israelites were forbidden to go twice over the vines or the olive-trees. What they gathered in the first gathering was their own, but what they passed by oversight remained for the widow, the orphan, and the stranger. I may also remind you of the commandment,—'Thou shalt not muzzle the ox that treadeth out thy corn on the floor.' God had mercy on the dumb beast that laboured for man.

Such was the constitution God gave when He legislated for His people in the political order. The instances I have given will warrant this conclusion, that the whole Jewish commonwealth was pervaded by the presence and will of God; its whole administration was carried out, as it were, in the sight of God; the spirit of mercy, justice, and compassion animated it throughout. This, then, was the commonwealth which God gave as a pattern in the Mount. He gave it as the example of what legislatures, kings, and rulers should do for the government of their people.

II. The Christian commonwealth is our next picture.

In the second chapter of the Book of Acts we read that the disciples had all things in common, that the multitude of those who believed were of one heart and mind, and that no man said anything which he possessed was his own; that those who had possessions and lands sold them, and brought the price and laid it at the Apostles' feet, distribution being made to all who had need.

Here we see the first foundations of the Christian commonwealth: all were brethren, and lived in common. Upon this, some who wrest, or do not know, the Word of God, have founded the monstrous error, that there ought to be no such thing as property among Christian men; that all things are to be thrown into a common stock, and all private rights extinguished. The very words of the Book of Acts prove the contrary. We read, in the case of Ananias and Saphira, that the Apostle said: 'Whilst it remained, did it not remain to thee? And after it was sold, was it not in thy power?'[2] Ananias held the property, and his right to that property was recognised. The Gospel never extinguishes any rights of man; it tempers, sanctifies, and protects them. It extinguishes none that are legitimate; and nothing which is illegitimate can be a right.

Next, we read in the Epistle to Philemon, the rich Christian of Colosse known to St. Paul, that the Apostle had found in Rome a runaway slave of the name of Onesimus. The Apostle converted him to the Christian faith: and instead of enfranchising or emancipating the slave, as, according to the Divine law, he justly might, he sent him back to his master, and

[2] Acts v. 4.

expressly told Philemon that he would not emancipate the slave because he desired the master to do it; that he wished it to be done, not so as by necessity, but by his free will; and that he sent him back not only as a servant, but more than a servant—as a brother in the Lord. Here we have the most positive proof that no right whatsoever was extinguished by any violent action of authority; but by the spirit of mercy and compassion infused into the whole political and social order of the world, men freely and unostentatiously did that which they knew to be prescribed by the perfect law of God.

We read also, in the first Epistle of St. Paul to the Corinthians, that Christians were commanded to lay by their contributions, of their own free will, on the first day of the week, according to the measure in which God had prospered them. Therefore it is evident they possessed their own, and gave of their own. The very injunction to give alms, which runs through the whole Gospel, proves the existence of property. For how can alms be given by those who do not possess? I say this in passing, that you may have an answer to guard you against the errors you will no doubt read and hear.

There was then a community and brotherhood among Christians. Christians did not account what they possessed to be their own for their own exclusive enjoyment. What they possessed they held from God as a stewardship of His bounty, to be distributed to those who had need, and to be shared in common with their brethren.

Nay, so marked is this, that a separate and sacred order, which exists in the Church of God to this day —the order of Deacons—was instituted specially for the care of the poor. In the Book of Acts it is expressly recorded that the seven deacons were ordained to distribute to the widows and others in need. The sacred order which assists in the holy Mysteries of the Altar took its rise from the law of charity. Such is the Christian commonwealth, or the Church; and the spirit of charity was infused by its presence, into the civil and political order of nations.

When what we call the world became Christian, it began to learn this spirit of mercy and compassion. The powers and rulers, who before were despotic, at once were limited by the divine law of justice and compassion. Next, the obedience of subjects was no longer constrained and forced, but glad and willing. Thirdly, rich men could no longer be exclusive, selfish, and luxurious, unless they violated conscience. Their riches were regarded as a trust. Once more, the state of poverty was sanctified and ennobled by the example of our divine Master, the first and greatest of the poor; poverty became a sacred state in life. Lastly, an equality was introduced among men. The distinctions of classes and the inequalities of the social order were mitigated by the spirit of compassion, which equalised all men, but did not level any lawful inequalities. It cast nothing down; it lifted the poorest to an equality with the rich, because they were created by the same Maker, redeemed by the same Saviour, sanctified by the same Holy Spirit, regenerated in the same Baptism, fed by the same Body and Blood of Jesus Christ at the altar. In the sight of God they were equal. They were to appear before the same Judge, to be tried by the same law, to be buried side by side in the same dust, which makes no distinction between crown and sceptre or spade and scythe. The great leveller is not man, but God. Grace and death are His weapons, that level all men; and the spirit of charity is that which equalises all classes upon earth, and binds them together in mutual compassion, kindness, and service. Such, then, is the Christian commonwealth. And where, dear brethren, does now it exist?

I will simply say, what I believe from my heart, and from the evidence of my own eyes: what therefore from my own experience I can affirm, that there does not, or rather did not, exist upon the face of the whole Christian world any civil government which in its principles, its laws, its spirit, its administration, was so closely conformed to the divine law given of old, and to the Christian law given by our divine Master, as the government of the Vicar of Jesus Christ over the city of Rome. I do not speak from hearsay; for six or seven years, from time to time, I lived in that city. I know it intimately. I know its people: I have lived among them, freely conversed with them—with men of every grade; both high and low; and I declare that I know of no government so just, so merciful, so benign, so compassionate; I know of no people so equal in their rights; no society in which the yawning chasms which divide class from class in all other people are so filled up by mutual sympathy; I know no race whatever that seemed to me to possess a commonwealth embodying principles of brotherhood, equality, and liberty so perfectly as the citizens of Rome. Nevertheless, it is against that city, government, and ruler that the antichristian revolution of the world has gathered and hurled all its assault; it is such a ruler and such a government that the princes and kings and ministers of the Christian nations of Europe have forsaken.

They have stood gazing—whether in fear or in secret treason it is not for me to say—betraying one and all the duties which they owe to the Head of the Christian world. You may ask me why it is that all governments have turned their faces from the government of the Sovereign Pontiff. I have no difficulty in finding a reason. It is the most explicit, the most luminous manifestation of the kingdom of God on earth. Rome is the seat of the Vicar of Jesus Christ, and therefore the throne of His Master among men; it is the city of the Incarnation, the city of the Blessed Sacrament, the city of our Blessed and Immaculate Mother; it is the Jerusalem of the new law; and therefore I am not surprised that an antichristian, anti-social revolution, gathering its numbers everywhere, an international conspiracy against God and His Christ, His Vicar and His King upon earth, should concentrate itself upon that one city and upon that one person. As I said in the beginning, the false principles set in motion twenty years ago have now simply completed their circle in the outrageous and sacrilegious usurpation of Rome, which belongs to God and Christendom, and not to men nor to Italy.

III. There remains now one more picture to draw, and that is the commonwealth without Christianity.

I have so fully, and I am afraid to your patience so tediously, in times past explained what the society of the world without God is, and whence it comes, that I will not repeat it to-day. I will simply remind you of one fact. For three hundred years all the governments and all the Christian nations of Europe have been withdrawing themselves, one by one, from the unity and authority of the Catholic Church. I say the governments; I do not say the people. I believe the people of Christendom are faithful, and that when thrones and governments are swept away, the people of Christendom will reconstitute the Christian commonwealth. The Christian world is not yet dissolved; thrones and sceptres are shattering every day; governments are being swept into the abyss they have opened for themselves; but the Christian peoples of the world still remain, and there is One Who looks upon them and says, 'I have compassion upon the multitude.' They will be gathered again round about His feet. But the action of the civil authorities and rulers and governments of the world, for three hundred years, has been faithless and apostate. The Pagan world was not Christian, indeed, but it was not apostate. The world once Christian has become antichristian. And the last state is worse than the first. We see a strange paradox — the civil powers become more absolute, and less able to govern. The State is deified. We have once more the Dea Roma and the Lex Regia of ancient Rome; but the very first principles of obedience, legality, and loyalty are dying out. Governments are compelled, in self-defence, to use a rigour and severity which the Christian law would condemn and restrain. We see the multitude of people turbulent and excited by insubordination and conspiracy against civil authority. We see a wide-spread hatred against every shadow of the sacred laws of faith. Obedience is no longer for conscience' sake, but for fear. Men conspire in secret against all authority that is over them. Riches become every day greater in the hands of those who possess them; poverty, festering in its wounds, day by day, grows more miserable. Rich men claim to be the lords and masters of that which they possess, so that they may, without limit or restraint, do, as they say, what they will with their own. We see lands cleared, homes pulled down, homesteads broken up, the roof-trees burned in the fire under which, from generation to generation, the poor, with all the sanctities and charities of home, have dwelt in peace from father to son. All this is done because the will of wealth is supreme. We see labour and capital warring against each other. Money makes law for labour, which to labour becomes intolerable. We talk about the 'labour market,' as if men were to be bought like cattle or like slaves. We see, on the other side, labour maddened, rising violently, or conspiring in the dark to overthrow the just and legal rights of property.

There are, no doubt, corruption and injustice on both sides. But men are not cattle to be sold in the market, nor chattels to be worn-out in the using. There is a limit to the strength of men and to the hours of honest labour. The men who toil from twilight to twilight have no time to fulfil the duties of fathers to their homes. The poor-law, which ought to lighten poverty, pauperises those whom it relieves. And yet, if there were not a poor-law in our country, God only knows what would have become of the people. He who has compassion on the multitudes because they have nothing to eat, has, in His providence, fed them in the midst of us. A poor-law is a duty of every Christian people, and woe to the people that ever abolishes it. Every man has a right to labour or to food, and no commonwealth can shut up its hand from those who are in need. We have indeed a poor-law; but what do we see in the administration of it? I bring no accusations against any man, but I say the administration of that merciful law is in the hands of those who are, above all men, interested to diminish to the utmost the amount given to the poor. Its administration has broken down in two ways. It lays heavy burdens on those who have to pay, and it does not adequately relieve those who are in need. And how do we regard the state of poverty? Is it sacred, ennobled, honoured amongst us? Are the poor regarded as the brethren of Jesus Christ? Are they treated as if they were the representatives of our divine Master? Time and my own will forbid me to draw out a picture of our workhouse charity and our official relief of paupers.

Let us turn next to our present social state. Look at the condition of morals. If I were to enumerate the mere heads of the moral corruption of our times, I know it would be boldly denied. Nevertheless these things are written in the book of God's remembrance, and with your eyes you see and know them. Where in our commonwealth is the unity of Christian brethren? The rich and poor parted widely asunder, the classes of society yawn and separate like the timbers of a sinking ship. The sympathies between Christian men are broken up; each class lives for itself, and fortifies itself in self-defence against all others. Such is the condition to which the commonwealth must inevitably tend when it has ceased to obey the law of God. You know well there is hardly left in the whole of Christian Europe a government which has not declared the state as such to have no religion. The state as such, therefore, is not Christian. The people are Christian as individuals, but the state is Christian no longer. We in England have not indeed yet reached such a candid declaration as this, but we are tending to it; and unless men who have their hand on the helm of power are governed by the fear of God rather than by the fear of man, or by the desire of popularity, or by the craving for power, to this we shall come at last, and who knows how soon? And now, if I go on farther, I shall be forced to speak upon what I declared I would not touch; I shall therefore only deal with one other point.

Some months ago, when speaking to you in this place, I made a mistake. I said that Liberalism, as it is called, is first-cousin of the Commune. I was in error, but only in the degree of consanguinity; for Liberalism is the elder brother of the Commune. Liberalism, which rejects, in the order of politics, the authority of the Church, the unity of worship, the unity of religion, and religious education, is the elder brother of the atheistic Commune, which was manifested the other day in Paris. God grant it may never root itself elsewhere. I say then that Liberalism is the elder brother of the Commune for this reason : Liberalism consists in casting off the public religion of the state, and Communism consists in casting off the public government of the state. They who begin by casting off Christianity set the example of casting off government; because they who cast off Christianity, in casting off the Church cast off the supernatural society which God has founded; and they who cast off government complete the revolt by casting off the civil society of the world, which God has ordained in the order of nature. Therefore it is that the Communist is more logical, consistent, and complete in his arguments than the man who calls himself a Liberal Catholic. Those who are out of the unity of the faith and of the unity of the Church have no principles that are definite and fixed; but, as I said in the beginning, God has given to His Church a constitution so inflexibly precise, that no man can depart from it. But it is this that the Liberal Catholic does. To show you why I call the Commune atheistic, I will read to you a few words copied out of a declaration made by the chief secretary of that anomalous government some months ago. It completely sums up what I have said: and will suffice to convince you, that in what I have said I have drawn nothing from my imagination, nor made any departure from the truth.

At an assembly of the Commune in Paris, the secretary expressed himself, in the midst of tumultuous applause, in these words:

'We must conquer or die. To that end we must boldly deny God, family, and country. We must withdraw our children from the stupefying influences of priests, of kings, and of nationality. To deny God is to proclaim man the sole and veritable ruler of his own destinies; it is to slay the priest, and abolish religion. In the denial of Divinity man only asserts his own strength and independence. As to the family, we reject it with our utmost might in the name of the emancipation of the human race. To the idea of the family it is that we owe the enslavement of woman and the ignorance of children. The child belongs not to his parents, but to the state; it is for the state to instruct him, to rear him, to make him a citizen. To deny family is to confirm the independence of man even from his cradle, to snatch woman from the thraldom in which she has been cast by the priest and by a putrid civilisation.'[1]

[1] Paris Correspondent of the *Daily Telegraph*.

We see then to what the throwing off of Christianity brings the civil order of man. It abolishes government; it abolishes family; it abolishes home; it casts the child upon the public alms of society. Shall the children of Christendom be workhouse boys, reared as cattle by the state? To this then we come. And what is the emancipation of woman? A degradation, a demoralisation, an abandonment of the law of Christ; a relapse into the state in which woman was of old in the heathen world—the tool, the sport, the prey of man. Such is the tendency of civilisation without Christianity. And where the equality and liberty and brotherhood of such a state may be, you will easily conclude.

The antichristian, anti-social power, which is conspiring in the dark everywhere, which is reaching its arms over all frontiers and all seas, binding itself together into one with a world-wide organisation, with an unity of will, and a vast concentration of power, as sure as the sun will rise to-morrow, will gain in strength until it comes into ultimate conflict with the Kingdom of God on earth. I said in the beginning, that in Rome the Vicar of Jesus Christ is hemmed in by an antichristian revolution. There is at this time a dead-lock in the state of Rome. Men and governments are looking on in wonder to know who shall make the first move. That lock has three keys. The first key that would unlock it would be an European war; the second, the rising of antichristian revolution which should overthrow the monarchy of Italy; the third, both war and revolution together. This last seems to be the most likely, indeed the almost certain, destiny of the future.

I have said these things upon Rosary Sunday, because it is our usual day of intercession for the Vicar of our Lord. I have called on all the faithful of this diocese, through the clergy, to make to-day once more a day of special prayer. We are not, however, only to pray; but we must learn to act. I call on you, therefore, one and all, to study and to practise the compassion of Christian brotherhood one with another, and above all with the poor. Secondly; to strengthen and uphold the authority of home, and to sanctify your families. Lastly, to educate your children, and to promote by all the power you have the Christian education of the children of the poor. Here is the root of the whole question of the day. The root of society is in the child; the education of the child is the first obligation of the law of God on men. Satan knows well, that if he can separate religion from instruction, he has cut through the roots of the Christian civilisation of the world. For that reason, all the art, all the wiles, all the frauds, all the false politics of this day, are directed to what is called secular education, national education, imperial education — anything you like, only not Christian education.

Be firm, then, and inflexible; not only in your own homes and for your children, but use all the power you have by word and deed to hinder and to render impossible the de-christianising of the education of our country. The education of these kingdoms is traditionally Christian still; and if you are faithful, and stand firm, it will never lose its religious character. But we are now at a crisis, in which the tide seems to hang wavering between ebb and flow. Remember that the children of to-day are the prophecy of the future. A generation of men brought up without Christianity, and England will be under an antichristian commonwealth. As the harvest springs from the seeds, and every seed bears its own fruit, so education without Christianity can have no other harvest. The Jews had two proverbs: the one, that the state is upheld by the breath of the school-children, that is, by the prayers and obedience of its youth; that the state is solid where the children of a people are educated in the fear and love of God. Again, they used to say that even the building of the Temple must be stayed, that the children may be educated; that is, money is squandered, wasted, cast away, while children are uneducated, even though applied to the building of the material House of God.

I have tried to draw out before you a mere outline of three pictures, and in one word the result from them is this: Without God there is no society; without society there is no commonwealth. There may be a crowd of men told by the head; but the united and organised life of man—the social order of mankind—is impossible without the love, fear, and law of God. Where these things are not, there is anarchy, disorder, confusion, the deliberate suicide of government and of nations.

The Vicar of Jesus Christ is at this moment in the hands of an antichristian rebellion, and the world is full of joy, believing that it has gained the victory at last. You perhaps are cast down and sad, because of the insults and outrages heaped upon him. Sad we may be; but cast down never. The Vicar of Jesus Christ has sat for eighteen hundred years upon that throne, and he has seen a Roman empire pass away; he has seen the empire of Constantinople disappear; he has seen a Frankish empire melt and cease to be; I know not how many empires—Saxon, Suabian, Bavarian—descend from Germany and pass over the earth as shadows. He has seen two French empires; and where are they? He has seen United Italies go to dust like the bodies of the dead. He has seen before now at least a score of kings of Rome. He has seen also two-and-twenty anti-popes—for I took the trouble to count them. He has seen a multitude of sacrileges; and now he sees one more. That, which Peter sitting calmly in his boat has seen these eighteen hundred years, he sees at this hour—gusts, storms, tempests, currents, whirlwinds, waterspouts; the rising of the great deep of men's iniquity. Round about him kingdoms and empires are foundering and going to pieces; races and people are scattered as the foam before the wind. There he sits unmoved, and there he will sit even to the end. Be not afraid, then; for, walking upon that same great deep is the Son of God, holding Peter's hand. And Peter is safe, not only because he is upheld, but because Peter no more can doubt. His faith cannot fail; and his successor is infallible. Though the night be dark in the heaven above, the Star of the Sea is bright, and the lights of the firmament are a multitude which no man can number, and the Father of Lights is in the midst of them, and His watch and power are over His Church.

The words of Jesus, then, are not spoken now to Peter, nor to his successor, but to you: 'O thou of little faith, why didst thou doubt?'[2]

[2] St. Matthew xiv. 31.

IX.

THE TRIUMPH OF THE CHURCH:

St. Mary's Church, Liverpool, Sunday September 22, 1872.

THE TRIUMPH OF THE CHURCH.

> We give thanks unto God, who maketh us always to triumph in Christ Jesus, and manifesteth the odour of the knowledge of Him by us in every place. For we are a good odour of Christ unto God both in them that are saved and in them that perish; in the one indeed an odour of life unto life, in the other an odour of death unto death. 2 COR. ii. 14-16.

SUCH was the confidence of the Apostle in the face of all that was most hostile, mighty and triumphant in the judgment of this world. He was confident that through God his mission in the world was being accomplished, that the word of God was triumphing over all the power of men. They may well have said to him, 'What is this triumph you speak of? If this be triumph, what is defeat? You were stoned the other day at Lystra; you were imprisoned at Philippi; you were scourged at Jerusalem; you were saved out of the hands of the people only by Roman soldiers; you were confounded by the philosophers at Athens; and you were refuted out of the Holy Scriptures by the Jews of Berea. If this is triumph, you are welcome to it.' Such, no doubt, was the lordly and confident language of men in the face of the Apostles of Jesus Christ then, and such is the language of confidence with which the world looks on the Catholic Church at this hour. It counts it to be a comedy played out, a stale mediæval superstition, and a name that is trampled in the earth. In every age the Church has been militant and in warfare. It is under the same law of suffering which crucified its Divine Head. His throne was a cross, and His crown was of thorns. Nevertheless He triumphed, and He triumphs still, and shall triumph to the end. And so at this moment, in this nineteenth century, in the century of modern civilisation, of light, of progress, of scientific affectation, the Catholic Church is derided. They say to us: 'Look at the Catholic Church in Germany; look at it in Italy; the Head of the Church dethroned; and not a spot on earth for the Incarnation to set its foot upon. If this be triumph, you are welcome to it.' Our answer is: 'Yes; even now we triumph always and in every place. The Catholic Church is triumphing now in America, and in Ireland, and in the Colonies of the British empire; aye, and in the midst of the confusions in Spain, and in France through revolution after revolution, and in the furnace of infidelity; aye, and in Germany, in the midst of all that the might of man can do against it; and in Italy too, where the Head of the Church is morally a prisoner, it is triumphing even now.'

But how can I verify this assertion? It would be enough indeed to quote the words of the Apostle, but I hope to do more. The world esteems the triumph of the Church to be in wealth, power, glory, honour, public sway over empires and nations. There was a time indeed when the world laid these things at the feet of the Apostles of Jesus Christ. There was a time when the Catholic Church and the Christian world knew how to sanctify the society of men; but there is this difference—the world then believed, and the world now is apostate. Nevertheless, there is a triumph in the Christian world, and there is a triumph in the antichristian world; and what is it? It is that the Church in every age and in every condition, and in the midst of all antagonists, fulfils its mission and accomplishes its work, and no power of man can hinder it. Men may, as we shall see hereafter, to their own destruction, resist the mission of the Church, but its work will be accomplished nevertheless, and accomplished even in them; and its work will be a good odour of Christ unto God both in those that are saved and in those that perish.

The world has neither tests nor measures by which to understand what the mission and the work of the Church are: but they who see by the light of faith have both. Let us examine, then, what is its mission, what is its work, and how it is fulfilled.

1. First of all, the mission of the Church among men is this—to be a witness for God, and for the Incarnation of God in the face of the world. Our Divine Lord said of Himself: 'For this was I born, and for this came I into the world, that I should give testimony unto the truth.'[1] As it was with Him, so it is with His Church; and therefore He said to His Apostles: 'You shall be witnesses unto Me;'[2] and St. John said: 'That which was from the beginning, which we have heard, which we have seen with our eyes, which we have looked upon, and our hands handled, of the word of life: for the life was manifested, and we have seen it, and do bear witness, and declare unto you, the life eternal which was with the Father, and hath appeared unto us;'[3] —that is to say, the manifestation of God in the flesh, the Incarnation of the Son of God. The Church was the witness of this Divine fact to the world: and it is witness to this hour. I may say it is an eye-witness. It was eye-witness of what it

---
[1] St. John xviii. 37. [2] Acts i. 8. [3] 1 St. John i. 1, 2.

declares. It was an ear-witness of what it affirms. I may say in truth that the Church of God, which testifies at this hour, saw the Son of God, and heard His words, and was witness of His miracles. So St. Peter expressly declares, speaking of His Transfiguration: 'We have not, by artificial fables, made known to you the power and presence of our Lord Jesus Christ; but we were eye-witnesses of His greatness. For He received from God the Father honour and glory; this voice coming down to Him from the excellent glory: This is My beloved Son, in Whom I am well pleased; hear ye Him. And this voice we heard brought from heaven, when we were with Him in the holy mount.'[4] More than this: it was a witness of the day of Pentecost, and upon it the Holy Ghost descended. It heard the sound of the mighty wind, and it saw the tongues of fire. The Church therefore testifies at this day as an ear-witness, and an eye-witness of the Divine facts which it declares. And how can this be said? Because that which the Apostles saw and heard they delivered to others who believed in them upon a full test and knowledge of their truth, and those who received their testimony held it as a sacred trust, and declared it to those who came after. From age to age the testimony of the

[4] 2 St. Peter i. 16-18.

Apostles has descended unbroken. The intrinsic certainty of their witness, resting on their own eye-witness and ear-witness of the facts, has not diminished by a shade, jot, or tittle in the lapse of time, and the external evidence of that fact has multiplied and extended throughout all time and throughout the world. Therefore the testimony of the Apostles to these Divine realities and truths is as living and fresh at this day as it was in the beginning. Then twelve men testified; now the nations of the world, united in one body by faith and by baptism, take up and perpetuate that testimony. And part of that testimony is this—that when the Son of God ascended into heaven, as they saw Him ascend, He fulfilled His promise that He would send the Spirit of truth, the Holy Ghost, to abide with them for ever; that when one Divine Teacher had gone up to His Father's throne, another should come in His stead; that the world should never be without a Divine person and a Divine teacher in the midst of it; and that the Spirit of Truth by which they were united to their Divine Head in Heaven should unite them also to each other as His members in one mystical body, and should form to Himself a dwelling-place in which to abide for ever. As the soul abides in 'the body of the man, so the Holy Ghost abides in the body of the Church. It is the sanctuary in which He dwells: the organ by which he speaks, so that the words of our Divine Lord are fulfilled to the very letter—'He that heareth you heareth Me;' for the voice of the Head and that of the body, as St. Augustine sa͏́ys, are one and the same voice. As they make one moral person, so their voice is identical, and the assistance of the Holy Spirit keeps the voice of the Church always in perfect harmony with the voice of its Divine Head, fulfilling the promise of the Lord by His prophet: 'My Spirit which is upon thee, and My word which I put in thy mouth, shall never depart out of thy mouth, nor out of the mouth of thy seed, nor out of the mouth of thy seed's seed from this time and for ever.' Thus, then, the mission of the Church is fulfilled always; whether the world believe or disbelieve, whether it gainsay or assent, it matters not; the testimony of the Church for ever triumphs in every place.

2. Another part of the mission of the Church is this—to teach the doctrines of Jesus Christ in the midst of all the controversies and contradictions of men. In the face of all the errors and heresies of men there is one Divine teacher perpetually declaring the same immutable truth. In the clamour and confusion of the human voices of philosophers and

human guides, of the scribes and pharisees of the new laws, there is one Divine voice—articulate, clear, and piercing—which cleaves through all the confusion, and is to be heard above the clamour of men and of nations—the voice of that one Holy, Catholic, and Roman Church, spreading from the sunrise to the sunset, immutable in its doctrine, teaching the same truths identically in every place, and abiding always the same unchanging teacher in every age. This is a fact legible in human history. I need not offer proof of it from histories written by ourselves: it is proved by histories and controversies of those who are most opposed to us. There is an accusation which is repeated from age to age against the Catholic and Roman Church; and what is it? That it always persists in its old errors. I accept the accusation. Its persistence proves its immutability, and that which they account error we know to be the doctrine of Jesus Christ; because, as I have already shown from the word of God, neither can the Catholic Church ever err in believing, nor can the Catholic Church err in teaching. These are two impossibilities, and they descend from one and the same Divine truth. God the Holy Ghost, abiding for ever in the mystical body of Christ, illuminates the whole body of the faithful from the time of their baptism. From the time that the graces of faith, hope, and charity are infused into their souls, they are illuminated with the light of faith as the world is illuminated by the splendour of the sun at noonday : and the faithful throughout the world continue passively in their persistence in that one baptismal faith wherewith they were enlightened from their earliest consciousness. And further, they can never err in believing; because the Church which teaches them can never err in teaching. The Episcopate throughout the world, which is the college of the Apostles multiplied and expanded among all nations, has always the assistance of the Spirit of truth to guide and preserve it, so that the errors of men and infirmities of our intellect never prevail over the light of faith by which the whole Episcopate of the Church is sustained in the revelation of the day of Pentecost. And more than this : nineteen General Councils, from the first which declared the coequality and consubstantiality of the Son with the Father and the Holy Ghost, down to the last which declared the Infallibility of the Vicar of Jesus Christ,—those nineteen Councils have been the organ of the Holy Ghost, preserving the truth in all ages ; and the Pontiffs, two hundred and fifty-seven in number, have also been guided and assisted by the same Spirit of truth ; so that no doctrine of faith and morals from their hand and from their lips has been out of harmony with the revelation of Jesus Christ. For these reasons the Church is fulfilling its mission, always and in every place, and it can say in every age, with a Divine certainty of knowledge and with a Divine authority of teaching: 'It seemed good to the Holy Ghost and to us.'[5]

3. Once more, and lastly: there is another part of the mission of the Church which never fails, and is never baffled—and that is, that the Church judges between the truth of God and the errors of men, and gives decision with Divine certainty what is truth, what is falsehood, what is light, and what is darkness. Here again the world, in the confusion of its discordant witnesses, bears testimony to our truth. The world disclaims altogether the presence of any Divine teacher in the midst of us. It derides the very notion. There is not a sect, or a communion, or a so-called church, which lays claim to this Divine guidance. They say infallibility exists nowhere but in God. As the Pharisees said: 'Who can forgive sins but God only?' thereby acknowledging the Divinity of Him who forgave the palsied man. And while they say: 'We have no infallibility in us; we do not claim it; we deny its existence on the face of the

[5] Acts xv. 28.

earth,' the one Teacher, who never varies in His voice, says: 'He that heareth Me heareth Him that sent Me. It seemed good to the Holy Ghost and unto us that we should claim that infallibility, and we cite you before the tribunal of God to answer for your denial of that truth.' We say further that no man knows that any revelation was ever made to man except through our testimony. You never saw the Word made flesh, you nor your forefathers; and you have no unbroken succession of witnesses who trace upward these eighteen hundred years to the day when the Holy Ghost descended with wind and fire; you are not in contact with the original revelation of God. How can you rise up and say: 'This was revealed upwards of eighteen hundred years ago,' when you have no proof to give, except that which you borrow from me, that the Son of God ever came into the world? You take my witness for the fact of Christianity, and you then contradict me when I teach you what the doctrines of Christianity are. And if men appeal to the Scriptures, our answer is the same. How do you know the Scriptures were ever written? How can you prove that there ever was a book called the Word of God? You had it from me; you snatched it out of my hand, and you then read it and interpret it in contradiction to my teaching. How do you know that there were four greater prophets and twelve less in the Old Testament; that there are four evangelists and fourteen epistles of St. Paul in the New? Who told you all these things? You had them all from me—from me alone, to whom these Scriptures were committed in custody and in guardianship; from me, who preserved and handed them on to this day. You, who are denying the inspiration of this book and of that, of this text and of that text, and who are gnawing away as a moth fretteth a garment the whole written word of God: you rise up and tell us: 'This is the meaning of the Holy Scriptures,' and you reject the Holy Catholic faith.

Dear brethren, it needs great patience to hear these things; nevertheless the judge is always calm and patient while he is fulfilling his work among men, and that because it is a grave thing to be the odour of life unto life and of death unto death to the eternal souls of men. And when men appeal to antiquity, and tell us that 'this is not the primitive tradition:' the Church answers: Were you ever in antiquity, or any that belong to you? I was there; and as a perpetual witness, antiquity is to me nothing but my early days. Antiquity exists in my consciousness to this hour, as men grown to riper years re-

member their childhood. Men of the world know
that the cotemporaneous interpretation of a law is
the most authentic and certain interpretation. But
I have the cotemporaneous interpretation of Holy
Scripture; and more than this, men who practise
before human tribunals know that the continuous
usage of a country is the interpretation of its laws
written and unwritten. But I have the cotemporaneous and the continuous usage of the Church
of God. The seven Sacraments are institutions of
Jesus Christ, and every one of them interprets a
cluster of truths. The existence of the Church itself
is an interpretation of the words: 'Thou art Peter,
and upon this rock will I build My Church, and the
gates of hell shall not prevail against it.' The
jurisdiction that I have over the world, which the
hearts of men recognise, and to which their consciences respond, is the interpretation of the words:
'Receive ye the Holy Ghost: whosoever sins ye forgive, they are forgiven unto them; and whosoever
sins ye retain, they are retained.'

But, lastly, there is another appeal which men
make in this day. We are now told that scientific
history is the test of truth; and I saw the other
day in a document having great pretension from
a certain body of men who are troubling Germany,

and attempting to trouble even England, with the name of Old Catholics—that the way to know the pure faith of Jesus Christ is to interpret history by science. Alas, as I said before, the world is full of pretensions to science; but those who claim to be Catholics, and who yet appeal from the living voice of the Catholic Church to any other tribunal whatsoever, are all of them identical in their principle, and that principle is heresy. Luther appealed from the voice of the Catholic Church to Scripture, and thereby became a heretic. There are others who appeal to antiquity; and the appeal is the same—it is an appeal from the living voice, from the divine authority of the Church, to something of their own choice and creation. It matters not to what the appeal is made. That which constitutes both the treason of the act and the heresy of the principle is, that they appeal from the living voice, that is from the Divine voice. This it is that is being done at this moment by a body of men who profess to be, and to intend to live and die Catholics; and what is more, to purify and reform the Church by staying in it. What is their appeal? Their appeal is to history, to scientific history; that is, to history interpreted by themselves. Luther was much more direct, and much wiser. He appealed to a book which is certainly written by the Holy Ghost; they appeal to I know not what books, but to books certainly written only by men, and not by the Spirit of God; to human history, the authenticity of which, and the purity of the text of which, no one can guarantee; and even this they interpret for themselves.

Now bear with me further if I dwell a few moments longer upon this. At the time I speak, in the old Catholic city of Cologne there is assembled together a number of these men—some four or five hundred—with a handful of unhappy priests, perhaps six or eight, of whom the greater part had already the note of unsoundness upon them before they took their deadly step. And what are they? What are these men who are rising up to purify the Church? What do they believe? Some believe all the Council of Trent, but not the Council of the Vatican. Some believe the Church to be infallible, but not its Head; others propose to reject the invocation of saints, and purgatory, and compulsory confession, and I know not what. Others again are either half or altogether rationalists. And who have they to assist them? Excommunicated Jansenists from Holland, and members, I grieve to say, of the Established Church from England; and those chosen, as it were, by a happy fatality, one, the most extreme of old-fashioned high-church orthodoxy, an estimable and excellent man, whose person I both respect and love; and another whose advanced rationalism is such that even his own brethren can hardly forbear protesting against him: so that we have assembled in this congress, which is to reform and purify the Catholic and Roman Church of all ages, men so irreconcilably in contradiction with themselves, that they cannot touch a religious doctrine without discord, and they cannot find anything on which to unite, except in opposition to the one immutable truth. There was a day when all the Scribes, and all the Pharisees, and all the Herodians, and all the hypocrites, and all the men who could never agree in anything else, or at any other time, were united together in one conspiracy, and though their witnesses did not agree together, and their discordant voices could not be combined, they all had one will and one purpose against the Son of God and against His truth. These men, I bear witness—many of them at least—have no such intention; but we know, from the Word of God, that neither had they who crucified our Divine Master a knowledge of what they did: 'Father, forgive them: they know not what they do.' 'Which none of the princes of this world knew; for if they had known it, they would never have crucified the

Lord of Glory.'[6] But they are at this moment fulfilling the very words of the Apostles: and to some the testimony of the Church is life unto life, to others death unto death.

Such, then, is the mission and the work of the Church—to bear its witness, to teach and to judge; and in doing this, whether men will believe or whether men will not believe, it is accomplishing its triumph in the world. The world forgets that there is not only salvation, but there is also judgment; and God, the just Judge of all, is putting men on their trial. The Church is fulfilling its office by proposing the way of salvation to men, visibly to the eye by its own presence, audibly to the ear by its own teaching, clearly to the intellect by the evident truth of its doctrines. It is putting men upon trial, and applying the test to their hearts. It tests their faith, to see whether men will believe; it tests their candour, to see whether they will choose God above all things; it tests their courage, to know whether they are ready to take up their cross and follow their Divine Master. The Church says to the men of this day: 'Whosoever will save his life shall lose it, and whosoever shall lose his life for My sake and the Gospel shall save it.' And

* 1 Cor. ii. 8.

in saying this, God is separating between nation and nation, and between man and man. His 'fan is in His hand, and He will thoroughly purge His floor, and gather His wheat into the garner, but the chaff will He burn with unquenchable fire.'[7] 'He that believeth and is baptised will be saved; but he that believeth not is condemned.' 'We thank God, who always maketh us to triumph in Christ Jesus, and manifesteth the odour of Him by us in every place;' for we now, at this hour, in the midst of this nineteenth century, in the midst of science and progress, are the odour of life unto life and the odour of death unto death. For the purpose of God in the world is this—to gather out, as He did of old, a people for His name. Among the Gentiles of the old world He chose Israel; so now amongst the nations of the new world He chooses those that believe. He knows the number of His elect, and He calls them all by their name. He proposes to them the way of salvation, and puts all things necessary— truth and grace—within their reach. God is putting them on trial, and the Church in this is fulfilling its mission and accomplishing its work.

The world is on its probation now. It has been for generations and generations driving God and

[7] St. Matt. iii. 12.

Christianity out of its public life. Christianity is cancelled from its public law; Christianity is silent in the legislature; Christianity at this moment lingers in education, but men are endeavouring to close the doors of the schools against it, and so to shut Christianity out of the knowledge of the rising generation. Woe to the people the tradition of whose Christian education is cut asunder! Woe to your children and to your posterity if they are brought up without the knowledge of Christianity! The world is labouring with all its might, and all its fraud, and all its riches, and all its public authority, to accomplish this end. I do not say that the men who are doing it know what they do; but I affirm that they are doing what I say. Unbelievers like those who created the infidel revolution of France in the last century knew well what they were doing. 'Let us destroy the accursed one,' was the language in which they frankly spoke of Jesus Christ. Men are more refined in the present day. They talk only of the religious difficulty. 'Let us evade or get round the religious difficulty;' and, under this plea of evading the religious difficulty, Christianity is to be excluded from our schools; that is to say, because grown men choose to controvert and contradict each other, as to what is the truth of God, the little ones of Jesus Christ are to be robbed of their faith. Again, the world is separating its civil powers, its public authority, from the unity of the faith and of the Church everywhere. It is making it a part of high and perfect legislation, of what we hear called in these days 'progress and modern civilisation,' to separate the Church from the State, and the school from the Church. Progress has deposed the Head of the Church; it has put in derision a crown of thorns upon his head; and it believes that, at last, it has the whole world to itself.

This indeed is the triumph of the world. But meanwhile the Church is triumphing, though men know it not. The Church was never more widespread than at this moment, never more luminous in the eyes of men, never more explicitly known in its faith; never more united, vigorous, pure, and confident in its work. Its kingdom is not of this world: that is, it is not derived from it; the foundation of its jurisdiction is in eternity; the source of its truth is the Holy Ghost; and its imperishable head is the Son of God at the right hand of the Father. His kingdom is in the world, but not of it. The world may prosper and go its way; it may stop its ears against the voice of the Divine witness to the truth; nevertheless, that witness will be the odour of death unto death.

And England also is on its probation. I bear witness that in England errors are vanishing away, as the snow melts before the sun — passing away, as the hard frosts before the coming of the spring. The errors which were once dominant, lordly, confident, and persecuting—where are they now? At this day men are proclaiming that they are not certain of what their forefathers bequeathed to them; that they cannot precisely tell what was the doctrine which was intended in the Thirty-nine Articles, and was incorporated in statute laws. They are no longer certain of these things; and I bear them witness that a gentler spirit and a kindlier disposition is working in the hearts of many. In the midst of this darkness, truth is rising again, and the old Catholic Church and faith, for which Ireland has stood inflexible as a martyr, with the aureola upon her head, at this day is multiplying the children of faith here and throughout the world. Here too in Lancashire, where the faith of England has never been extinct—where to this day the little children of our flock are the descendents of those who were martyrs and confessors some three hundred years ago—the lingering tradition of faith once more is embodied in the perfect hierarchy of the Church of God, in its perfect order, perfect unity, perfect jurisdiction, perfect authority. And, what is more, the men of England have learned to know it better. They have heard it speak; they have seen it worship; they have even knelt together with us before the same altar, perhaps hardly knowing what they did; and that because the Spirit of God is working for His truth, and multitudes will be saved. We are only in the twilight of the morning; but we can see Jesus standing on the shore, and there is a net in the hands of His Apostles let down in the water. But when we are long gone to our rest, who can say what shall be the great draught of souls which shall be miraculously taken in England?

I must bear witness that in England there are tokens full of hope. England never rejected the holy Catholic faith. A tyrannous and guilty king, a corrupt and covetous court, men full of the conceit of false learning, schemers and intriguers, men that hungered to spoil the Church for their own enrichment —these tyrannised over the people of England. The people of England held to their faith and died for it. The people of England never rejected it. They were robbed of it; they were deprived of their inheritance, and their children were born disinherited of their faith; every century, from that hour to this, they have gone farther and farther from the light of the one truth. Poor English people! Bear with them—I speak as an Englishman—bear with them; they know not what they do, in believing that we worship images, that we imbrued our hands in the massacre of St. Bartholomew. Let the men who write these things look at their own hands: there is blood enough upon them. But the English people do not believe these things now: they are passed away. And there has come in the place of these impostures a desire after truth—' Only let me find it;' a craving after unity—' Can we never make an end of these divisions?' a thirsting for the presence of Jesus Christ upon the altar—' Where can I find Him?' And what are all these aspirations? They are the evidences of the good odour of life unto life.

And if so, then, dear brethren, you that have the inheritance of faith are on your probation too. You are called to let the light of your faith shine like the day. The silent, penetrating, convincing light of a man who, knowing the faith, speaks it calmly, without controversy, without bickering, without contention, sheds a grace around him. As men that possess the greatest gift of God, and who desire to make everybody else share it to the full, so let your faith shine. And next, as you have faith, so you ought to have the warmth of charity. Where there is light, there is warmth; and where there is greater light, there is greater warmth. Where there is perfect truth, there ought to be perfect charity. You who have the whole revelation of God, ought to have the whole charity of God in you. Let your neighbours who are round about, even those who are not of the faith, feel that there is something in you —a warmth, a kindness, a sympathy and generosity which they find in no other men. And lastly, let there be the fragrance of a holy life. This is the good odour of Christ unto God, and this diffuses life unto life wherever you go. You are upon this probation. Be worthy of the great gift which has been given to you. You have it in its fulness. Be, then, worthy of its fulness, in faith and in charity.

And now, dear brethren, in the midst of all the lordly triumph of the world, of all that which no doubt we shall hear to-morrow, be of good heart. As they said to the Apostles so they will say to us: 'If this be triumph, what can be defeat? We do not quarrel if you are content with these victories.' Overhead there is a throne, and round about it there are those whom no man can number; the powers and prerogatives of Him who sits upon that throne are working mightily in the world. There is One who sits above the water-flood, with all its confusions, whose voice penetrates through all the jangling contradictions of men.. He is bringing to its fulfilment the purpose which from all eternity He has predestined. He knows His own by number and by name, and He will gather them out, as the shepherd gathers his flock, and He will separate the goats from the sheep. He must reign until the whole of that work is accomplished. When it is done, and when the last of His elect has been gathered in, and the last of His redeemed has been made perfect, then He will manifest Himself to all men, and the world shall then know that He has triumphed always and in every place.

X.

THE GLORY OF THE CHURCH ALWAYS PROGRESSIVE:

At the opening of the Church of St. Francis of Assisi, Manchester,
Thursday Sept. 26, 1872.

THE GLORY OF THE CHURCH ALWAYS PROGRESSIVE.

Thy Throne, O God, is for ever and ever. PSALM xlv.

THESE are the words of the Eternal Father, investing His Incarnate Son with the royalties of His kingdom. They speak not of the eternal kingdom which He had with the Father before He was made man, but of that same kingdom which the Archangel, in the salutation of His Immaculate Mother, foretold, saying that the Lord should give unto Him the throne of David His father, that He should reign over the house of Jacob for ever, and that of His kingdom there should be no end. It is the kingdom of which in the Creed we make profession of our faith, 'Cujus regni non erit finis;' the kingdom of Jesus Christ, the King of kings, Lord of lords, deriving its authority from eternity, but here present in this world. It was of this kingdom that Jesus spoke when He said to His Apostles, 'All power in heaven and in earth is given unto Me; go ye therefore;' 'I dispose to you, as My Father has disposed to Me, a kingdom.' The royalties of that kingdom He committed to Peter when He said, 'Thou art Peter, and upon this rock I will build My Church, and the gates of hell shall not prevail against it.'

The Appian way by which Peter entered Rome has on either side the sepulchres of kings, consuls, and patricians, the memorials of a kingdom, of a republic, and of an empire. And as the Apostle, lone and weak, passed between these shadows of departed greatness to found in Rome the Throne of God, which shall be for ever and ever, he foreshadowed the course of the Church through the path of time. Empires, kingdoms, and commonwealths lie on either side its road, and the shadows of departed greatness, and of majesty that is here no longer, hover, as it were, about the path of the Church. The ever-living Kingdom of God moves steadily on to the amplitude of its dominion, and to the accomplishment of its purpose, undying, imperishable, and divine, fulfilling the promise of the Eternal Father: 'I have set my King upon My holy hill of Zion;' 'Sit Thou at My right hand until I make Thy enemies Thy footstool.'

I have chosen these words to-day because we

are in a time in which the world, and the powers
and the tongues of the world, multitudinous and innumerable, are for ever exulting over the clouding
of the light of the Church of God, and the unfolding
splendour of the majesty of man. It is good, therefore, that we should meet these empty and confident
vaunts by a bold and fearless declaration that the
Church of God, its royalties and its prerogatives, its
lights and its powers, are not only what they were in
the beginning, but that they are expanding in their
maturity, unfolding to their fulness, and that the
Church of God is culminating, from age to age, to
the amplest manifestation of its splendour. There are
men who tell us every day that the Church had indeed
a golden age of unity and authority, to which they appeal in the past, seeking the living amongst the dead.
There are others who tell us that the Church, in its
greatness and its unity, is a Church of the future,
seeking the Church that is among the things that are
not. We affirm the Church to be here now, living,
mighty, energetic, the Throne of God in the midst of
the world, extending its circumference, accumulating
its powers, and rising perpetually towards its perfection. This, then, is the one thought which I desire
somewhat to unfold; and I think it is a thought full
of courage, and that the time is opportune to dwell

on it. In this nineteenth century the intelligence of men, and the tongues of men, and the pens that write what the intelligence conceives and the tongue utters, so as to spread it to the ends of the world—all these agencies of human antagonism to the one Faith and the one Church, are in perpetual activity. They fill the atmosphere on every side; we cannot draw breath without inspiring their influence; they hover about our dwellings, we cannot pass our threshold without meeting them. No man can go through a day but his ears and eyes are filled with triumphant proclamations of the expiring power of Pope Pius the Ninth, the dethronement of the Sovereign Pontiff, the routed hosts of the Church, the majesty of new empires, and I know not what boastings of this world and what anticipations of the downfall of all that God has founded. In answer to this I will affirm, that at no time in the history of the Church have its notes been so resplendent or so manifest as in this nineteenth century. At no time has the note of its universality so nearly approached its fulness. At no time has its unity, both within and without, been so complete. And as the consequence of these things, our confidence of faith ought to turn the balance of these bold vauntings, and to restore our courage, if in any it has failed. Nations and men may conspire together, but the foundation of God is imperishable, and the throne which rests upon it cannot fall.

I. First, then, there never was a time in the history of the Church in which its universality was advancing so near to the full circumference of the human race. I shall be told: 'Your Christianity is the religion of a fragment, after all.' I answer: 'The Church, in its action upon the races of mankind, is not to be estimated by mathematical dimensions.' Who can say that the prophecy of the universality of the Church signifies that it should ever be simultaneously and mathematically universal? The Gospel of the Kingdom is to be preached to all nations before the end comes. Its witness shall have been universal. Let us look at the facts. There was a time when the universal Church was contained in a guest-chamber; nevertheless it was potentially universal even then. In a little while it spread to Samaria, then to Antioch; then it passed to the Hellenistic dispersion, from them to Rome, then to the Gentile nations of the world. It became the Church of the nations of which Rome was the centre. Then the great Roman empire disappeared from the earth, and a new Christian world arose, spreading beyond the boundaries of the old civilisation of Rome. When the

East apostatised, the nations of the West were given to the Catholic unity. When Saxony and England fell from the unity of the Church, a new world was opened in the West; and now that the old Christendom of Europe seems to be sapped by unbelief, and poisoned by animosity against the Church, God has opened a new world in the Southern seas. At this moment the universality of the Church occupies, I may say, five continents of the world. Europe, and America in all its length is Christian; Africa is unfolding its gates, our Evangelists are there; Asia is being penetrated on every side; at this time Japan, the mother of martyrs, is beginning to open its boundaries; and Australia, the cradle of an empire, it may be, greater than the world has ever seen, is now added to the unity of the Church. It never showed the note of universality so luminously as now. But the other day, round the throne of the Vicar of Christ there were seven hundred Bishops, representing some thirty or forty nations, races, and tongues—a number never assembled before; and gathered too from an extent of the earth's surface never before represented in any Council. Though England be out of unity, some hundred and fifty were English-speaking Bishops. Of these between eighty and a hundred were sons of St. Patrick. If St. Augustine of Canterbury has been shorn of his glory, St. Patrick has inherited it. I therefore say, as my first answer to the vaunts of the world, the Church is not pent up within your four seas or limited to a nation; nor is its heart feeble; but the pulsations of that mighty and undying life are ever sending out the light and the grace with which the Sacred Heart of Jesus inspires it even to the ends of the earth. It is accomplishing its mission, always and to this day, fulfilling to the letter the commandment of its Divine Head to ' Go ye into the whole world and preach the Gospel to every creature.'[4]

II. But once more it is certain that there never was an age in which the unity of the Church both within and without—I mean both its external unity of organisation and its internal union or unanimity— were so resplendent as now. The Church has had to pass through times of dissension, periods of internal intellectual conflicts of every kind. During the great Arian heresy, not only were there separations and external disunion, but there were the evils of internal and intellectual confusion. So also the Nestorian heresy sowed broadcast the germs of intellectual errors which disturbed the Church within. So in the whole line of speculative subtilties with which

[4] St. Mark xvi. 15.

the Oriental mind, fruitful of heresy, perplexed the faithful. These were periods in which the Church was tormented from within, until, by the vigour of its life and by the action of its unerring authority, it cast out everything contrary to the divine, inviolable faith. Next came the period of the Christian world; and no sooner was the world Christian than secularity began to taint the members of the Church. Byzantine emperors, German kaisers, Franks, Swabians, Saxons, Bavarians, tainted the Church by their patronage, oppressed it by their protection, and strove with it in the audacity of their pride. There was never a period, down to the vanishing away of the last of those great empires, each in its turn, in which they did not wrestle foot to foot with the Vicar of Jesus Christ. After this came the period of nationalities, when the unity of the Church was torn asunder into what, with a keen irony, were called obediences. Even the very Conclave was divided by it. Three doubtful elections for the Head of the Church reduced the faithful to doubt as to who had claim on their fidelity. This again passed away into a perfect unity, which from that day to this has never been broken. Then came the time of royal supremacies and national separations, and, what is worse, of nationality absorbed into the unity of churches, throwing out Gallicanism and Josephism, and endless domestic and national evils.

But, all these—where are they now? During our own lifetime we have seen three manifestations of the unity of the Church which have effaced the last traces of them all. The definition of the Immaculate Conception, against which the world has never ceased to rave, was received with an acclamation of faith from sunrise to sunset, which revealed and confirmed the supernatural unanimity of the Mystical Body of Christ. A few years after, the Church was in full conflict with the powers of the world and with the subtilty of the revolution. The Temporal Power of the Vicar of Jesus Christ was the ball at the foot of statesmen, and journalists, and mockers, and Liberal Catholics, and half-hearted men, who sought to serve both God and Mammon. The Bishops of the Church met once more around the throne of the Vicar of our Lord, and with one voice proclaimed that God in His providence had so ordered the world that, as long as it was Christian, His Vicar could never be the subject of any human authority; but sovereign over all; the chief of sovereigns, the first of kings, according to the promise of the Father. From that hour to this the whole body of the faithful, harassed as it had been, and perplexed by the confident assertions even of men Catholic in name, has been united in the defence of this truth. The Catholic people of the world know that they have in this declaration a sure guide for Catholic thought, which, though it did not create a dogma of their faith, traced for them a law and a principle of certainty even in matters of the political order where the Church comes in contact with the world. But, lastly, the other day we had a still more luminous and wonderful manifestation of this unity without and this unanimity within the Church. In the midst of scorn and mockery, of reviling and accusation, of hostility and intrigue, the great Vatican Council assembled. You know what men have said and written against it, against its freedom, its independence, its wisdom. You know that there is not a stone which could be gathered from the mire which has not been hurled against it, not an imputation which could sting the hearts of honourable men that has not been launched against it. It was said that the Bishops of the Church were divided, that a majestic minority was about to check the extreme pretensions of the Vicar of Christ, and to curb the encroachments of Rome. What was the result? With a unanimity which included even those who, exercising their freedom in perfect liberty, believed that the time was not come to define the Infallibility of the Roman Pontiff, the definition was promulgated. After its promulgation the whole Episcopate received it. In all the world, even to the last unit of the number, with true Catholic hearts they adhered one by one to what the Church of God had defined. Through them the whole priesthood of the Church, and the whole Catholic people, pastors and flock, at this hour recognise in the article of their baptismal creed, 'I believe in the Holy Ghost, the Holy Catholic Church,' the doctrine that the successor of Peter and the Vicar of Jesus Christ, when, in the plentitude of his authority, speaking from the chair of Peter, and teaching the universal Church, he defines anything in matter of faith and morals, has the assistance of the Holy Ghost promised to Peter, and in Peter to all his successors, and therefore can never err.

For these reasons, then, I affirm that there never was a time when the external unity and the internal unanimity of the whole Catholic Church upon earth were more complete. The world knows it, and frets at it; it is chafed by it; it cannot endure the spectacle of unity in the midst of its contradictions. Heretical men see in it the ruin of their hopes. They thought to raise a bulwark against the spread of the one imperishable faith, to construct a battlement from which to hurl stones and arrows against its unity. But never in past time was the whole Episcopate of the Church so inseparably united to its Head. Pius IX. sees around him his brethren in the Episcopate, bound to him by faith, by love, and by fidelity, with an intimate closeness such as no Pontiff ever knew. As a consequence of this there never was a moment when the whole flock upon earth was so closely united to its pastors. And further, no more splendid example of that unity is to be found than in Ireland, England, Scotland, America, and the Colonies of the British Empire; that is, amongst the freest peoples of the earth, where thought, and will, and act, have their most perfect liberty. There was never an age in history when the whole laity of the Church—men, women, and children—were in so close a bond of fidelity and charity with the pastors who are immediately over them, and with the Vicar of Christ, who is the common Father of us all. In truth, the flock is united to its parish-priest, the clergy is united to its Bishops in the measure and in the proportion in which the parish-priest is obedient to his Bishop, and his Bishop to the Head of the Church. The busy pens that day by day are so fast in criticisms never venture to deny the entire fidelity which binds you to your clergy, and the enduring bond of fidelity and trust which binds the clergy to their Bishops, and the Bishops to the Successor of Peter.

III. But once more : never was there a period in the Church's history when the whole Catholic faith was so explicit, so luminous, so clearly defined. If you recite your baptismal creed, and take the pages of Christian history, you will see that every article of our baptismal faith, from the first to the last, has been disputed by some sect, beginning with the heresy of the Gnostics, and coming down to the heresy of scientific historians in our day. Every article has been successively attacked, and has been successively defined. There is not a single article of the baptismal creed which has not been made a subject of explicit definition to expel or to exclude some heresy. And now an event has come to pass in our time which puts the keystone into that explicit declaration of faith. As every particular doctrine has had its definition, the liberty of error has been narrowed, and the field of truth expanded; and now the infallible authority of the Church speaking by its Head, and the infallible authority of its Head in virtue of the assistance specially promised to him who sits in the Chair of Peter, has been defined. This last definition has tied together in indissoluble unity the whole structure of faith. As the keystone of that arch put in the other day completed the solidity of this sanctuary, so is it with our Creed. That which the Council of Constance prepared, and the Council of Florence implicitly defined, and the Council of Trent would have defined explicitly if national jealousies had not intervened, the Council of the Vatican, in the fulness of its divine authority, has formally declared. The definition of the infallibility of the Head of the Church is now incorporated in the faith of the Catholic world, and can never pass away.

IV. The effect of this has been to cut to the root the principle of heresy. Without the gift of prophecy, I may say that we shall never have again a Christian heresy. We shall have a multitude of antichristian errors; but a Christian heresy—that is, a fragmentary Christianity—is a thing which belongs to the past. Where are the old heresies now? Where is the dominant Arianism which tormented the Church for centuries? Where now is the heresy of Nestorius? Where that of Eutyches? Travellers and antiquarians may find a few relics of them; but there are no other proofs of their ever having been. Where are the heresies that tormented the Church in its youth? Where are the heresies of the Middle Ages? You do not know them by name. What has become of the fragmentary Christianities of three hundred years ago? They do not exist as a form of intellectual thought; as a precise form of erroneous doctrine they have no existence. They have mouldered and fallen piecemeal; they have run to seed, and followed the law of their own creation; they were formed upon the principle of destruction, and they have destroyed themselves. I will not now speak of England or of Scotland; but I will recite the words of an adversary of the Catholic Church, and above all of the Vatican Council, who three years ago, writing from Berlin, declared—unconscious of what he was doing, and that we could read and make use of his words—that in Germany three-fourths of educated men believe no Christianity which either Luther or Rome would acknowledge to be such. This was denied at the time by men who desired to refute it; but even they showed that these words are substantially true. The testimony of an impartial and disinterested person, writing from Dresden, gave these facts. He said that he was present at a meeting of ministers of religion in that country, when they unanimously affirmed two things—his own being the only dissentient voice—first, that Arius was as good a Christian as Athanasius; secondly, that the Lord's Prayer was creed enough for Christendom. And again, at an assembly of ministers of religion it was publicly declared that 'the atonement of our Lord Jesus Christ was a superstition of the Middle Ages.'[5]

Where, then, I ask, is the work of Luther? Where is the error which for a little while bore his name? Men have played out the comedy. They know that to reject a few doctrines and retain others is not worthy of intellectual men. They are now more thorough-going, more courageous, more consistent, more consecutive. They have rejected the whole fable. Holy Scripture, inspiration, books of the supernatural order: all these are swept away. They know that the real issue, and the only issue, is between faith and unbelief, between authority and license, between the teacher speaking in the name of God and the boundless freedom of each man to test for himself the revelation of God by his own intellectual measures. Men are coming to see, with a clearness which equals our own, that there is but one barrier against unbelief—the authority of the Holy Catholic and Roman Church; there is but one basis of faith—the divine tradition of the Church of God, founded upon a rock, indefectible in its life, and infallible in its voice.

As a farther proof of this, at this moment there

---

[5] *Religious Thought in Germany.* Appendix A. Tinsley, London, 1870.

is gathered together at Cologne a strange assembly of men. It is worth noting how they are watched here in England; what hopes are laid up in the future of their action; and how men believe that out of the meeting of what are called 'Old Catholics' there may come some new rays of light for those who will not obey the voice of the Catholic Church. Bear with me if I very shortly describe what is there taking place. The heads and leaders of that Congress began with the simple rejection of the Nineteenth Council of the Church. They professed to believe the other eighteen with all their hearts, and, above all, to believe in the Council of Trent, in all its dogmas, and in the infallibility of that Council, in virtue of the infallibility of the Church. In the midst of them there was, indeed, already a virus of Rationalism, which was eating away the doctrines of the faith. Many from the first were for rejecting confession, invocation of Saints, and other revealed truths. They have now aggregated to themselves members of the Anglican body; and the first proposition made to them by these new friends was to reject the Creed of Pius IV. and the twelve chief definitions of the Council of Trent, together with the infallibility of that Council, and therefore the infallibility of the Church itself. As if this were not enough, one of them invited their allegiance to the Church of the future—a Church never yet seen, and therefore not founded by Jesus Christ —a something hanging in the atmosphere—a nebula that has not yet attained solidity or shape—an expression which is to come out of the unity of men's intellects; and when they have agreed to agree upon that which they do not yet know, then they will frame a doctrine, and from that doctrine will issue an authority. And, as if this did not suffice, they aggregated to themselves one who learnedly discoursed upon the Greek Church, and of the first seven General Councils, as the sole rule of faith, inviting them back to the Byzantine heresy. How these irreconcilable things are to illuminate the hopeful Protestantism of England, we, in our simplicity, cannot understand. It may well, then, be affirmed, that there never was a time when the right of private judgment and the principle of heresy were so discredited in the judgment of reasonable men as they are now; I may say, so completely effaced from intellectual and consistent minds.

V. I will add but one other proof of the visible progress of the Church towards its final victory. It is one of contrast. Look at the state of the Christian world. Was there ever a time since the world became Christian when it was so profoundly conscious of its own aberrations, of its own disorders, of its own impotence to govern and to sustain itself? If we look upon the Christian world, or rather on the world that was Christian till its rulers and its kings separated themselves from the Church of God, we shall see the fulfilment of the words of the prophet Isaias: 'As he that is hungry dreameth and eateth, but when he is awake his soul is empty; and as he that is thirsty dreameth and drinketh, and after he is awake is yet faint with thirst. . . . So shall be the multitude of the nations that have fought against Mount Zion.'[6] So shall it be with the nations once gathered into the unity of the Church by the mission of the Apostles, if they shall separate themselves again from that unity, and return into the divisions and the darkness of the natural order. All those who fight against the Church fight against Mount Zion and against Him who sits thereon, and they will receive their condemnation, passed by their own lips and executed by their own hands. Look at the political order of the world, and at the thrones overturned one after another. We could count them the other day; now they are innumerable. Look at the charters which have been written, re-written, and torn to shreds. Look at the revolutions which have

[6] Isaias xxix. 8.

scourged every people. The revolutionary fever is in the blood of the nations; it may be intermittent, but it never ceases to run in their veins. And the rulers and the princes, and the legislators who talked the other day of civilisation and Christianity as if they were the creators of the Christian world, cannot hold together that Christian society which the Church created and they are destroying. Look at the religious teachers who, rejecting the Divine authority of the Church, and breaking up of the unity of the faith, have never continued for one generation identical in their belief. They have been in perpetual flux and change, varying from each other and from themselves, thereby incurring a twofold penalty, the loss of authority over their people, and the loss of those very people themselves, who, wandering to and fro in the darkness, have either found the path which leads into the perfect light, or are losing all faith in their Redeemer. Look, again, at our philosophers. There was a time when they were Pantheists, believing God was everywhere and in all things; but that is too pious, too mediæval, too superstitious, now. The philosophers of these days are Secularists, who believe in the world because they can trample upon it, and in created things because they can make them the subjects of their chemistry; but of anything beyond sense they deny the existence. There are next those whom men call Sceptics, doubtful of everything except their own self-sufficiency to judge, destroying the imposture of their own philosophy by their certainty that nothing can be known. And to complete the circle of error, the Sophists of the old world are come again to teach us the philosophy of contradictories: that the highest truth is to affirm and to deny the same things under the same categories. To us the Secularist seems to be a pollard tree, whose stature is stunted, and its dignity defaced. Scepticism we are simple enough to believe to be an intellectual palsy; and sophistry to be the aberration of an idiotic brain.

From all this we learn a great and solemn lesson. There was a time when reason revolted against the authority of the Church of God, destroying the unity of the faith. Now unbelief has risen up and avenged the wrongs of faith. It has destroyed the basis even of natural belief in the existence of God, the authority of conscience, the distinctions of right from wrong, the being of the soul, its spirituality, its immortality, and its future. These truths of the natural order our Secularists, our Sceptics, and our Sophists reject, because by their philosophy they cannot prove them. Their disciples are obliged to come back to the Church of God, to receive from its infallible voice a proof of these very truths of the natural order which their natural reason has lost, because their teachers have depraved it.

Let us, then, sum up the argument that I have used, and the facts I have asserted. There never was a time when the expanse of the Church's reign upon earth was so near its fulness; there never was a time when its unity without and its unanimity within were so luminous and undeniable; never a time when the holy Catholic faith stood so clear in the sunlight of revelation, as a mountain against the blue sky; never a time when the very principle of heresy was so discredited, or clear-headed men so ashamed of the folly of the human reason in erecting itself in judgment against the Divine authority of the Church of God. Reject the truth of God altogether or believe it altogether; but to walk wavering between these paths of Christ and Antichrist is contrary to reason. Never was the world so conscious of this in its political and in its religious order. Never was it more unstable or more full of fear. The Church of God, then, is not in decrepitude. If not in its youth, it is in the vigour of its manhood. It is ever renewing its strength. Like its Divine Head, in the midst of this world it is visible to faith in the fulness of its prerogatives, in the splendour of its notes. The true progress of mankind is by faith. The Church is ever going onward. In the midst of the sepulchres and tombs of departed human greatness, of thrones which have already fallen or will fall to-morrow, it stands solid and changeless, resting upon the basis God has laid, indefectible as is the light of the firmament, pure as the waters from the springs of the earth, imperishable as the Throne that is for ever and ever.

XI.

THE DAY OF THE LORD:

Rosary Sunday, 1872, in the Franciscan Jubilee of our Holy
Father Pius IX.

THE DAY OF THE LORD.

> Thy dead men shall live; My slain shall rise again: awake and give praise, ye that dwell in the dust: for thy dew is the dew of the light, and the land of the giants thou shalt pull down into ruin. Go, My people, enter into thy chambers; shut thy doors upon thee; hide thyself a little for a moment, until the indignation pass away. For behold, the Lord will come out of His place to visit the iniquity of the inhabitant of the earth against Him : and the earth shall disclose her blood, and shall cover her slain no more. ISAIAS xxvi. 19-21.

WITH all my heart I would rather speak to you on things which bear upon our own interior life before God than upon the topics which Rosary Sunday brings before us year by year. Nevertheless every time has its needs; and the necessity of the days which are upon us compels us to speak of matters which must be distasteful to us all: I mean of the disorders of this world and its conflicts against the Church of God. But we are set as watchmen upon the walls of Jerusalem; and the prophet has warned us in the name of the Lord, that, if the watchman shall see the sword coming, and shall not give warning, the blood of the slain shall be required at his hand. We therefore are compelled by fidelity to our duty to speak openly on the great principles by which we shall be tried.

I can easily understand that those who, when they hear the name of the Church, can see in it only a mere human creation or human society, must turn away from such subjects in the sanctuary as out of place; but they who know that the Church of God is the mystical Body of Jesus Christ; that He is its Head; that the Holy Ghost inhabits it, and is its life; that it is compacted of the souls of His elect, and that every wound inflicted upon it is received by Himself; that it is the channel of our sanctification, and the divine order whereby we are saved;—they who have this light of faith and the spiritual instincts which spring from it, intuitively see that the conflict of the Church and the world is the conflict of God and of Satan, of Christ and Antichrist.

Now, for the last five or six and twenty years we have been watching the continual advance of an Antichristian revolution against the Vicar of Jesus Christ. I remember, and so perhaps do many of you likewise, how, in the year 1847, subtil and insidious men thought to use the name and the power of the sovereign Pontiff for the accomplishment of their revolutionary designs. Failing of this, they turned against him; and in twelve months, by treason, by menace, and by murder, they drove him from his throne. During the years that followed, the revolution, infidel at its heart, unjust in all its actions, has gradually risen like a flood, until it has covered the whole face of Italy, and finally has occupied the city of Rome. We have come therefore to a time of crisis: the flood has risen above the banks, and has submerged the Christian institutions of Italy. The tide is now, as we may see it often in the sea, hanging in a balance before the ebb begins. This is a time of momentary calm—how long it will last, God only knows; but when the ebb begins to run, confusions, which the world has never seen as yet, will surely come. For never from the beginning of the Christian world were the moral powers of law, order, government, and society, so weak as now. Never since there was law, order, or government among Christian men and Christian nations was the basis and foundation of that order so undermined. As the moral powers of the world have become continually less, the material powers of the world have become continually greater. At this moment the whole of Christian Europe, from east to west, is one wide camp in arms. Between six and seven millions of men are standing in line, nation against nation; and the skill and the science of mutual destruction are raised and developed to a pitch and a perfection, which in the history of man was never known before. The prophecy of the Christian world was this: that men 'shall turn their swords into ploughshares and their spears into sickles,' and the nations shall not 'be exercised any more to war;'[1] but the world has falsified that prophecy for itself, though it cannot falsify it for the Kingdom of the Prince of Peace. As for the world, once Christian, never from the beginning of time were men organised and drilled to slay with such an intensity of energy and of aim, as if the end of life were mutual destruction, as at this moment. The day will come when the barriers which hold in these fiery floods must give way, and the devastation that will follow no man can conceive. It will be a convulsion that will shake, it may be destroy, the nations of modern Europe. In the midst of this array of hostile arms stands the Church of God, without weapon, without defence, without protector, forsaken and alone. To-day, therefore, we make a solemn intercession for the Head of the Church of God on earth; because in him and in his person are summed up all things that affect the Church at large, all its interests, all its fortunes, all its future: as he is, so it will be.

[1] Isaias ii. 4.

My purpose, then, is to take these words of the book of Isaias and make an obvious application of them to this moment. God, speaking by the prophet, told Jerusalem, that is the Church of old, that though its desolations were near to come, and though its desolations should be terrible, yet they should not be for ever; that 'its dead men should live again;' that though the people of Israel should be, as the prophet Ezekiel saw in vision, like the 'dry bones,' scattered 'and very dry,' utterly dead, there should come once more the spirit of life, 'and My slain shall live again;' that the weak, and those that had been trampled into the dust of the earth, should be as the dew of the morning, and should see the overthrow of the mighty—'the land of the giants thou shalt pull down in ruin;' the world, with all its massive strength and all its material power, shall come to nothing before the unarmed Church of God. Again, he said, 'Go, My people, enter into your chambers,'—that is, into the chamber where you pray before your heavenly Father, who seeth in secret,—'shut your doors about you,'—as the Apostles did when the world had crucified their Master,—'hide yourselves a little for a moment,'—it is but a short time that this tyranny shall endure,—'until the indignation pass away; for the Lord will come out of His place,'—there is none other to take up His cause; He will therefore answer for Himself—'the Lord shall come out of His place to visit the iniquity of the inhabitant of the earth,' —that is, the nations taken in their whole array against him,—' and the earth, which has covered over with its dust the blood of the just unjustly slain, shall disclose the proof of its guilt; and its slain shall be hid out of the sight of the Judge no more. There shall come a day when God will require the innocent blood shed from the beginning at the hands of the world, pagan, Christian, and apostate. This prophecy applied first to Jerusalem of old, and was fulfilled in its final desolation. The spiritual Jerusalem, which now is, inherits both the desolation and the resurrection here promised. The fulfilment is not yet complete, nor is the prophecy yet exhausted; the warfare of the spiritual Jerusalem shall never cease until the world's end. But after the desolations which are visibly coming on the Catholic and Roman Church shall come also the resurrection of its power; 'the Lord shall come out of His place' to judge the nations which have fought against Mount Sion.

There can be no doubt that, at the moment in which we are, the Christian world has either silently withdrawn itself from, or has risen in open antagonism against, the Christian Church and the Christian faith. It is like the multitude in Jerusalem who had forgotten the coming of Messias, and had forsaken the Law and the Temple of God. Of this fact, visible before our eyes, there can be no doubt. What, then, are the designs of God in permitting this apparent undoing of His own work?

1. First of all, I would say that the separation of the world from the Church seems to be intended to bring out more visibly than ever the note of sanctity. He is purifying His Church throughout the world. Inasmuch as it is the fountain of the sanctification of man, the enmity of the world from the beginning has always been busy in the endeavour to choke it; or, if it cannot choke it altogether, at least to poison or to taint it. Therefore it has striven by heresies and schisms, by worldliness and infidelities and false philosophies, by every imaginable deceit of man and of Satan united, to fill the Church with its own leprosy; sometimes by falsehoods against the faith, sometimes by impurity in morals, sometimes by perversion of its laws, sometimes by the pestilence of corrupt public opinion. The world cannot indeed taint the Church; because its sanctity flows from the Holy Ghost, who dwells in it. Therefore the means of sanctification are incorruptible,—the doc-

trines of the faith, the laws of divine morality, and the fruits of the Spirit which have been perpetually multiplied from the beginning, not only in the Saints and the innocent, but in the penitent, and even in those who, like ourselves, are but humble commonplace Christians hoping to attain eternal life, striving with no high degree of sanctity indeed, but yet with sincere and upright hearts. Nevertheless, from the beginning, the world has been endeavouring to poison and taint, if it cannot altogether dry up, this supernatural fountain of sanctity. Even in the first ages of the faith, though persecutions purified the life of Christians, and the hatred of the world helped them to love one another, and to have their life hid with Christ in God, even then many walked 'as enemies of the Cross of Christ.'[2] But when the world began to clothe the Church with possessions and power, then began the subtilest dangers of taint and of poison, not only to private men one by one, but to the Hierarchy and to the Priesthood of the Church. In cleansing the leprous world the hands of many were stricken with the leprosy. To be always in spiritual contact with sin needs special grace; 'for who can touch pitch and not be defiled?' Much more when the Church was invested with the pow-

[2] Philippians iii. 18.

ers of the world and entered upon the civil life of kingdoms. Then the breath of the world began to tarnish, not indeed the divine creation of the Church, which is immutable in its sanctity, but the men that bore office in it, and its members mingled in the world. Riches, titles, patronage, offices of state, royal supremacies, imperial favours, filled the air with worldliness, love of wealth, of power, of honour, of influence; 'the concupiscence of the flesh, the concupiscence of the eyes, the pride of life,' and of all things 'which are not of the Father, but of the world.'[3] These things hung in the air; they were breathed with the atmosphere; they entered and poisoned the life-blood of men. Read the history of the empires and kingdoms and courts of mediæval and modern Europe. How many Saints are there in these last eight hundred years? How many followers of Ananias and Sapphira, of Judas and Caiaphas? How many national churches, royal theologies, and conspiracies against the Vicar of Jesus Christ? And now it seems that God has jealously separated His Church everywhere from this contact with the civil powers of the world which have already renounced Him. For their own suicide and destruction they have put the name of Christ out of their laws, and the name of

[3] St. John ii. 16.

God out of their statute-book; and they treat Him as an outlaw in the commonwealth, an intruder among men. They try to be rid of His name, that they may govern the nations of the world without Him, and be rid of the 'religious difficulty' which He has made for them by His Revelation and by His Presence. They claim to govern by the sovereignty of their own will, and by human legislation in the natural order. We may see, then, first a sheltering grace bestowed on the Church in this separation from the civil powers of the world, though it be a heavy judgment upon the world that withdraws itself from the Church of God. If the world be sinking, the Church is cut loose from it, that it may float in safety like the ark upon the waters. All this fulfils the words of the prophet: 'Go, My people, enter into your chambers, and shut thy doors upon thee,' even as the patriarch when the fountains of the great deep were broken up. The Church is returning again into its own internal unity, separate from the world in the last days as it was in the first. And though this separation is neither by any act nor by the will of the Church, nevertheless the Church derives from it many graces. Its pastors will be poor. They will receive nothing from princes, or courts, or governments. They will re-enter their apostolic liberty and detachment from all things:

they will live of the altar by the oblations of the faithful. This also will rekindle the zeal, charity, and generosity of the Catholic peoples of the world. Germany and Italy will become like Ireland, England, and our colonies, where the Catholic Church lives in the hearts, and is supported by the hands of the flock. Pastors and people are held together by an intimate bond of charity and generous reciprocal service which consolidates the Church with the closest unity, and multiplies its power sevenfold. The world and society, and the millions who are out of the Catholic unity, all alike will suffer by this separation from the influences and the guidance of Christianity: but the Church is purified by its freedom from all contacts with a sinking world.

2. Next, in so doing, God is manifesting His one only Church to mankind in a fulness of light which has never been so unfolded on the world till now. In the first centuries, while as yet the world was heathen, the Church was hid. Its divine worship was in secret; it held no Œcumenical Councils; its Pontiffs spoke to the faithful, not to the world. It was made up of individuals here and there; they were lost in the great multitude of men. When the world became Christian, the hierarchy of the Church was clothed with judicial powers and imperial offices for

the sanctification of society; but those things often disguised it under the aspects of the world, so that men, when they looked for the Bishops of the Church, could hardly see their pastors through the robes of electors and of princes. The world hung its trappings between the light and splendour of the Church and the multitude of the people. Feudalisms and palatinates and baronies masked the Apostles of the Lamb. Secularity and ambition, betrayal of the Church, and swerving from the faith, are the fruits of the world, as sanctity is the fruit of the Church. But God has put forth His hand to heal. He has permitted the world to cast off the mystical Body of Christ. It is calumniated, assailed, and persecuted in every place; and now in the most august of sanctuaries, in Rome itself, where until a year ago the Vicar of Jesus Christ reigned as sovereign. The world now sees the Church standing out into the nineteenth century with its four notes visible to the eye: its universality spreading throughout the earth; its unity within and without, perfect and in every place; its apostolic tradition of authority and truth in unbroken continuity from the beginning beyond denial; and its sanctity acknowledged even by its enemies. That is to say, there is in the world a body of men who are bound by a divine law to love and practise poverty of spirit, which is in direct contradiction to the spirit of the world: secondly, not to seek themselves, but with generosity which goes beyond the bounds of worldly prudence, to give, to forgive, and to return good for evil: thirdly, not only to love their friends, but to love strangers, and to love their enemies; and this threefold law was promulgated by a Legislator who said, 'You have heard that it hath been said, thou shalt love thy neighbour and hate thy enemy; but I say unto you, love your enemies, do good to them that hate you, and pray for them that persecute and calumniate you, that you may be the children of your Father who is in heaven, who maketh His sun to rise upon the good and bad, and raineth upon the just and the unjust.'[4] And these three notes of the Christian law are at this moment visibly manifested in the Church, as distinct from political society of the world. Take, for example, the pontificate of Pius IX. For six-and-twenty years he has endured an unintermitting enmity with every kind of contumely. His whole pontificate from the amnesty on his accession has been one of forgiveness and of mercy. The world has never ceased to fight against him. In this there is a contrast between the Church and

[4] St. Matt. v. 43-45.

the world which cannot be denied. Between the two systems there is a direct spiritual antagonism. The world treats us as foolish, and we do not think the world to be wise. Take, for example, the opinions and actions of journalists and statesmen on the Vatican Council. And at this very time, when there is between the spirit of the world and the spirit of the Church more visibly and more sensibly than ever an irreconcilable contradiction, the world is crying to the Church to conform itself to its worldly rules, and clamouring to the Sovereign Pontiff to follow the progress of modern civilisation. The answer of Pius IX. to this clamour was the Syllabus, which shows all hope of compromise to be vain.

There are three plague-spots which at this moment are marked upon the face of the world, growing darker and broader every day. They are brought out more visibly by the very contact that the world has with the Church. These are, first its unbelief. The words of our divine Lord are being manifestly fulfilled before our eyes: 'When the Spirit of Truth is come, He shall convince the world of sin; of sin, because they believe not in Me; of justice, because I go to the Father, and you shall see Me no more; of judgment, because the prince of this world is judged.'[5]

[5] St. John xvi. 8-11.

There are at this moment two operations continually going onward; the one throughout the nations, a departure farther and farther from all Christian faith; the other throughout the Church, a more fervent and devoted return to the faith and love of Jesus Christ; and as these diverging lines part asunder, the contrast between belief and unbelief is made more visible every year.

Next there is a contrast between justice and injustice. Where in all the Christian world does there exist such a thing as international law? The law of nations was a sacred code of public morality. But it is dead and buried. Does justice protect the frontiers of states? Does equity restrain or rule the material powers of the world? What defence have the weak against a stronger neighbour? Look at Italy and Germany, where might makes right. Does justice anywhere restrain commerce? Look at the double weights, and deceitful measures, and adulterated products, and false balances, and commercial bubbles, and gamblings, and tricks, and speculations with which merchants and traders, buyers and sellers grow rich in a day. There are indeed just men to be found; but they are individuals lost in the mass, powerless to resist the stream which carries the society of men farther, year by year, from public and private justice. We are like Jerusalem in the days of Isaias: 'Judgment is turned away backward, and justice hath stood afar off: because truth has fallen down in the street; and equity could not come in.'[6]

Thirdly, there is another contrast between the Church and the world. While it was yet Christian in its public life, it had a grace of piety or the love of men for their Maker, and the love of disciples for their Redeemer. Men were not ashamed of public intercessions in their disasters, and public thanksgivings in their prosperity. Where is that now to be found? The other day when England made public prayer and public thanksgiving the world wondered. Look at the capitals of the nations; every shrine and sanctuary, and wayside cross, and token of redemption, is clean gone. The city which till the other day was the capital of Christendom—blemished it may be by secret sins which are inseparable from mankind—nevertheless in its public life, in its public manifestation, had everywhere, and in every place, and at the corner of every street, the memorials of our Divine Redeemer. Rome at this moment is filled with impiety. As when the Son of God was upon earth, Satan came visibly to tempt Him, so wherever that which is Divine is manifest, that which is dia-

[6] Isaias lix. 14.

bolical is nearest. The city of Rome at this moment is the haunt and home of impiety. There was sold publicly in the streets on last Good Friday a caricature of the Crucifixion of the Son of God. Why does He permit these things? His arm is not shortened, neither do His eyes slumber. He is leaving the world to work its will, for men to see that unbelief, injustice, impiety, are the natural growth of its own soil; that faith, justice, and piety grow in another soil, which sin has never cursed; and that by its own hatred against these notes of the Divine Presence the world may condemn itself.

4. And farther, God has a purpose in these things which comes intimately home to each of us, one by one. God said of old by the prophet, 'And it shall come to pass at that time that I will search Jerusalem with lamps.'[7] That is, as the master of the house, when he doubts of the safety of his dwelling, lights his lamp, and goes from chamber to chamber, and from the roof to the foundation, and casts the light of the lamp upon his servants one by one, that he may know whether his house is in safety and his servants watching—so is God doing now with us. The other day, when the great Council assembled in Rome, the light of the Divine Presence was thrown

[7] Sophon. i. 12.

first of all upon the chief pastors of the Church, to see whether they were faithful to their trust; through them it fell upon the pastors who are labouring under them in the sheepfold throughout the world; through them again upon the whole flock. We have therefore all been searched by the light of the Divine Presence, to see whether we are faithful, and conformed to the mind of our Divine Master. The Apostle says that 'judgment should begin at the house of God.'[8] Those will first be tried who are in the full light and authority of the Church; after them, all the faithful. One by one, you will be tried to know whether you are faithful to the truth of Jesus Christ in which you have been reared, whether you have the courage to stand for that truth, whether you have the spirit of self-sacrifice to lose all things rather than to forfeit that Divine gift. You remember how our Divine Lord searched the Seven Churches; how He said to one, 'Thou hast left thy first charity; .. be mindful therefore from whence thou art fallen, .. or else I come and will remove thy candlestick out of his place;'[9] to another He said, 'I have against thee a few things;'[10] and to another, 'Thou art lukewarm, and neither cold nor hot.'[11]

[8] 2 St. Peter iv. 17.   [9] Apoc. i. 4, 5.   [10] Ib. 14.
[11] Ib. iii. 16.

Every flock with its pastor will have its searching trial. He will first try the Bishop above all, then the Priests will be tried, then the people; aye, and the faithful in every household, to know whether they are true to the light that He has given them. There was a time when Ireland was searched out; and because the priests of Ireland were stedfast and vindicated their faith by suffering, it has been preserved inviolate to this day. England by its side was likewise tried; and because its chief pastors gave way, and its priests were full of fear, the people were robbed of their inheritance. At this moment the judgment has begun again at the house of God. In Italy Bishops and priests are standing firm, with peril to their life about them. Of all the Bishops of Italy only one man was found, and he has gone to his account, who wavered in his fidelity. Of the priests of Italy, a hundred thousand men and more, only a handful have been found to waver. Now the same trial is beginning in Germany, and innocent untried men, without accusation, are driven by despotic violence from their homes and country. Bishops are arraigned as disloyal and threatened with penalties, because they will not prostitute the spiritual authority of the Church, and subject the supreme power of the Keys, whereby sin is bound or loosed, to the cognisance of the civil power. These are but the first drops of the storm, faint preludes of the trials which are coming. The Lord is sitting as the refiner of silver. He is casting us into the furnace, and we shall be tried. Happy will they be who shall be found pure in that day! Let us, then, rouse ourselves up, and be ready for our turn. We also may be compelled to answer for the authority we hold from Jesus Christ; and you too may be tried whether you have courage to stand fast and firm by your pastors in the day when they shall bear their witness to the Truth.

5. Lastly, God is permitting all these things to come upon His Church that He may manifest His own sovereignty. In the vision of Daniel, the stone that smote the great Antichrist was cut out of the mountain without hand of man. It was the work of God alone. A Divine power took it from the mountain-side, and launched it against the whole might and mass of human power. All agency of man was excluded, that the power of God might be revealed. So will the manifestation of the sovereignty of God be now. There is not on the face of the earth a power of man that has the will to intervene to protect the Church of God from wrong. The whole heart of society has so departed from faith in Jesus Christ,

the whole public opinion of Christian Europe is so poisoned by the spirit of the world, and so blinded by infidelity, that it has not the will to use either its authority or its power to protect the Christian faith against its open enemies. And still more wonderful, those who are the strongest, the mightiest potentates of Europe, if they had the will, have no longer the power to do it. Their mutual jealousies hinder them alike from banishing Mahometanism from Christendom, and from restoring the Vicar of Jesus Christ to his right. The gigantic material powers of Europe are mighty for mutual destruction, but they are impotent to protect the Church of God. God has so permitted for their humiliation. He is showing them the impotence of strength. God is teaching them that He alone can defend His Kingdom. The nations of the world, by forsaking God and His Christ, have locked themselves in a mutual struggle, out of which there is no issue but to destroy or be destroyed. They have suffered and encouraged Italy as a nation to commit sacrilege against Rome. As nations they are accomplices. They have admitted Italy into the Council of European nations; under the new code of international injustice which consecrates the supremacy of wrongs when done, and of impiety when it seems to prosper. The old code of

Christian justice has departed from the world. Usurping dynasties cannot administer it without self-condemnation. The maxims, axioms, principles, of justice would reverse the whole order, which is founded on wars of ambition and revolutionary treason. In 1848 the secret political societies of Europe were in the streets; they are now in cabinets and congresses and on thrones. Therefore no man can lift a hand for justice. They have made a compact with death; and they must move onward in the path of progress and modern civilisation which leads to Armageddon. Their mutual ambitions, hatreds, and intrigues are preparing for the day of the Lord. It was but a small thing that not long ago a great empire in the east was crushed in seven days; and last year a still mightier in the west went down in a few months in utter ruin. The suddenness of their wreck is a sample of what will be when the armies of Europe are driven together by the just judgment of God. Because the nations like Jerusalem of old have said: 'Let the Holy One of Israel cease from before us. Therefore thus saith the Holy One of Israel: Because you have rejected this word, and have trusted in oppression and tumult: and have leaned upon it: Therefore shall this iniquity be to you as a breach that falleth, and is found wanting in a high wall: for the destruction thereof shall come on a sudden when it is not looked for. And it shall be broken small as the potter's vessel is broken all to pieces with mighty breaking, and there shall not a shard be found of the pieces thereof wherein a little fire may be carried from the hearth, or a little water be drawn out of the pit.'[12] 'He shall rule them with a rod of iron, and break them in pieces as a potter's vessel.' They shall fall upon each other as the mountains, and shall be shaken by revolutions under their feet, and wasted by mutual destruction, and by blind fury, and by the Angel of the Lord. 'Their land is filled with silver and gold, and there is no end of their treasures, and their land is filled with horses, and their chariots are innumerable. Their land is also full of idols: they have adored the work of their own hands, which their own fingers have made'—the civilisation they have created without God, and the civil power which they deify. 'And man hath bowed himself down, and man hath been debased, therefore forgive them not. Enter thou into the rock, and hide thee in the pit from the face of the fear of the Lord, and from the glory of His majesty. The lofty eyes of man are humbled, and the haughtiness of man shall be made to stoop; and the Lord alone shall be exalted in that day.

[12] Isaias xxx. 11-14.

Because the day of the Lord of Hosts shall be upon every one that is proud and high-minded, and upon every one that is arrogant, and he shall be humbled. And upon all the tall and lofty cedars of Libanus, and upon all the oaks of Basan; and upon all the high mountains, and upon all the elevated hills; and upon every high tower, and every fenced wall; and upon all the ships of Tarshish, and upon all that is fair to behold. And the loftiness of man shall be bowed down, and the haughtiness of man shall be humbled. And the Lord alone shall be exalted in that day.'[13] 'And I saw, and behold a white cloud, and upon the cloud one sitting like to the Son of Man, having on His head a crown of gold, and in His hand a sharp sickle. And another angel came out from the Temple, crying with a loud voice to Him that sat upon the cloud: Thrust in Thy sickle and reap; because the hour is come to reap, for the harvest of the earth is ripe.'[14] The harvest is ripe indeed. The pride of man is ripe for judgment, and the ambitions, and the covetousness, and the injustice, and the wrongs, and the luxuries, and the lusts, and the falsehoods, and the betrayals of the just, and the shedding of the innocent blood, and the hypocrisies in high places, and the mockery of the Lord

---

[13] Isaias ii. 7-17.   [14] Apoc. xiv. 14-16.

Jesus in His servants, and in His Vicar upon earth—all these are ripe and rank: and yet the Reaper still tarries, and the sickle abides its time. There is silence in heaven, and waiting, and patience, if by any means men will repent before it be too late.

If you ask me how this reaping shall be accomplished, I answer, no man knoweth. It will be either by some chosen weapon of God's chastisement, like Cyrus of old, or by a more direct and personal intervention. There are already tokens of this harvest visible to the eye. The anti-Christian revolution has pushed on the governments of Europe to their present deadlock. They cannot turn back, for the revolution is behind them: they dare not go on, for the pit is open before. They mutually mistrust and hate each other. The unjust can conspire: they can never combine. The false cannot unite. Injustice and falsehood dissolve all bonds, and inspire mutual hates. They will, therefore, reap each other down with the sickle of the judgment of Almighty God. But now, for a time, Christ and Antichrist are standing face to face, that the kingdom and the sovereignty of Jesus, springing from eternity, and sustained by His own Presence, may manifest itself visibly to the world: and that no human hand may touch it for its support. 'The strong man, and the man of war, the judge, and the prophet, and the cunning man, and the ancient, . . . and the counsellor, and the skilful in eloquent speech,'[15] are loud and lordly in all tongues rejoicing over the desolations of the Church. The temporal power, they say, is fallen, and the spiritual cannot long endure; and all nations have cast off the old superstition, and the Church is weakened in every place and is fast vanishing away. So of old men sent gifts to each other, and rejoiced when the Church in catacombs and deserts seemed to be swept off the face of the earth; but it was then, at that very hour, that the whole face of the world was silently changing, and the kingdom of Jesus Christ was nearest to be revealed. So will it be again. God will intervene to do His own work in His own time, and by His own power.

This, then, is what we meet to pray for to-day. On Rosary Sunday, with full trust in the prayers of our Immaculate Mother, we look the world in the face; calmly, firmly, and without fear; bearing a string of beads in our hands, glad to be despised by the world as our forefathers have ever been.

I would therefore say to you that there are two things which you must do.

The first is to keep as closely as you can to the

[15] Isaias iii. 2 3.

Sacred Heart of Jesus. Be faithful to His law. Cherish every particle of His truth, every commandment, every counsel of His will, every inspiration of His grace. Conform yourselves generously in all your reason, in all your conscience, to the mind of Jesus Christ. Unite your whole heart with all its love and all its affections to Him, to His kingdom, to His interests upon earth, to His poverty, to His sufferings, to His contempt, and to His cross. Say, 'God forbid that I should glory save in the cross of our Lord Jesus Christ, by whom the world is crucified unto me, and I unto the world.'[16] Keep close to Him in prayer. Whensoever you have to choose between the maxims of the world and the counsel of your conscience, which comes to you from the Spirit of God, and from the holy faith, and in every doubt dictates to you what to do, choose the safe way of the Cross. This is the first lesson. The second is to ask earnestly that the prayers of the Mother of God may obtain for us once more the victory as they have obtained so often in the past. She stands at the right hand of her Son, who stands at the right hand of His Father; and the right hand of her Son is almighty, and the prayers of His Blessed Mother never fail. They never fail, because

[16] Gal. vi. 14.

she never asks amiss. They never fail, because she knows the will of her Divine Son. They never fail, because it is His joy and His glory to grant the thing she asks. The Immaculate Heart of Mary intimately knows the Sacred Heart of Jesus. She has no interests so dear, no desire so ardent, as that His elect should be gathered out, that His mystical Body should be made perfect; that even through fire it may be purified, and that the sovereignty of her Son may be at last revealed.

Never from the time the great warfare which began when Michael and his angels fought in heaven against the Dragon and his angels, and prevailed over them until those once glorious splendours were cast down as flakes of fire to wither the earth — never from that hour to this has the warfare between good and evil, God and Satan, been stayed. It burns at this moment fiercer than ever, and will burn more fiercely yet, until the day that 'the Lord shall come out of His place to judge the iniquity of the inhabitants of the earth against Him.' The Church in the midst of the world is the bush that burned with fire and was not consumed. The stem of the bush is inveloped in flame, and the fire which is winding about it spreads through every branch, and reaches to every spray; but the bush is imperishable because it is of

God. It is as if you should see upon the face of the deep the splendour of a light tossed by the motion of the waters, beaten by the storms, and hemmed in by whirlwinds, but never for a moment failing to shed its steadfast rays, never for a moment wavering or slackening in its intensity. Such is the Church of God. At this moment in the world all things are hostile: but God is 'a wall of fire round about, ... and the glory in the midst thereof.'[17] All human powers are at this time in array against it; but all the invisible powers of the world to come are with it; God and His holy angels, Jesus and His Saints. The Vicar of Jesus upon earth stands, like Eliseus, upon the mountain. When the prophet's servant, seeing the armies of Syria about the city, in fear cried out, 'Lord, what shall we do?' the prophet answered, 'Fear not, there are more with us than with them.' Then he prayed and said: 'Lord, open his eyes, that he may see,' and he saw that 'the mountain was full of horses and chariots of fire round about Eliseus.'[19] So is it at this time. Pius IX., a poor Franciscan, like Francis in absolute poverty, spoiled and stripped of all things, living upon the alms of his children, stands upon the mountain with uplifted hands, praying to the Sacred Heart of His Master

[17] Zach. ii. 5. [18] 4 Kings vi. 15-17.

through the prayers of the Mother of God, confident that He will intervene in His own time when the hour is come. Never doubt that he will see the day-spring of the Church's deliverance, though the full splendour of the noon-tide may be for those that come after. Therefore 'go into your chambers;' pray earnestly, wait in patience, be not cast down, and fear nothing. The Church cannot fail: your hope can never be disappointed. Be faithful, humble, charitable, and patient. Pray for the enemies of God and of His Christ; pray for those who wound His Church, as He prayed for those who crucified Him. Pray for them, for they know not what they do. Pray that the light of faith may be poured out upon them, that when the Lord shall come to take reckoning with them, multitudes may beat upon their breast, and fall down penitent at the feet of Him whom they have pierced, not knowing what they did. This is our prayer to-day before our Divine Master, who, under the Veil of His Sacramental Presence, is in the midst of us. Pray to Him with all your faith; for prayer is our strength, and our hope is in the Lord our God.

INDEX.

Abbasso Cristo, the cry, xcix., ci.
Abbasso il Governo dei Preti, xiii.
Achitophel, lxxxvii.
Acts, Book of, 198.
Adultery, 196.
Æmilius, 48.
Alms, 200.
Ambassadors, xliv.
America, 2.
Ananias, 199, 283.
Anglicanism, 31.
Animosity against the Pope, xii.
Ανομος ὁ, of St. Paul, lxxxiii., 154.
Anti-catholicity, lxxii.
Antichrist, liii., 80, 191, 276, 299.
Anti-council of Naples, xxxi.
Antioch, 105, 123.
Antiquity, 232.
Apostles, 226, 279.
Appian Way, 249.
Arbues, ciii.
Aristocracies, xlvii.
Arius, 124, 261.
Armageddon, 296.
Articles, the thirty-nine, 241.
Astolphus, 9.
Athanasius, 262.
Atheism, xcii., 40, 83.
Athens, 221.
Augsburg Gazette, xxxiii., xl.
Augustine of Canterbury, St., 253.
Australia, 253.
Austria, xiii., xlvi.

Authority, xlvii., 86, 117; key of, 109.

Baptism, abolition of, lxxi.
Barnabites, lxxiv.
Bartholomew, massacre of St., 243.
Basan, 298.
Bavaria, xxiv.
Belgium, xiv.
Berea, 221.
Beust, Count von, xxxii.
Bible, 94.
Bishops, xix.
Bismarck, xlvi., liv., lxi.
Bones, the dry, 279.
Boniface VIII., lxxi.
Braunsberg affair, lix.
Brest, scandals at, cv.
Brotherhood, 200.
Bull *Unam sanctam*, lxxi.

Cæsar, cviii.
Cæsarism, 26.
Caiaphas, 283.
Calvinism, lxxviii.
Camillus, 48.
Canada, 58.
Canterbury, St. Thomas of, 145.
Capital of Christendom, 57, 65, 92.
Carcassonne, scandals at, cv.
Caricature of the Crucifixion, 291.

Castelfidardo, 166.
Catechismus ad Parochos, 101.
Celibacy, xli.
Cemetery of Rome, ix.
Censures, 82.
Certainty of faith, xcii.
Chalcedon, Council of, 170.
Chargés d'affaires, xliv.
Charity, 193, 243.
Charles, St., 103.
Chastity, 42.
Chemistry, 267.
Christendom, capital of, 57, 65, 92; public law of, xcvi.
Church, one, xxi.; visible, 4; mission of, 224.
Churches, the Seven, 292.
Cincinnatus, 48.
Civilisation, modern, 85, 96.
Civiltà Cattolica, xxvii.
Civinini, the Italian deputy, xcix.
Clement XIV., lxxxvii.
Clergy in elections, lix.
Cologne, Archbishop of, lxxx.; assembly at, 263.
Commandments, the ten, 83.
Commonwealths, the three, 194.
Communism, 83, 177, 209.
Community, 200.
Compassion, 193; for the poor, 197.
Conception, the Immaculate, xli., 168.
Conclave, the next, lvii., lxxvii., lxxx., 255.
Concupiscence, 283.
Confession, xli.
Confessional, 83.
Confucius, 48.
Conscience, 5.
Constance, Council of, 172, 261.
Constantine, donation of, 9.
Constantinople, emperor of, 8; history of, 24; council of, 170.
Constitution of the Church, 193.

Corinthians, Epistle to, 200.
Corruption of morals, 208.
Councils, of Chalcedon, 170; of Constantinople, 170; of Trent, 103, 235, 261; the nineteen, 229; of the Vatican, xviii., xxiii., xxxix., lxxx., lxxxix., 235.
Cranmer, 145.
Credulity of Englishmen, xii.
Crisis, time of, 277.
Cross, way of the, 301.
Crucifixion, caricature of, 291.
Curia, the Roman, xxxiv.
Curses, the seven, 147.
Cyrus, 299.

DANIEL, Book of, lxxxv.
Daru, Count, xxxii.
Deacons, order of, 201.
Deadlock of governments, 299.
Definition of the Infallibility, lxxxix.
Deification of the State, xcii.
Deism, xcii.
Democracy, 193.
Despotisms, 25.
Diary of the Council, xxxiv.
Difficulty, the religious, xcvii., 284.
Diplomacy, xxxv., 143.
Disestablishment, lxxxvi.
Divorce, xx.
Doctrine, key of, 169.
Döllinger, Dr. von, xxxi., xli., lxiv., lxx.
Donation of Constantine, 9.
Dore, Dr., lviii.
Dragon, the, 302.
Dresden, 63.
Duty of rulers, 18.

EAST, schism of the, cvii.
Ecclesia malignantium, 41.
Education, xx. 214.

INDEX.

Eliscus, 303.
Encyclical of Pius IX., xxvii., lxxxviii., xc., cvi., 45, 81, 85.
England, animosity of, xii.: history of, xlv.; probation of, 241, 293.
Englishmen, honesty of, 4.
Equality, 86, 239.
Equity, 193, 289.
Ermland, Bishop of, xlix., lx., lxv., lxxix.
Errors, 45, 241; eighty, 82.
Essence of the Church, lvii.
Eutyches, 261.
Ezekiel, 276.

FAITH, light of, 243; certainty of, xcii.
Fear, lxxii.
Fellow-feeling, 193.
Fenni, the Italian deputy, xcix.
Feudalism, 286.
Florence, Council of, xxxvii.
Fragrance of a holy life, 244.
France, 69.
Franciscan, 303.
Frederick II., lxxix.
Freedom of the Pope, 17; of the press, xii.; human, 41.
Freemasons, lxii., lxxiv.
Friedberg, Dr., lxviii.
Friedrich, Professor, xxxiv.
Fuor d' Italia gli Stranieri, xiii.

GALLICANISM, xi., lxxx., 173, 256.
Garibaldi, xiv., cii., 39, 49, 67, 69.
Garibaldians, ci.
Gazette, Augsburg, xxxiii., xl.
Geneva, 46.
Germanism, lxiv.
Germany, lvii.; probation of, 293; professordom of, xxxix.
Gibraltar, 58.
Gneist, Dr., lvii.

Gnosticism, German, xxxix., lxxix.
God, legislation of, 196; a leveller, 202; word of, 233; kingdom of, 249.
Gospel of rebellion, 158.
Government, 194; deadlock of, 299.
Greeks, schism of the, xxxv.
Gregory VII., 184.

HAGUE, Congress at the, lxxxiii.
Heart, the Immaculate, 302; the Sacred, 254, 301.
Hefele, Bishop von, xxxvii.
Henry II., 145.
Henry VIII., xlix.
Heresy, 6, 227, 261, 281.
Herodians, lxxxix., 236.
Hierarchy, lxviii., 282, 285.
Hilary, St., 138.
History, scientific, 233.
Hohenlohe, Cardinal, xliii.; Prince, xxv., xxx.
Honesty of Englishmen, 4.
Huguenots, ciii.

IMMACULATE Conception, the, xli., 81, 168, 256, 302.
Immutability, 228.
Impiegati, the Roman, xv.
Impiety, 195.
Incarnation, the, 40, 161, 204, 224.
Index, the Roman, xxxix.
India, 58.
Infallibility, 230, 258.
Infidelity, 70, 192, 295.
Injustice, 22.
Innspruck, lxv.
Inquisition, a liberal, liv.
Insubordination, 206.
Intercession, public, 290.
Intercessor, 33.
International, the, lxxxii.

Intoxication, mental, xxxvi.
Ireland, history of, xlv., lxxviii., lxxxvi., xciv., 241, 293; people of, 3, 7, 140.
Irishmen, 57.
Isaias, 276.
Israel, constitution of, 195.
Italy, Bishops of, 293.

JANSENISTS, xli., 235.
Janus, the book called, xxix., xlviii., lxxxix.
Japan, 253.
Jeremias, 184.
Jerusalem, 105, 204, 221, 275, 296.
Jesuits, xlvi., xlix., lvii.
Jews, proverbs of the, 214.
Josephism, 256.
Judas, followers of, 283.
Judge, the Church as, 41.
Julian, policy of, xxi.
Junta, the Italian, ix.
Justice, 41, 193, 195, 289.

KAISERS, German, 255.
Key of doctrine, 169.
Keystone of Christianity, 23.
Kingdom, the Italian, xii.; of Jesus, 248.
Knowledge of Christianity, 239.

LABOUR-MARKET, 207.
Lancashire, 241.
Lasker, Dr., lx.
Law, international, xxvi., 289; weakness of, 276; of Moses, 105, 195.
Lawlessness, 154.
Legislation of God, 196.
Leo, St., 176.
Lepanto, 79, 84, 134.
Leveller, God, 202.
Libanus, 298.

Liberalism, modern, lx., lxxiii., 84, 96, 177, 209.
Liberals of Europe, x., lii.
Light of faith, 243.
Liguorian Brothers, xlix.
Lima, Roman Journal, civ.
Litany of the Blessed Virgin, 61.
London, population of, 146; seven curses of, 147.
Lorenzo, San, cemetery of, ix., xcv.
Luther, reformation of, x., 234, 262.
Lutheranism, lxxviii., lxxxvi.
Lycurgus, 48.
Lystra, 221.

MADRID, 63.
Mahometanism, lxxxiv., 56, 79, 191, 295.
Majority of a people, xiii., xlvii.: of the Council, xxxvii.
Malta, 7, 58.
Mammon, 256.
Marriage, civil, lxvi., lxxi.
Marx, Karl, lxxv., lxxxii.
Mary, the Blessed Virgin, 33.
Massacre of St. Bartholomew, 243.
Matrimony, Sacrament of, xx., 84, 91.
Mayence, lxxv.
Mayer, Dr., lvii.
Mazzini, xiv.
Mediator, 33.
Menabrea, General, xxxii.
Montana, ix.
Mercy, 193.
Merlin, the President, 49.
Messias, 281.
Michael, St., 302.
Milan, 104.
Minority of a people, xiii., xlvii.; of the Council, xxxvii., 257.
Miracles, 225.

INDEX. 309

Mission of the Church, 224.
Monarchy, 193.
Money, 207.
Moniteur of 1793, 47.
Monte Rotondo, 69.
Morals, corruption of, 203; of society, 83.
Morte al Papa, c.; *ai preti*, e.
Moses, law of, 105, 195.
Mother of God, 301.
Munich, xxiii., xxiv.
Murder, 132.
Mysteries of piety and impiety, 40.

NAMZANOWSKI, Mgr., lii.
Naples, anti-council of, xxxi.
Nationality, spirit of, 173, 255.
Nero, 50.
Nestorius, 261.
Numa, 43.
Nun of Cracow, cii.; at Picpus, cv.

OBEDIENCE a duty, 7, 18, 42, 86, 201, 206.
Obediences, 255.
Olozaga, xxx.
Onesimus, 199.
Oppression of truth and justice, xii.
Orders, religious, 42.
Organisation, xvii.

PAGANISM, xcviii.
Palatinates, 286.
Pall-Mall Gazette, 133.
Pantheism, 83.
Papacy, the, liv., lxxvi.
Patrick, St., 254.
Patrimonies, the twenty-three, 11, 67.
Pentecost, day of, 120, 225.
Pepin, 9.
Peter, St., 225, 240 258; centenary of, xviii.

Peter's pence. liii.
Petitio principii, xci.
Petrucelli della Gattina, xcix.
Pharisees, lxxxix., 236.
Philemon, 199.
Philippi, 221.
Phosphorus, 47.
Picpus, nuns at, cv.
Piety, 195.
Pilate, 129.
Pius IV., 103.
Pius V., 81.
Pius IX., ix., xviii., xxv., xciv., cv., 25, 35, 38, 50, 64, 73, 163, 251, 259, 276, 287.
Plebiscite, 7, 134, 152.
Poland, liii.
Politics, 83.
Polytheism, 40.
Pontiff, the Sovereign, xvii.; 229, 257.
Poor, the, 197.
Poor-law, 207.
Population of London, 146.
Postulatum of the Bishops, xxxii.
Poverty, 42, 201.
Power, the temporal, 5; ordained of God, 7; rightful, 8; of most ancient tradition, 12; specially sacred, 14; never oppressive, 18; guardian of public order, 145; the liberty of the Church, 183.
Press, freedom of the, xii.
Priesthood, the, lxviii., 43.
Prim, General, 67.
Princedom, the civil, xi., 25
Probation, 238.
Professordom, xxxix., xcvii.
Progress, modern, 41, 84, 96, 117, 240.
Property, 150, 196, 200.
Protestantism, cvii., 265.
Proverbs of the Jews, 214.
Providence, Divine, 4, 7, 10, 23, 36.

Purity, 41.

QUEBEC, 63.
Question, the Roman, 143.
Quirinal, the, liv.

RATIONALISM, xcii., 83.
Ravenna, 9.
Rebellion, 6, 19, 158.
Redemptorists, lxxiv.
Reformers, Protestant, xcvi.
Reichensperger, Dr., lx.
Reichstag, the German, li., lviii., lxxiii.
Republic, 193.
Retrogression, 118.
Revolution, xxi., 24, 212.
Riches a trust, 201.
Rights of man, 48.
Rome, empire of, 6; occupation of, ix.; people of, xii.
Rosary Sunday, ix., 3, 31, 79, 189, 275, 300.
Royalties of the Church, 250.
Rulers, duties of, 18.
Russia, 59.

SACRAMENTS, the seven, 41, 233; city of the blessed, 204.
Sacrilege, 13, 295.
Sadducees, lxxxix.
Sanctity, note of, 281.
Saphira, 199, 283.
Satan, work of, lxvii., 213, 231.
Saxony, 253.
Scepticism, 268.
Schism, the Greek, xxxv., 6.
Schools, xxi., 214.
Schleswig-Holstein, lxxiii.
Schrader, Father, xxxviii.
Science, xxxviii.; German, xxxv.; religion of, 46.
Scipio, 48.
Scotland, 4, 7, 259.

Scribes, 228, 236.
Scriptures, 231.
Secularists, 267.
Seminaries, 411.
Sepulchre, the Holy, 56.
Shaftesbury, Lord, 146.
Slaves, 207.
Socialism, 83.
Society, tendency of, xx.
Solon, 48.
Sophists, 268.
Standard newspaper, ciii.
State, the, lviii., 214; deification of, xcii., 206; schools, xxi.; life, lxvii.
Stephen II., Pope, 9.
Subjects, duties of, 18.
Suffrage, universal, 7.
Sugar, 47.
Syllabus, the, xxvii., lxxxviii., xc., cvi., 45, 81, 98, 175, 283.

TARSHISH, 298.
Teacher, the Church as, 41, 226.
Telegraph, the *Daily*, 134.
Temple, the Jewish, 215.
Testimony of the Apostles, 226.
Thanksgiving, public, 290.
Theatres in Rome, ci.
Theocracy of Rome, x., xciv.
Theology, candlestick of, xxxvi.
Thomas, St., of Canterbury, l., 145, 184.
Thought, 47.
Tithes, 150.
Tocqueville, De, cvi.
Torquemada, ciii.
Tradition, 12.
Transfiguration, the, 225.
Treason, 6.
Trent, Council of, xli.
Triumph of the Church, 221.
Truth, oppression of the, xii.; immutable, 227.
Tyranny, 19

ULTRAMONTANISM, xi., xl., li., lxi.
Unanimity of the Council, 257.
Unbelief, 288.
Unbelievers, 239.
United States, 58.
Unity, craving after, 243.
Univers, the, xxxviii.
Utrecht, Jansenist Archbishop of, xlii.

VATICAN, Council of the, xviii., xxiii., xxxix., lxxx., lxxxix, 235, 257.
Vesinier, lxxxii.
Veto, xciv.
Vicar of Christ, xi., 71, 88, 97, 99, 137, 157, 169, 171, 177, 255, 259.
Victor Emmanuel, King, liv., ci.
Vienna, 63.
Vincent de Paul, St., lxxiv.
Virtues, extinct, 42.
Voice, the living, 234.
Volk, Dr., lv.
Voltaire, 47, 165.

WAGENER, Herr, lv.
War against society, xlvii.
Warmth of charity, 243.
Weakness of law, 276.
Wealth, supreme, 206.
William, the Emperor, xlviii.
Windthorst, lvi., lxx.
Witness, the Church as, 41; of the faith, 176.
Woman, emancipation of, 212.
Word of God, 233.
World, probation of the, 238.

ZION, hill of, 249, 266.
Zoroaster, 48.
Zouaves, the Papal, 39, 132.

THE END.